'Round Lake Huron: A Bicyclist's Tour Guide

Harvey Botzman

Harvey Botzman

Cyclotour Guide Books
Rochester New York

2002

‘Round Lake Huron: A Bicyclist’s Tour Guide

Cyclotour Guide Books
PO Box 10585, Rochester, New York 14610-0585
cyclotour@cyclotour.com
http://www.cyclotour.com

Other books by the author
Erie Canal Bicyclist’s & Hiker Tour Guide
Finger Lakes Bicyclist’s Tour Guide
Long Distance Bicycle Touring Primer
Great Lakes Bicycle Touring Series:
‘Round Lake Ontario: A Bicyclist’s Tour Guide
‘Round Lake Erie: A Bicyclist’s Tour Guide
‘Round Lake Michigan: A Bicyclist’s Tour Guide
‘Round Lake Superior: A Bicyclist’s Tour Guide (2004)

Disclaimers

The author; publisher; wholesale and retail purveyor; library owner; of this book and its contents; and government units/agencies on whose roads you bicycle are not responsible for your riding habits, bicycle and any accidents which might occur. They encourage users of this *Guide* to wear a helmet; use a mechanically correct bicycle; use reflectors; use lights even during daylight hours; wear clothing which is readily visible to motorists, pedestrians and others; watch for other vehicles and pedestrians; position yourself and your bicycle correctly on a roadway or trail; and obey all traffic laws, rules and regulations.

Road and trail conditions change. The routes suggested herein may be altered due to road and trail work; surface conditions; or your need to explore. Every effort has been made to provide accurate information.

Library of Congress Catalog Card Number: 99-90014

ISBN: 1-889602-11-6 [Perfect Bound]
ISBN: 1-889602-12-4 [Coil Bound]

10 9 8 7 6 5 4 3 2 1

To Alex, Jordan and Zachary

The constraints of your mind
Are the only things which prevent
The accomplishment of your goals.

'Round Lake Huron: A Bicyclist's Tour Guide

Harvey Botzman

Contents

ACKNOWLEDGEMENTS

Without my father and mother, Samuel and Lillian Botzman teaching me how to explore the world; and the encouragement my sister and brother in law Gail and Gerry Robinson; nieces Randi Robinson; Bonnie Cimring, her husband Mark, great-nephews Alex, Jordan and Zachary this series of books would have stopped long ago.

The business advice and traveling experiences of Joe and Sylvia Baron. Uncle Abraham and aunt Celia Aaroni's enthusiasm for this endeavor lead me to continue writing.

My *Detroit* cousins in particular Joe and Nancy Pearl; and Arnold Pearl who need this book to traverse the lakeshore on their periodic trips home from the Pacific Coast.

It was my friends and their children to whom I owe immense gratitude for their support, criticism and ability to take me away from staring at a computer monitor! Thanks, Ed, Martha, Eli and Emmy Awad; Jim, Becky, Jenny and Jimmy Parks; Bob, Mary, Nathanel and Tommy Howe; Jeff Schwartz; Pat Townsend, Gervase Pevarnik; Lori Cooley; and others.

My cycling partners Tom Knapp and Doug Weimer; bike club members Rich DeSarra and Dick Burns all have helped me pedal through the writing process.

Boyhood friends who started me on the bicycling phenomenon Larry Fiebert, Barry Kasdan, Ron Lichtman, David Weisenfreund might be the originators of this series of tour guides.

Thanks.

Harvey

PREFACE

This book has taken an interminably long time to research, write and publish.

The distance involved in circumnavigating Lake Huron is equal to traveling across half the width of North America. A long trip which once started can not be significantly shortened.

Then there were the inevitable political and economic changes. The responsibility for maintaining some roads in Ontario were transferred to municipalities necessitating a change in road numbers and sometimes road names. New telephone area codes kept popping up every six months. Ah! The travails of tour guide writers!

Finally *'Round Lake Huron* was finished. Then the master computer disks were stolen from my car.

Now it is done and ready for you to use.

Unlike my most recent tour guides I've had to eliminate the narrative portions of the tour guide. The geographical information, personal philosophy, stories, and bicycling advocacy stuff simply added too many pages (read extra weight.) Some folks will be sad that this information is not included. Others will be overjoyed. I am planning to post this information on the web for cyclotourists to read and download.

Have fun. Ride with delight. Spin your mind as you spin your pedals.

Harvey Botzman
March 1, 2002

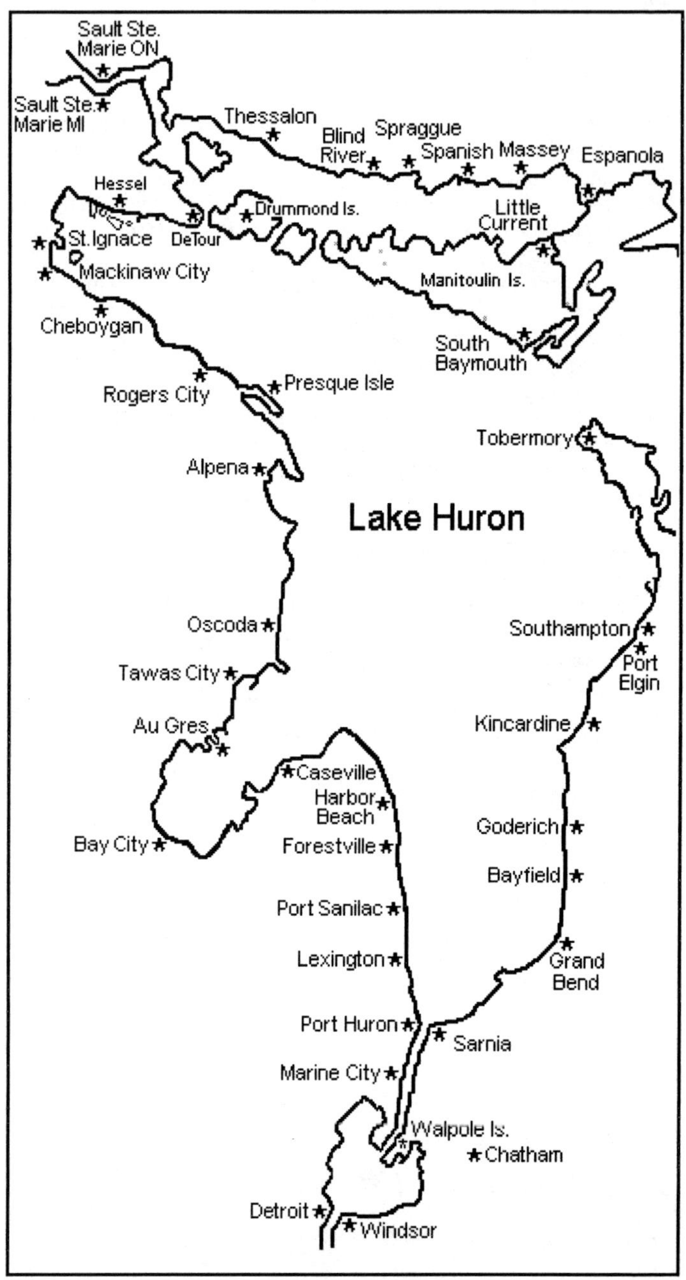
Sault Ste.
Marie ON
Sault Ste.
Marie MI
Thessalon
Blind
River
Spraggue
Spanish
Massey
Espanola
Hessel
Drummond Is.
Little
Current
St. Ignace
DeTour
Mackinaw City
Manitoulin Is.
Cheboygan
South
Baymouth
Rogers City
Presque Isle
Tobermory
Alpena
Lake Huron
Oscoda
Southampton
Port
Elgin
Tawas City
Au Gres
Kincardine
Caseville
Harbor
Beach
Goderich
Bay City
Forestville
Bayfield
Port Sanilac
Lexington
Grand
Bend
Port Huron
Sarnia
Marine City
Walpole Is.
Chatham
Detroit
Windsor

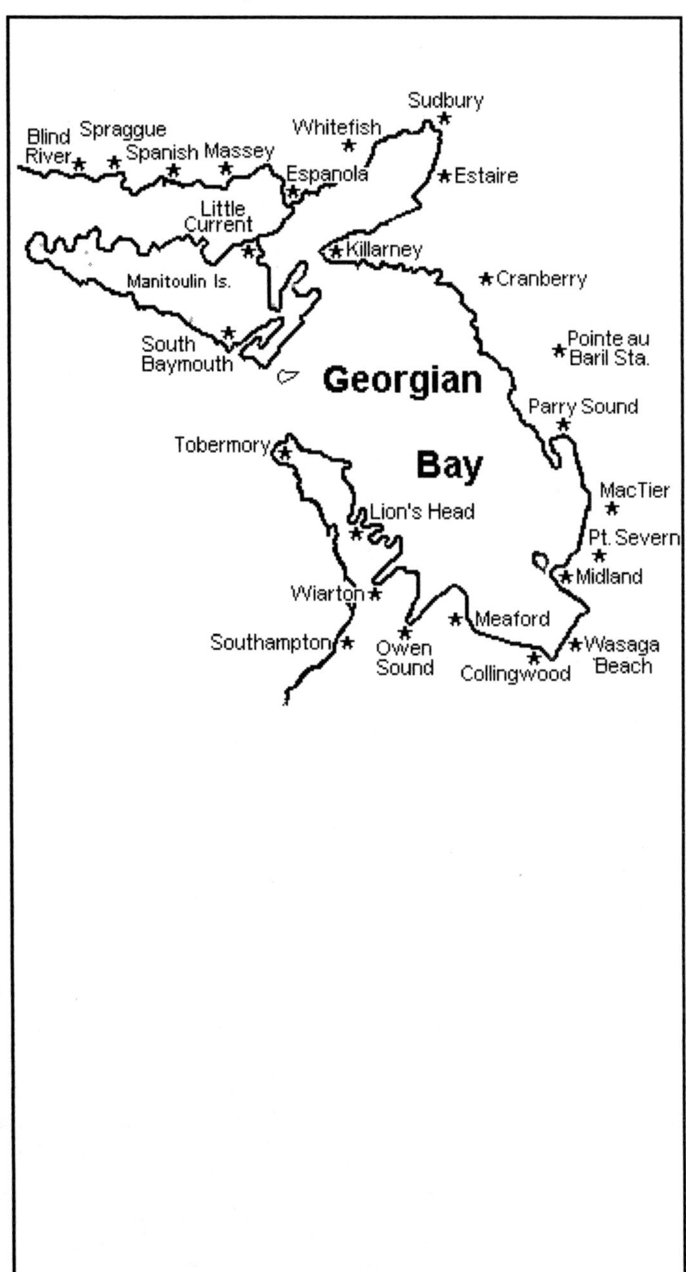
Sudbury
Blind River
Spraggue
Spanish
Massey
Whitefish
Espanola
Estaire
Little Current
Killarney
Manitoulin Is.
Cranberry
Pointe au Baril Sta.
South Baymouth
Georgian
Bay
Parry Sound
Tobermory
MacTier
Lion's Head
Pt. Severn
Midland
Wiarton
Meaford
Southampton
Owen Sound
Collingwood
Wasaga Beach

TOUR PREPARATION

Tour Preparation Contents

Traveler Note

This chapter, *Tour Preparation*, has grown from 12 pages to 25 pages. You really do not need to carry these pages on your cyclotour or hike along the Canal.

If you purchased a coil bound copy of this *Tour Guide* then carefully bend back the end of the coil. Unscrew the coil binding, remove these pages. Screw the coil back into the holes. You've lost some weight! You can replace these pages when you return home from your cyclotour.

If you purchased a bound copy of this *Tour Guide*, then rip out these pages and paste them back in when you return home.

Types of Bicycle Touring

I travel as a self-contained bicycle tourist. I cyclotour in this manner to view the world at its level as well as for economic reasons. The philosophical concept of self-reliance has a direct bearing on my mode of travel.

Other people cyclotour with only a credit card, an emergency repair kit, some snacks, and a few pieces of clothing. Still others travel with a sag wagon containing all their equipment, friends or family members. Some people travel alone others with family or friends. Many folks prefer to cyclotour with commercial or non-profit organized tours.

It really doesn't matter how you define your form of cyclotouring. You made a choice to travel by bicycle rather than by car or public transportation. You will meet people who state, *...since I first rode a bicycle I've always wanted to bicycle tour.* You're cyclotouring and they're still waiting to bicycle tour!

In American and Canadian society we tend to define and classify what we do. In my mind bicycle touring is cyclotouring is bicycle touring. For others the following definitions of cyclotouring can help to sort out the type of bicycle touring which best meets their needs and wants.

Self-contained (self-reliant) Cyclotouring is when the bicyclist, (alone or with others) carries sufficient equipment to maintain the bicyclist(s) for the entire tour period. The equipment includes but is not limited to camping gear, clothing, personal gear, tools, and food. Obviously, consumables (food, *etc.*) will be replenished as the tour progresses.

Partially Loaded Cyclotouring is when the bicyclist carries emergency sleeping/camping equipment, basic repair equipment, a limited amount of clothing and personal items, snacks, or one meal's worth of food. A combination of commercial lodging and preparing one's own food or camping and eating in restaurants is considered partially loaded cyclotouring.

Credit Card Cyclotouring is for bicyclists who want to be least encumbered with *stuff!* A credit card or debit card is necessary! Travelers checks will suffice! Only small panniers are needed along with a lock; a wallet with credit cards; and a small amount of cash! Meals are eaten in restaurants. Lodging is at motels, b&bs or hostels. The cyclotourist travels by charging everything to the credit card or paying cash. Hopefully the tourist doesn't forget to pay the bills!

Segment Cyclotouring is completing a long distance tour over a period of time with breaks to return home. The bicyclist starts each segment at the point where the previous segment was completed.

Personal Sag Wagon Cyclotouring is a touring mode in which the food, camping and bicycle specific equipment is carried in a sag wagon. A spouse or friend functions as the sag wagon driver. The bicyclist(s) carries the minimum amount of snacks, water, repair equipment, and some rain gear. Many times lodging for sag wagon bicycle tourists is at motels or b&bs rather than campsites. Bicyclist(s) and sag wagon meet at predetermined places for food, fun, and lodging.

Day Tripping is when an individual or a group travel for one day on a short round trip tour of a specific area. Usually these travelers carry the bare minimum amount of equipment and eat in restaurants. Sometimes a day trip includes an overnight stay at commercial lodging.

Arranged Cyclotouring is when all long distance touring arrangements (with or without sag wagon support) are made by a non-profit or commercial bicycle tour company. Cyclotourists who participate in arranged touring have memorable experiences less the hassles associated with making all the arrangements themselves. They usually enjoy meeting and interacting with people who have similar interests.

Bikepacking is off road cyclotouring. Usually the object is to establish a camping spot and mt. bike on trails from that base camp.

Guerrilla Camping is finding a beautiful secluded place, off the road and using it as your camp site. The guerrilla camper makes every effort to obtain permission to camp if there is an indication that the site is on private property.

Friends, Family and the Passionate Cyclotourist

How to convince your non-cycling family members or friends to help you exercise your cyclotouring fantasy without breaking up the relationship!

1. Make certain all family/friends have bicycles.
2. Plan your tour so that the first few overnight stops are 20-30 miles apart. This will allow you to spend time with your loved ones or friends while you tour.
3. The *passionate cyclotourist* bicycles to each overnight stop. At the overnight stopping point, the dedicated cyclist joins the other members of the touring group for an hour or two of recreational bicycling. Enjoy your vacation!
4. The passionate cyclist suggests to the other vacatíoners that one semi-dedicated bicyclist accompanies him/her on a portion of the next day's ride between overnight stops.
5. The sag wagon meets you and the co-rider at an intermediate point; picks up the co-rider who normally would not want to bicycle the entire distance between stops. You, the experienced cyclotourist, continues riding the entire distance to the next overnight stop.
6. Continue doing this for a few days and your family and friends will start enjoying *total* bicycle touring with you.
7. Alternatively, purchase a tandem!

Breakdown Cruise

At least two weeks before your tour begins take a short trial tour. Pack everything you *intend* to take on your long distance cyclotour. Include, in your panniers, what you *think* might be needed on your cyclotour. Ride twenty or thirty miles to a nearby campground. Stay overnight. Make notes on how you and your bike traveled.

When you return home, toss out everything which was superfluous to your weekend trip. Be vicious! Be heartless! "***Less is more***," Mies Van der Rohr said. Truer words were never stated in regard to cyclotouring. The less you load into your panniers the lighter your bike and the more enjoyable your tour will be!

Equipment

I'm frequently asked what I take on a tour. There are many bicyclists with more miles under their toes than me. They might carry more equipment than I do. My needs are very basic while cyclotouring. Your needs are different.

One bicycle, kind of essential and I use an old one:
18 speed, triple crank (24/40/52 x 13/34).

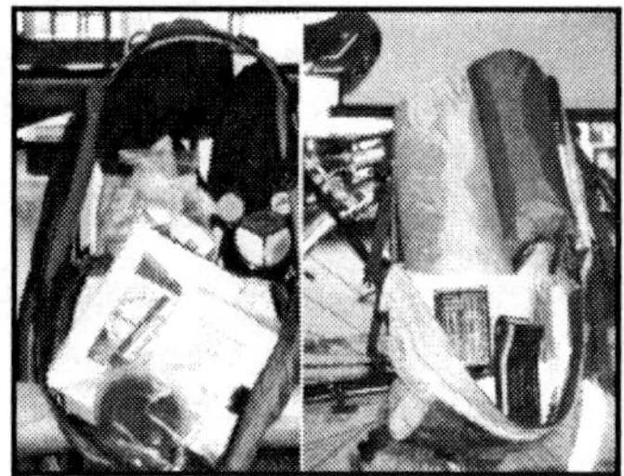

The panniers are packed as follows:

Right Rear Pannier	Left Rear Pannier
Tent	Stove inside a 1 qt. pan
Tent Poles	Fuel Bottle
Mattress Pad	First Aid Kit
Tools & Lights	Maps, misc. papers
Personal Items	Personal Items
1/2 "U" lock	1/2 "U" lock

Sleeping bag on top of the rear rack.

Right Front Pannier	Left Front Pannier
Clothing	Food

Total weight = ~37 lb./17 kg. including panniers.

For aerodynamic and theft reasons, I try to have very few items *blowin' in the wind*!

The load is balanced, left and right sides, front and rear. I shift items between panniers to better balance the load.

I use both sets of panniers because I'm small and light weight! If all the weight is on the rear wheels I lose some steering control.

This pannier set up changes if I do not use front panniers. Then the rear panniers are balanced by a handlebar bag containing a limited number of heavy items: "U" lock, camera, snacks (fruit weights a lot), rain wear, towel, and bathing suit.

Roads

State Highways in Michigan in are smooth asphalt. Usually these roads have a striped paved shoulder of at least 4 ft. (1.2 m.) These roads are termed, M [Road number] in the text.

Provincial Highways (King's Highways) in Ontario are major roads with an asphalt or cement surface. They may or may not have a paved shoulder. These roads are termed PH [Road number] or Hwy. [Road number]

Michigan and Ontario county and municipal roads used in this book usually have a chip sealed surface. These roads may have a shoulder and then again they may not. If there is a shoulder it will be small and either gravel or mowed grass. These roads are termed CR [Road number] or have a name.

The trails used in this *Tour Guide* are usually surfaced with stone dust. Technically stone dust is <.125 in. (<.32 cm.) in diameter. Generally the stone used is shale or ground metamorphic rock. The stone dust comes from two sources, quarries and street sweepings. The street sweepings have the added advantage of containing minute non-polluting amounts of salt left over from winter road salting. This small amount of salt inhibits the growth of vegetation on the trail.

Bicycles

Your Bike vs. a Touring Bike

For most cyclotourists their tried and true bike will suffice for this tour. We do suggest that you use new slightly wider tires for this tour. There are several sections of the route where you might have to ride on a gravel or grass shoulder. A wider tire with a slightly more defined tread pattern will provide more steering control in such instances.

It is *fit* not the type of bicycle which is important for successful cyclotouring (or any type of bicycling). An improper fit of your body to a bicycle will make your bicycle tour a horror. A proper fit of your body to a bicycle will make your tour a joy.

You can use any type of bike, with some modifications, for this or any other cyclotour. You can place racks, panniers, lights, fenders, different tires, and different gearing on a hybrid, sport tourer, mt. bike or even a racing bike and still successfully tour! Traditional touring bicycles with long chain stays and a full range of gears are a rare sight in bike shops. Only a few major bike manufacturers make touring bikes. An additional fifteen or so custom builders make touring bikes. If you think you really need one, have your local bike shop order it.

The primary differences between a touring bicycle and a recreational bike or mt. bike are in the chain stay length; head tube angle; frame flex; sufficient frame strength to carry a load; and stronger or more spokes; and having sufficient busses for attaching racks, water bottles, *etc.*

A touring bike usually has chainstays which are ~18 in./45.7 cm. or more in length. The head tube angle on a touring bike tends to be ~73°. Yes, all these technical specifications do make for a more comfortable long distance ride.

Bicycle manufacturers put all sorts of *do dads* on recreational bikes to make them appear as touring bicycles. Do a bit of research if you are planning to purchase a touring bicycle.

Mt. Bikes

A mt. bike makes a fine touring machine! Yes, traditional touring bike riders, they do! True, a few modifications are necessary to make a Mt. bike a more efficient touring bike. None the less, they make comfortable touring bikes.

A mt. bike with a front suspension fork generally can not use front panniers. This means that all the weight of your *stuff* will be on the rear wheel. Use a handle bar bag and place some of the weightier items (U lock) in it to help balance the load.

Or change the front fork! If you do this, make certain that the new suspension fork has busses for attaching front racks. Several manufacturers now make front forks specifically designed for attaching front racks. Front panniers really are not necessary if you limit the amount of *stuff* you take on your cyclotour! *Less is More!*

A number of rack manufacturers make special Mt. bike front and rear racks which can be used with front and rear suspended frames. Ask about these racks at your local bike shop or send Cyclotour Guide Books a letter or email. We try to maintain information files to answer your touring questions.

Mt. bikes with short chain stays may present a problem with rear panniers. Your heels may continually strike the rear panniers as you pedal. If this occurs on your bike, move the panniers a few inches or centimeters rearward. Carefully pack your rear panniers with the heaviest items centered over the axle.

Mt. bike handle bars and handle bar mounted shifters are designed for constant shifting on difficult terrain. In general cyclotourists do not shift often but need to change their hand positions often to relieve numbness.

Don't go out and purchase a new set of shifters or handlebars! A simple and inexpensive mt. bike modification is to add bar ends.. These bar ends will allow you to use your current shifters and provide additional hand positions to relieve numbness. A new type of bolt on Mt. bike bar end even has the traditional dropped curved section. A number of cyclotourists use bolt on aero bars to provide even more hand positions.

Tires

I suggest that you use a set of the multipurpose touring tires These multipurpose touring tires are efficient for negotiating smooth asphalt, stone dust and will allow you to successfully explore the rural dirt roads which strike your fancy.

Slick no tread tires are not suitable for touring. Occasionally you might have to go off the roadway and onto a gravel or grass shoulder. Slicks on such surfaces will provide a greater chance for you to wipe out!

A set of fairly wide, >28 mm. (~1 in.), touring or hybrid tires with a well defined (but not knobby) tread pattern will be well worth their premium price by having sufficient tread to slough off roadway irregularities. Their well defined tread pattern will provide excellent traction and the smoother central road tread pattern will provide low rolling resistance.

Although mt. bikes make fine touring machines for this tour, knobby treaded Mt. bike tires are not useful for traveling on asphalt or chip seal. Knobby tires have too much rolling resistance and wear out very fast touring on road surfaces.

Gearing!

A triple chain ring with a relatively small inner chain ring is useful for traversing hills.

Mt. Bike gearing usually provides a full range of choices for street and off road use. Mt. bikers might find that the higher gears used for road travel are not on their bike. One relatively easy way to obtain a more suitable gear configuration is to change the chain rings. Simply bolt on a large chain ring with more teeth (Don't forget to remove the current chain ring!). You might have wider steps between some gear stops but nothing which presents undue problems. Keep the small chain ring, you'll need it for the hills!

Given the chain rings on newer bikes (road and mountain), this might not be such a simple modification. Check with an experienced bicycle mechanic at a good bike shop before replacing the chain rings or freewheel.

Other Bits & Pieces

A first aid kit is a necessity.

Rain gear for the inevitable rain shower is a must.

Warm clothing for chilly mornings/evenings and after a rain shower will help prevent hypothermia.

Clothing is bulky and surprisingly weighs a lot. Do not take too much clothing, Laundromats are available.

H_2O must be carried. Dehydration is the prime malady of bicyclists. Drink at least 8-12 fl. oz. (235-355 ml.) of water per half or three quarters of an hour. It is far better to drink more water than less water. You can add those high energy/ electrolyte replacement substances/drinks to your water bottle but good old H_2O and some fruit will be just as effective for the majority of cyclotourists.

Equipment Lists

Do not take too much! ***Less is more!*** Excess weight due to excess equipment, clothing, tools, and food make a bicycle tour a drudgery rather than a pleasure. There are sufficient supply depots along the way. A Post Office is always available to send *stuff* home!

The *Equipment Lists* can help you plan and choose the items you need on your tour. The *Lists* are simply provided. You make the decision what to pack in your panniers. Base your equipment decisions on the type of cyclotouring you are doing—fully loaded to credit card—and your need for *stuff*. You will be able to purchase *stuff* along your route. You will be able to send home anything which is superfluous.

The Equipment Lists are particularly useful when crossing international borders. The Customs agent may want to see a list of what is in your panniers. Simply show the agent the Equipment Lists and have the agent stamp the Lists. You'll save time upon reentry.

Balance your load, front and rear; right and left sides.

Do not overload your bicycle.

Climate

During the summer (June-September) the climate of Lake Huron is perfect for bicycling. It is in the marginal months, March-May and October-November when the climate presents the most notable problems.

Wind! The bane of cyclists! Generally the wind blows from the Northwest or West.

A climate factor called, *lake effect* influences the land mass surrounding large lakes creating micro-climate areas bordering a lake. Lake effect areas have a different climate than a location one or two miles away from a large body of water. You might notice these micro climates as the route verges away from the Lake. Lake effect also contributes to the betterment of humankind by creating ideal conditions for growing wine grapes and certain fruits like apricots in the northern latitutes.

Precipitation and Temperature

Snow and cold weather may buffet the northern end of the Lake during the marginal Spring and Autumn seasons. Plan accordingly. This is a long tour.

In April and May the day time temperature range is from 45-70°F (7-21°C) with rain a few days week. Rarely does it rain all day.

Days during June, July and August most likely will be sunny and clear with temperatures in the 73-85°F (23-30°C) range. It rains during the summer about once a week but rarely for more than an hour or two. Evenings in late August can drop the temperature to the high 50s° F (10s° C.) Early

September days usually are warm with clear cloudless skies.

In late September the day time temperatures begin to descend to the 50-70°F (10-21°C) range. Mid-October brings precipitation similar to September with slightly chillier day time temperatures. The added bonus of fantastic Fall foliage in mid to late September makes Lake Huron a prime cycling destinations for locals and visitors from afar.

Snow will most likely be falling and covering the ground in early March and late October. The snow during these months is heavy and wet. It may disappear after a day or two as the temperature rises and then again it might not.

Don't think snow hinders bicyclists from using the routes bordering the Lake. Road cyclists switch to mt. bikes with knobby tires or simply use tires with a more pronounced tread. They'll put on a few more layers of clothing to ride all year long. Mt. bikers claim that snow is like mud except colder.

Fuel for Body and Mind

I carry very little food. Some pasta, dehydrated sauce mixes, cereal, snacks, fresh fruit, and two bottles of water. Some type of food can be obtained readily along almost the entire route. There are several sections of the described route when you will not pass at least one small local grocery or convenience store. These areas are noted in the text.

Perishable products such as meat, cheese, milk or ice cream (the exception is yoghut) do not travel well in panniers. It is best to buy perishable products on a daily basis within a half hour of stopping to cook and eat them. Salmonella and other gastro-intestinal diseases can turn a delightful tour into a miserable experience. With a little common sense and care you should have few problems.

Without preaching, eating is important. Bicycling is a strenuous activity when you are touring everyday for a few weeks. Food and the correct foods to refuel and rebuild your depleted carbohydrate and protein supplies is of utmost importance.

I tend to eat more vegetables and carbohydrates (primarily pasta and rice) and less meat on my tours. These foods are relatively simple to store and prepare on a backpacking

stove. I do eat my requisite beef, fish and chicken protein sources.

Fresh vegetables and fruit can be bought at roadside stands. you will be missing a vital and satisfying culinary experience by not purchasing and eating fresh fruit and vegetables from the many farms and homeowners along the way.

Bananas and most citrus fruit, which tend to be staples of bicyclists, will have to be bought in groceries.

Take your fishing pole! Yup! There are fish in Lake Huron. Happy fish. You will encounter fisherpersons and they eat the fish they catch! Excellent trout, whitefish, bass, and other fish are found streams flowing into the Lake and the Lake itself.

If you are a fisherperson make certain you contact Ontario and Michigan for the proper regulations and licenses.

Take a chance eating at what appears to be a non-imposing restaurant or tavern. In most cases, you will be pleasantly surprised with a fine, hearty meal and a friendly atmosphere. Similarly, the village bakeries (real bakeries, not the supermarket variety) have superb delights!

A notation is made in the text of grocery stores, convenience stores, gas stations, and the more permanent farm stands along the route. In urban and suburban areas only the last supply depots before entering a relatively long stretch of road where there are few stores are they noted.

Many campgrounds have small stores which cater to campers. Usually, their selection is limited. Bear in mind that the concessionaires stock what is needed most by the campers in a given park. If the park has a large number of RV campers then there will be fewer groceries. Most RV campers come, to the park, prepared and have little need for purchasing groceries. Make life easy for yourself, plan ahead, stop at a grocery which is within a half hour of your next meal. Use the *Food List* to help plan your needs.

Keep everything light. Try not to buy canned goods. Use dehydrated sauces and fresh foods which will be consumed in a day or two. Price will rarely be a factor for the small quantities you will need.

A short paragraph about dehydrated food. You are not going to be traveling in an area which is totally isolated from civilization. Only a few 50 mi. (80 km.) stretches of the route are relatively devoid of humanity. Trees, grains, fruits, deer, and cows being the dominant inhabitants. Expensive backpacker type dehydrated food packets are not necessary. Search your everyday grocery store for items like packets of sauces, veggie burgers in dehydrated form and pasta.

Dehydrated foods—both those specifically designed for backpackers and those off the shelf in a grocery store—should be bought prior to the trip and tested for taste and preparation ease. There is nothing worse than looking forward to an easily prepared meal, making it and then discarding it for its foul taste.

One interesting *new* food available in your local grocery store is tuna fish in packets rather than cans. The packet tuna weighs half as much as the canned tuna.

You might find that pasta with locally made cheese is just as easy to prepare as an expensive box of macaroni and cheese. It probably will taste better, too!

Carrying food

Plastic freezer bags are the simplest and easiest way to carry foods. Purchase freezer rather than normal plastic bags, they hold up better. You'll probably need a few different size bags.

Recently I've switched to carrying most of my food in plastic containers rather than plastic bags. I thought there would be a significant weight and space difference but that does not appear to be true. Plastic containers have the advantage of being easy to seal securely, not ripping open and being more moisture proof.

Recipe Ideas

Basic foods which are always in my panniers:

Pasta (spinach or avocado noodles, macaroni, etc.)
Rice
Cereal
Coffee, fresh ground, in a plastic container
Spice mixtures (commercial packets) or in 35 mm film cans
Yogurt. Yogurt keeps for several days.

Breakfast

Cereal w/yogurt
Fresh fruit
Coffee (ground or regular)
MSR® and Melita® make backpaker coffee makers

Eggs, milk and other perishable items should be bought and used within an hour of purchase. Pancake mix is fine but fat (oil) is usually needed. Fats become rancid very quickly in warm weather. Besides clean up is much more difficult with these foods and you want to start riding as soon as possible.

Lunch

Sandwiches: Rolls or pita bread are easier to use and store than a loaf of bread. Peanut butter, jelly, cheese, fruit all on one sandwich. Packaged or fresh cut luncheon meat from a grocery is fine but remember that luncheon meat spoils very quickly. Use hard or semi-soft natural cheeses (cheddar, Swiss, parmesan) rather than soft or processed cheeses. The hard varieties will keep for several days.

Dinner

Pasta or rice.

Salad. Remember that lettuce and other vegetables are heavy and spoil baking in your panniers.

Soup:An easily prepared soup or stew can be made by dumping farm fresh vegetables along with a piece of chicken, ground beef or tofu into one pot.

Without the chicken (chicken stock spoils quickly) you can keep the soup overnight and use it for lunch the next day. If you make a vegetable soup and plan to use it for lunch the next day, boil it down to thicken the soup for over night storage and transport in you panniers. Of course you will need a container which seals securely. You can always thin the thickened soup with water.

Meats: If you're at a grocery within a half hour of making dinner, have the butcher put the meat into a plastic freezer bag then place that bag into a second bag packed with ice (usually the butcher supplies free ice). Do not use any ice which has come in contact with uncooked meat.

Sauce

Sauces make meals interesting. Instead of carrying bottles or cans of pasta sauce use packets of different varieties of dehydrated sauce mixes (marinara, pesto, alfredo, Thai noodle, sweet and sour, *etc.*). These are found in almost any grocery store. They are lighter and easier to use than bottled sauce. A packet of sauce can be used for two or three meals! Simply roll over the packet top and place it in a small plastic bag to store for another dinner or lunch. The dehydrated sauce mix can be sprinkled on top of sandwich *fixins* to provide additional taste treats.

Most commercial sauce mixes contain too much salt for my taste. Bulk spices can be found in many grocery stores.

One Pot Cooking: Drain the pasta but leave a bit of water in the pan. Add some of the sauce mix, stir and eat! Yogurt and peanut butter can be added to the pasta to make a sauce! Real simple preparation for hearty meal. Little clean up.

Gourmet eating at its finest!

Watch your calories; your carbohydrate, fat, and protein balance!

Drink sufficient water!

Eat enough carbohydrates to refuel your bod. Do not BONK!

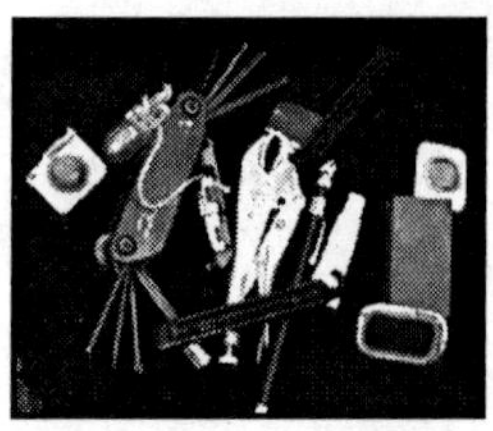

Tools

I'm a fanatic about tools. I probably bring too many. After being stuck in some desolate places without a nut or screw of the right size or thread I try to be prepared for almost anything.

There are several sections of this route where you will be more than 75 mi. (120 km.) from a bike shop. The Post Office, UPS or a friendly motorist can easily transport a vital item to your campsite or lodging.

Although bicycle shops are located in major cities and towns, hardware stores and mass merchandisers abound. Most of these *substitute* bike shops will have something you can use for an emergency repair.

See the *Tool List* and make your own selection. Tools weigh a lot! Use discretion. The newer multiple use tools are great, provided they meet your needs. Test the way your tools work before loading them into your panniers. Combine tools; unscrew or cut off parts of tools you don't think you'll need.

Three patch kits, two spare tubes, a pump, hex wrenches, and screw drivers are the bare minimum. A spare tire is unnecessary on this trip. If your tire degenerates to the point of no return, simply call the nearest bike shop and have them mail you a new one.

Personal Health & Safety

First Aid supplies are absolutely essential on a long distance tour. You can purchase ready made kits or you can assemble your own first aid supplies. Large and small adhesive gauze pads and bandages; adhesive tape; a triangular bandage; a general bacterial agent; sun screen; headache and muscle ache pills; are the basic items. At some time on a tour you will probably use all of these items. It may take two or three years before you do but you will use them!

Be familiar with the danger signs associated with heat and muscle exhaustion; dehydration; hypothermia; and just being tired. Rest. Take care of yourself. Stop riding. If necessary go to a physician or hospital for treatment.

Helmet! Helmet! Helmet! Always wear one! Even on rural roads and urban bikeways. If you have something to protect, your brains, wear a helmet. Pros wear bike helmets, amateurs don't.

Bicycles must be equipped with a rear red reflector (a flashing red rear light is OK if it also is a passive red rear reflector); a front reflector and a front light; aural warning device; and other basic safety equipment.

During the day, the rear red flashing light should be on. It helps to make you more visible to motorists. It marks you as an experienced safety conscious bicyclist.

Wear bright clothing. When riding into the sun, wear clothing which will make you very visible to vehicle drivers. A t-shirt with dark stripes or a patterned shirt is perfect. When riding with the sun at your back wear a top which will make you stand out from the scenery and sky. Use lots of reflective clothing during dusk, dawn and at night.

These safety items could save your life.

Lodging

All known bed & breakfasts and campgrounds are listed in the text with their complete address and telephone numbers. There may be some recently established lodgings which are not listed. Conversely, there may be some listed lodgings which no longer are in operation. These changes are the bane of tour guide writers and are unavoidable. I have tried to keep the listings up to date.

Consult the local tourist information office for a current lodging list if you have any questions.

Lodging facilities are not rated.

Use care to plan your overnight sojourns. Some villages and hamlets along the way simply do not have formal places to sleep. Guerrilla campers have a distinct advantage in this regard.

Maps

The maps in this book provide more than sufficient information for you to cyclotour the route circumnavigating Lake Huron.

You can purchase large scale maps at most grocery or bookstores along the route or have your hometown bookstore order them. I recommend you cut up the large sheet regional maps. You only need the panels which show the area nearest the Lake. You will save weight and space by cutting the large sheets.

People

Meeting people and speaking to them is part of the joy and accessibility of cyclotouring. Unlike the Pacific Coast Bicycle

Route, a touring bicyclist is generally a rare sight around the Great Lakes. People will ask about your trip. People will offer help. Answer their queries with delight! Provide stories. Weave tales which will make them jealous.

Public Transit

A very efficient and enjoyable way to begin and end your cyclotour is to travel to your start point or from your end point home via train, airline or an inter-city bus. Of course if you live near the Lake, just hop on your bike. This *Guide* is designed so that a cyclotourist can begin and end at any point along the route. Directions to and from the major train stations, airports and bus terminals are provided in the text.

General Public Transit Rules

Each carrier—airline, bus and train companies—has specific rules regarding the transport of bicycles. All carriers specify that bicycles must be boxed and shipped as baggage. Trains and the airlines will sell you a box at the terminal. US bus companies do not stock bike boxes or bags at their terminals. Ontario Northern bus terminals do stock bike bags.

If you are traveling to Lake Huron via public transportation then purchase the carrier's box. These boxes are designed so that you only have to turn the handlebars and remove the pedals to fit a bicycle into the box. Very simple! You **must** have your own tools. Bicycle tools are not available at any terminals.

Using the carrier's bike box assures that the carrier can not claim your box was too weak for holding a bicycle. Amtrak's bicycle boxes cost ~US$7.00; VIARail charges a standard CN $15.00; the airlines charge US$15.00.

Airlines

In general commuter airlines do <u>not</u> have facilities for the transport of bicycle boxes.

You will also have to pay an *extra* baggage charge on domestic United States and Canadian airline flights. This charge can be as high as US$ 80.00. A way of avoiding this ridiculous charge is to fly to Canada from the United States or vice versa. Airlines do not charge extra for bicycles on international flights.

Trains

Long Distance Trains

Amtrak and VIARail do not charge extra for transporting your bicycle, just for the bike box itself.

Port Huron and Sarnia are stops on the *International* train between Chicago and Toronto; a direct train goes from Chicago to Detroit; Windsor is the terminus for trains from

Toronto; and Sudbury Jct. is on the main VIARail cross Canada train route.

Amtrak and VIARail only carry bicycles in baggage cars. This is significant! Not all Amtrak and VIARail trains and stations have baggage facilities! Make certain that both your originating and terminating train and station have baggage facilities. Otherwise your bike will be at one station and you at another.

Of course you could just carry your bike on to the coach if you have a folding bicycle, a Japanese *rinko bukuro* (bicycle bag, 2m.x2 m./6 ft.x 6 ft.).

Other Trains

The Algoma Central Railway encourages bicyclists to travel on its routes North from Sault Ste. Marie, ON by having facilities for carriage of unboxed bicycles.

Bus

Bus travel presents a different problem. Greyhound-USA and Greyhound-Canada bus stations do not stock bicycle boxes. Bikes must be boxed for carriage on either Greyhound companies' buses. Ontario Northland bus terminals do stock bike bags. Although the smaller offices may not have the bags. You will have to do one of the following:

Obtain a bicycle box from a bike shop;

Construct your own box from two or more smaller boxes;

Put your (unboxed) bike into the baggage compartment when the driver's back is turned. Many drivers suddenly disappear with the implication that you should do this heinous crime!

Tandem and Recumbent Bicycles

Tandem and long wheel base recumbent bicyclists must check the carrier's rules and regulations. In general these *over size* bicycles can be transported on public transport if they are boxed. Which means more disassembly of the bicycle. A bit of astute questioning and making certain that you receive the answer in writing might be necessary.

Ah! To be back traveling in Africa (Peace Corps '66-'69) where bikes are simply placed on top of the bus or lashed to the wall of the train's baggage car. How simple! And rarely were the bikes damaged.

How to Box Your Bike

The first time I boxed my bike I did it at home. I inserted extra cardboard into the box to reinforce the long sides of the box. I double sealed all edges using reinforced packing tape. I loaded the bike filled box into my station wagon and brought it to the terminal the day before my departure. It took an interminably long time to do all this >2½ hours. What a chore!

Make life simple for yourself. Pack the box at the terminal. Allow an extra 45 minutes to pack the box.

I'm down to 15-20 minutes bike into the box time!

1. Before you start on your cyclotour take pictures of your bicycle with and without panniers. Open the panniers and take some pictures of the contents of the panniers. If any damage occurs in transit you might need these pictures to assert your claim.
2. Public transit terminals do not have bicycle tools. You will need the following tools (depending on the bolts on your bike.
   Cone wrench (pedals)
   6 mm hex wrench (stem/pedal bolt)
   Hex wrenches to loosen the brakes & for the new types of pedal & stem bolts.
   A roll or two of 2" wide filament reinforced packing tape
   Clothes line (for tying the handlebars to the top tube; and a crank arm to a chain stay).
3. Obtain a bicycle box.
4. Clearly mark the following information on four sides of the bike box. Use a black permanent marker. Write in big letters and numerals.
   Destination:
   Departure date:
   Train, bus or flight number:
   Ticket number:
   Your name:
   ↑ Pointing to the top.
5. Remove both pedals using a cone wrench. The pedals or cranks on new bikes are sometimes removed using a hex wrench. Tape or tie one crank (if not removed) to a chain stay. Put your pedals into one pannier.
6. Loosen the brake cables; loosen the stem; turn the stem or remove it so as to align the handlebars with the top tube. Wrap or tie the handlebars to the top tube or front rack.

6a. If you are transporting your bike on an airplane, reduce your tire pressure by at least half the normal tire pressure. Baggage holds on planes are not usually pressurized and the tube most likely will blow if you don't reduce the pressure.

7. Wheel the bike into the bike box.
8. Secure the bike by wedging your sleeping bag and a pannier between the bike and the box sides. Do not overload the box with heavy panniers. Carry the other panniers on to the train, plane or bus.
9. Seal the box with 2" reinforced packing tape.

10. Bring the filled bike box to the baggage room and obtain a baggage claim check. Keep the baggage claim check with you. You will not be able to claim your bike without this claim check.

At Your Destination

Claim your bicycle!

I have to preface this discussion of damage claims with the fact that my bike has never been damaged traveling via Amtrak and only once on a plane trip. Amtrak stores bikes in an upright position in its baggage cars. Airlines and bus lines store bikes on their side in baggage holds.

Check the exterior of the bicycle box for possible in transit damage. If you see any damage, to the exterior of the bike box, immediately take a picture of the damage and show the damage to the baggage personnel before you open the box.

Open the bike box. Check your bike for any damage or missing items. If damage occurred, immediately show it to the baggage personnel and complete the damage claim form.

After assembling your bike, take a short ride in the terminal to make certain there was no non-visible damage to the gearing, frame, wheels, etc. If you determine that there is some damage, immediately show it to the baggage personnel and take a picture of the damage. Ask for and complete the damage claim form.

Find a local bicycle shop (look in the phone book.) Purchase the part. Copy the receipt and make copies of your completed claim form. Send a copy of the receipt with the original claim form to the carrier. Mail home, the original receipt and one copy of the claim form. It takes 2-6 weeks for most airlines, bus lines or Amtrak to begin to settle baggage damage claims. Enjoy your cyclotour.

Postal Addresses

The proper form of addressing letters is important for your mail to arrive at its destination. The postal systems in both the USA and Canada are very automated. Barcodes are placed automatically on the bottom of envelopes and post cards. Even your handwritten addresses are optical character recognition read.

The clearer you address your letters the faster they speed to their destination. Print! Addresses should be printed in capital letters without punctuation.

Canadian Postal Codes cover a significantly smaller area than US Zip Codes. To conserve space many Postal Codes have been eliminated from the text.

Zip Codes and Postal Codes

N = Number; L = Letter

USA Zip Codes consist of five or nine numbers:

NNNNN or NNNNN-NNNN

Canadian Postal codes consist of a combination of two groups of numbers and letters separated by a space.

NLN LNL

Use two or three letters to abbreviate roadways and the State or Province.

street = ST; avenue = AVE; road = RD; drive = DR; boulevard = BLVD; *etc.*

Ontario = ON; Michigan = MI

A return address is placed in the upper left corner of the envelope.

The stamp goes on the upper right corner.

The addressee's address is centered on the envelope.

A ½ in. (1.25 cm.) blank space must be left at the bottom of the envelope or post card.

RETURN NAME
ADDRESS Postage
CITY ST NNNNN

NAME
ORGANIZATION
STREET
CITY ST NNNNN
NATION

Information Sources

Glossy tourist brochures with all sorts of information and discount coupons will be joyfully supplied by tourist information bureaus. I suggest that you write for them.

I have had to search, dig and cajole regional and local planners; transportation agencies; county and municipal officials for valid bicycling route information. I've biked around Lake Huron in both directions. A very time consuming and expensive endeavor, which is exactly why you purchased this book! You can simply cyclotour to your heart's mighty beat!

You should request bicycling information if only to make tourism officials aware that people do want to bicycle in their locality. Always request bicycling specific information and local maps. Mention that you obtained the address from *'Round Lake Huron: A Bicyclist's Tour Guide*. It helps!

If you circumnavigate the entire Lake you'll travel through many political units.

Do be careful as you cross a County border. Police may be hiding behind a billboard and if you're speeding, a ticket will be proffered. Passports are not needed when crossing County borders!

Abbreviations used in these listings: TO = Tourism Office; CVB = Convention & Visitors Bureau; CofC = Chamber of Commerce.

How to Read the Route Guide Entries

It's really easy! The entire route is divided into route segments of ~50 mi. (~80 km.)

The route descriptions are written as if you are proceeding clockwise around either Lake Huron or Georgian Bay.

At the beginning and end of each route section you will see, besides normal chapter titles, the following barred route heading:

Cyclotourists traveling **Clockwise** around Lake Huron
read the mileage on the left side of the page
downwards from the top of the page.

clockwise	**Wiarton to**	counterclockwise
↓ Read mi. (km.)	**Kincardine**	mi. (km.) Read ↑

Cyclotourists traveling **Counterclockwise**
read the mileage on the right side of the page
upwards from the bottom of the page.

The first line of an entry gives the cumulative distance in miles and kilometers (in parentheses) in either direction and a location intersection. Usually it is in the form of:

7.0 (11.3)   Hope Rd. @ M 25   37.6 (60.5)

Every effort has been made to be accurate in the distances noted. Mistakes might occur! If so, please send me a post card noting the error.

The distances are cumulative. You will have to do the subtraction to find the distances between entries.

The second line of each entry usually gives directions, Turn, Continue, Stop, Look, *etc.* and where to go. *E. g.*, Turn South on to Rt. 31. Cardinal compass directions are generally used. Left and right directions are rarely used.

Turn West on to Ferndale Rd./CR 9.

Special Instructions for Counterclockwise Cyclotourists

Travelers proceeding counterclockwise around Lake Huron are traveling in the opposite way the directions are written. Counterclockwise cyclotourists must ***reverse*** the direction provided in a text entry.

Turn North should be read as:

Turn **South**

This only becomes a problem if you have absolutely no sense of direction. Travelers rapidly get used to reading the mileage (kilometage [*sic*]) on the right side of the page and mentally reversing the directions. Use builds expertise!

Getting lost has always been a treat for me. I've discovered new and interesting routes, places and most importantly people. Think of it as part of the adventure of traveling.

The entries for cities, towns or villages with specific services appears like this:

GORE BAY

Info.:
Cycling Info.:
Services:
Attractions:
Lodging:

If there is no information then a category does not appear. State and Provincial abbreviations are not included when it is obvious which state or province applies.

Bed & breakfast and campground accommodations listings are complete with addresses and telephone numbers.

Motels are noted simply as *motel* without any other information. For motel accommodations you will have to use a phone book or write to the information source.

Restaurants are listed as, restaurant without a name.

If every bit and piece of information in my files was listed in this *Guide,* it would be more than 700 pages long and weigh over 3 lbs. (1.4 kg.). Thus a bit of research before you depart will allow you to follow the *Less is More* rule!

Of course you could be a *wanderlust* cyclotourist and let your front wheel lead you to wherever!

Segment	Mi.	Km.	Pg.
Georgian Bay Route			
Owen Sound to Tobermory	79.2	127.5	138
South Baymouth to Espanola	72.5	116.7	144
Espanola to Sudbury	45.5	73.3	148
Sudbury to Cranberry	47.4	76.3	154
Cranberry to Parry Sound	54.5	87.7	158
Parry Sound to Midland	67.8	109.2	163
Midland to Collingwood	41.0	66.0	168
Tiny Peninsula Loop	22.1	35.6	171
Collingwood to Owen Sound	39.6	63.8	178
Distance Summaries			
Michigan Segments			
Michigan Distance, using the Direct St. Ignace to Sault Ste. Marie Route	503.7	811.0	
Michigan Distance, using the Drummond Island Route	582.4	937.2	
Ontario Segments			
Ontario Distance using the Direct Manitoulin Island Route	437.9	705.0	
Ontario Distance using the Manitoulin Island Scenic Tour	578.1	930.4	
Main Lake Huron Distance using the Direct routes	941.6	1516.0	
Main Lake Huron Distance using Drummond Island & Manitoulin Island Routes	1160.5	1867.6	
Georgian Bay Route (Direct)	447.5	720.5	
Total Distance Summaries			
Total Distance using Direct Routes	1389.1	2235.5	
Total Distance using Drummond Island & Manitoulin Island Routes	1608.0	2589.8	

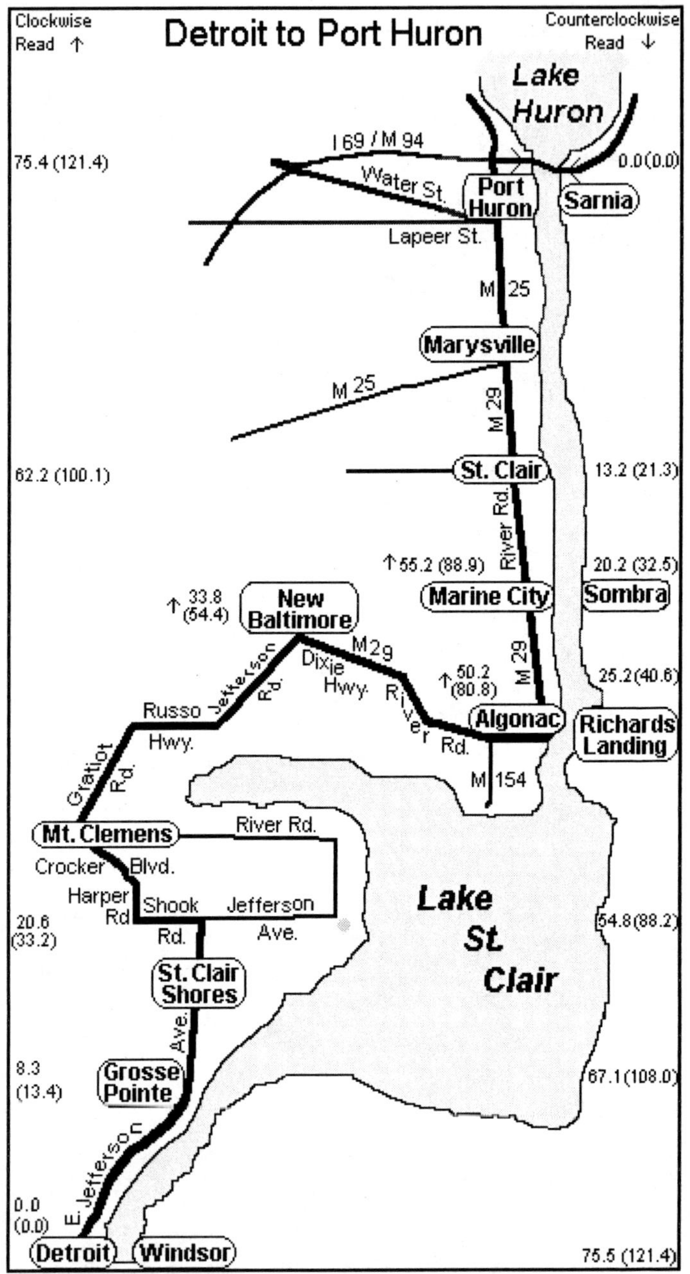
Clockwise Read ↑
Detroit to Port Huron
Counterclockwise Read ↓
Lake Huron
I 69 / M 94
75.4 (121.4)
0.0 (0.0)
Water St.
Port Huron
Sarnia
Lapeer St.
M 25
Marysville
M 25
M 29
62.2 (100.1)
St. Clair
13.2 (21.3)
River Rd.
↑55.2 (88.9)
20.2 (32.5)
↑33.8 (54.4)
New Baltimore
Marine City
Sombra
Jefferson Rd.
M 29
Dixie Hwy.
River Rd.
↑50.2 (80.8)
M 29
25.2 (40.6)
Russo Hwy.
Algonac
Richards Landing
Gratiot Rd.
M 154
Mt. Clemens
River Rd.
Crocker Blvd.
Harper Rd
Shook Rd.
Jefferson Ave.
20.6 (33.2)
Lake St. Clair
54.8 (88.2)
St. Clair Shores
Ave.
8.3 (13.4)
Grosse Pointe
67.1 (108.0)
E. Jefferson
0.0 (0.0)
Detroit
Windsor
75.5 (121.4)

DETROIT TO PORT HURON and SARNIA

Clockwise ↓ Read mi. (km.)	**Detroit to Port Huron**	Counterclockwise mi. (km.) Read ↑

Travelers Note: Highway Terminology

State maintained roads in Michigan are termed *M* __. Highways maintained with the use of United States federal government funds are termed *US* __ or I __. County maintained roads are abbreviated *CR* __.

0.0 (0.0)	Woodward Ave. @ E. Jefferson Ave.	75.4 (121.4)

Travel East on E. Jefferson Ave.

DETROIT

Info.: Detroit Metro CVB, 211 W. Fort St., Ste. 1000, Detroit MI 48226, 800 338-7647/313 202-1800, www.visitdetroit.com. Area Code: 313 unless otherwise noted. Zip Codes: Various. Windsor information is in the *Sarnia to Windsor* segment.

Services: All. Bike shops are mostly in the suburbs.

Transportation: It is difficult going by bike from Detroit MI to Windsor ON. Neither the Ambassador Bridge nor the Detroit Windsor Tunnel permit bicycles on their roadways. Buses which do use the Bridge and Tunnel do not have bike racks. Transit Windsor has a bus which is capable of transporting bicycles through the Tunnel. However this bus is inoperable. The Bridge Authority does have a pick up truck to transport you across the River, call: 849-5244. Telephone the following sources to acertain the availability a means to transport you and your bike across the Detroit River to Windsor. Transit Windsor, 519 944-4111; Detroit-Windsor Tunnel, 567-4422x200; Detroit DOT (local bus), 933-1300.
Amtrak, 11 W. Baltimore, 873-3442.

Attractions: Contrary to its reputation as a city devoid of attractions, Detroit is a great place to visit.

The Arts: Detroit Opera House, 1526 Broadway, 237-7464; Detroit Symphony Orchestra Hall, 3711 Woodward Ave., 576-5111; Fisher Theatre, Fisher Bldg., 872-1000; Gem Theatre, 333 Madison Ave., 963-9800.

Museums: African Bead Mus., 6559 Grand River, 899-1626; Automotive Hall of Fame, 21400 Oakwood Blvd., 240-4000; Charles H. Wright Mus. of African American Hist., 315 E. Warren Ave., 494-5800; Detroit Hist. Mus., 5401 Woodward Ave., 833-1805; Detroit Inst. of Arts, 5200 Woodward Ave.,

833-7900; Detroit Sci. Ctr., 5020 John R. St., 577-8400; Dossin Great Lakes Mus., 100 Strand Dr., Belle Isle, 852-4051; Gospel Music Hall of Fame, 18301 W. McNichols, 592-0017; Historic Fort Wayne, 6325 W. Jefferson Ave., 297-9360; International Inst. of Detroit, 111 E. Kirby, 871-8600; Motown Hist. Mus., 2648 W. Grand Blvd., 875-2264. Gardens: Anna Scripps Whitcomb Cons., Belle Isle, 852-4054; Moross House/Detroit Garden Ctr., 1460 E. Jefferson Ave., 259-6363.

Parks: Huron-Clinton MetroParks, 13000 High Ridge Dr., Brighton MI, 810 227-2757; Belle Isle Pk., Brdg. at Grand St. & Detroit R. (on your way to Port Huron), 852-4078.

Special Events: Many street festivals. International Freedom Fest., Downtown Detroit & Windsor, 923-8259; Detroit Jazz Fest., Hart Plz., 963-7622; Michigan St. Fair, Fairgrounds, 369-8250; Auto Grand Prix of Detroit, Belle Isle, 870-7223.

Sports: Tigers Baseball, 2100 Woodward Ave., 471-2555; Rockers Soccer, 2 Championship Dr., Auburn Hills, 248 366-6254; Football; basketball, hockey, harness racing.

Other: Greektown Entertainment Area; Eastern Outdoor Mkt., 2934 Russell St., 833-1560.

Nearby Attractions: Detroit Zoo, 8450 W. 10 Mile Rd., Royal Oak, 248 398-0900; Cranbrook Art Mus. & Sci. Ctr., 1221 N. Woodward Ave., Bloomfield Hills, 877 462-7222; Walter P. Chrysler Mus., 1 Chrysler Dr., Auburn Hills, 248 944-0001; Henry Ford Mus. & Greenfield Village, 20900 Oakwood Blvd., Dearborn, 271-1570; Holocaust Mem. Ctr., 6602 W. Maple Rd., W. Bloomfield, 248 661-0840; Michigan Renaissance Fest., 800 601-4848; Yankee Air Mus., 734 483-4030.

Lodging: Downtown, hotels and motels.

8.3 (13.4) E. Jefferson Ave. 67.1 (108.0)
@ Lake Shore Dr.

Continue traveling Northeast on Lake Shore Dr.

GROSSE POINTE

Info.: Grosse Pointe, Grosse Pointe Shores & Grosse Pointe Woods. www.thevillagegp.com; www.grossepoint.com.

Services: Bike shop in Grosse Pointe Woods. Grocery.

Attraction: Edsel & Eleanor Ford House, 1100 Lake Shore Rd., Grosse Point Shores, 313 884-4222.

12.7 (20.4) Lake Shore Dr. 62.7 (100.9)
@ Jefferson Ave.

Continue traveling on Lake Shore Dr./Jefferson Ave. The road's name changes as you enter Macomb Co.

16.2 (26.1) 11 Mile Rd. @ Jefferson Ave. 59.2 (95.3)
Continue traveling North on Jefferson Ave.
Info.: City of St. Clair Shores, 27600 Jefferson Cir., St. Clair Shores 48081.

20.6 (33.2) Shook Rd. @ Jefferson Ave. 54.8 (88.2)
Turn West on to Shook Rd. to go into Mt. Clemens.
Use Jefferson Ave. to go to Metro Beach Park

21.4 (34.5) Harper Rd. @ Shook Rd. 54.0 (86.9)
Turn North on to Harper Rd.

23.3 (37.5) Crocker Blvd. @ Harper Rd. 52.1 (83.9)
Turn Northwest on to Crocker Blvd.

24.1 (38.8) Gratiot Rd. @ M 3/Crocker Blvd. 51.3 (82.6)
Turn North on to Gratiot Rd.

MT. CLEMENS

Info.: Macomb Co. Dep't of Eco. Development, Admin. Bldg., Mt. Clemens 48043, 810 469-5285.
Services: Grocery & other retail stores.
Attractions: Michigan Transit Mus., Railroad Depot, 463-1863; Macomb Performing Arts Ctr., 44575 Garfield Rd.
Lodging: Motel.

24.3 (39.1) North River Rd. @ Gratiot Rd. 51.1 (82.3)
Continue traveling on Gratiot Rd.
St. Clair Metro Beach turn off bikers rejoin us here.

26.7 (43.0) Hall Rd./Russo Hwy. @ Gratiot Rd. 48.7 (78.4)
Turn East on to Hall Rd./Russo Hwy.

28.5 (45.9) Jefferson Rd. @ Russo Hwy. 46.9 (75.5)
Turn North on to Jefferson Rd.
You're back at the Lake Huron shore line.

33.8 (54.4) M 29 @ Jefferson Rd. 41.6 (67.0)

Turn East on to M 29.

35.1 (56.5) County Line Rd. @ M 29/Green St./Dixie Hwy. 40.3 (64.9)

Continue traveling on M 29. M 29 becomes Dixie Hwy. and then River Rd. going East from New Baltimore.
NEW BALTIMORE: **Lodging:** Motels.

50.2 (80.8) Algonac St. Pk. @ M 29 25.2 (40.6)

Continue traveling on M. 29/River Rd.
At Algonac, M 29/River Rd. turns North.
Side Route: 12.1 mi. (3.4 km.) SW of Algonac M 154, leads you 5.8 mi. (9.3 km.) to the end of a peninsula through the Clair Flats Wildlife Area.

ALGONAC

Services: Transportation: Ferry to Roberts Landing/ Walpole Is. ON is just North of Algonac St. Pk. Use this ferry or the one at Marine City if you are planning to cyclotour counterclockwise around the Lake. See Pt. Huron/Sarnia information about the Blue Water Bridge.
Attractions: Algonac/Clay Twp. Hist. Mus., 1240 St. Clair Dr., 810 794-9015; Algonac Theater, 810 794-2522.
Lodging: Motels. Camping: Algonac St. Pk., 8732 River Rd., 810 465-2160; River View, M 29, 810 794-0182.

55.2 (88.9) Plank Rd. @ M 29/River Rd. 20.2 (32.5)

Continue on M 29.

MARINE CITY

Info.: Marine City, 300 Broadway St., Marine City 48039.
Services: Transportation: Ferry to Sombra ON. If you are planning to travel counterclockwise around Lake Huron then cross the St. Clair River via the Marine City-Sombra Ferry or the Algonac-Walpole Is. Ferry. Then use the *Saria to Windsor* segment from Sombra.
Attractions: Museum.
Lodging: Motels. B&B: Heather House, 409 N. Main St., 810 765-3175.

62.2 (100.1) Rattle Run @ M 29/River Rd. 13.2 (21.3)

Continue traveling on M 29/River Rd.

ST. CLAIR

Attractions: St. Clair Hist. Mus., 308 S. 4th St. 810 329-6888.
Lodging: Motels. B&Bs: Clairmont House, 147 Brown St., 329-0047; Murphy Inn, 505 Clinton Ave., 329-7118; William Hopkins Manor, 613 N. Riverside, 329-0188.

65.7 (105.8) M 29 Jct. River Rd. 9.7 (15.6)
Southern Jct. point of River Rd. & M 29.
Either bear towards the Lake on to River Rd.
Or continue traveling on M 29.
68.9 (110.9) River Rd. Jct. M 29 6.5 (10.5)
Northern Jct. point of River Rd. & M 29.
Either bear towards the Lake on to River Rd.
Or continue traveling on M 29.

69.4 (111.7) M 29 Jct. M 25 6.0 (9.7)
Clockwise: Continue North bound on M 25.
Counterclockwise:: Continue South bound on M 29.
MARYSVILLE: **Attraction:** Hist. Mus. **Lodging:** Motels.

73.4 (118.2) Lapeer St. @ M 25/River Rd. 2.0 (3.2)
Continue traveling North to the Blue Water Bridges.
Actually you're in the heart of Port Huron.

Travelers Note

Transportation: Blue Water Bridge, 519 336-2720, www.bwba.org. The rules for having the Bluewater Bridge Authority help you cross the Bridge are: 1. You must be a *bona fide* tourist. 2. You must show a picture identification of your residence. The Authority suggests you use the ferry between Sombra, ON and Marine City, MI which is ~20mi. (~32 km.) South of where you are standing. No joke! They really suggested this to me.
My usual way of crossing a bridge who's operating authority has such an attitude is to stand at entrance to the highway leading to the Bridge and try to hitch a ride.
The Michigan DOT does have a pickup truck to transport you across this Bridge. Call 313 984-3131.

74.5 (119.9) M 136 @ M 25 0.9 (1.4)
Continue traveling North on M 25.

75.4 (121.4) Blue Water Bridges @ M 25 0.0 (0.0)
Hey! You're at the Southern end of Lake Huron.
Port Huron MI information in the *Port Huron to Harbor Beach* segment.
Sarnia ON information in the *Grand Bend to Sarnia* segment.

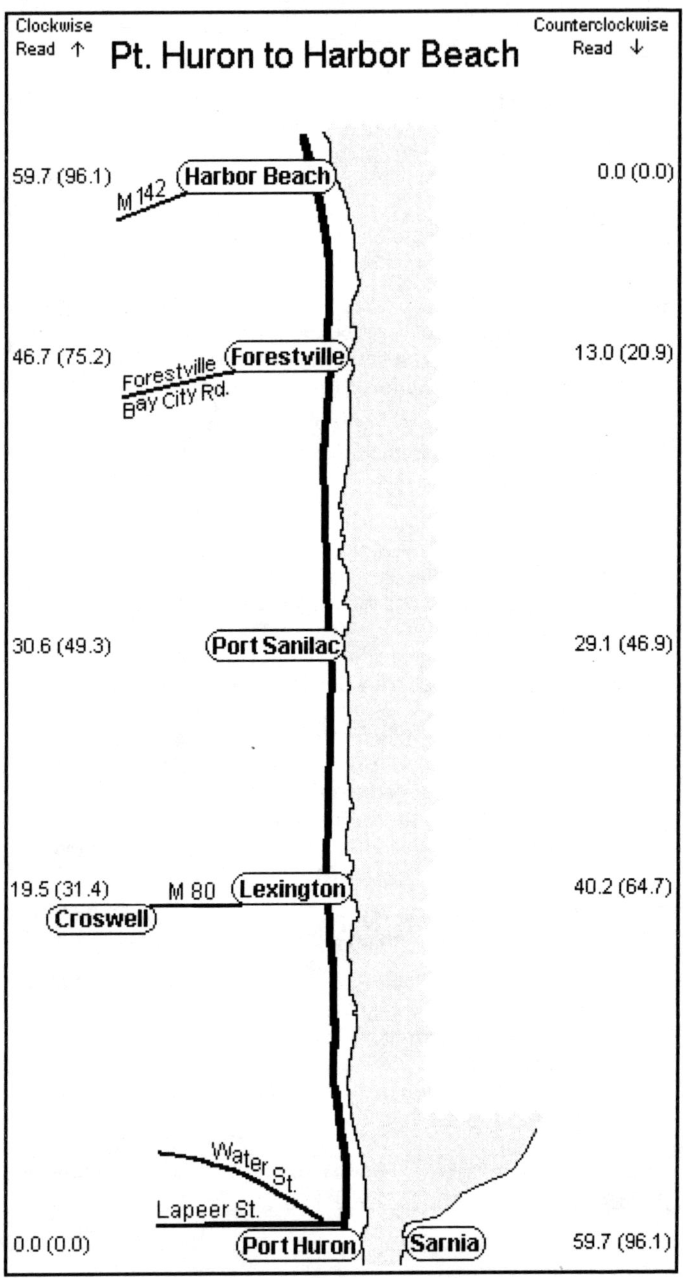
Clockwise
Read ↑
Pt. Huron to Harbor Beach
Counterclockwise
Read ↓
59.7 (96.1)
M 142
Harbor Beach
0.0 (0.0)
46.7 (75.2)
Forestville
Bay City Rd.
Forestville
13.0 (20.9)
30.6 (49.3)
Port Sanilac
29.1 (46.9)
19.5 (31.4)
M 80
Lexington
40.2 (64.7)
Croswell
Water St.
Lapeer St.
0.0 (0.0)
Port Huron
Sarnia
59.7 (96.1)

PORT HURON TO HARBOR BEACH

Clockwise ↓ Read mi. (km.)	**Port Huron to Harbor Beach**	Counterclockwise mi. (km.) Read ↑
0.0 (0.0)	Blue Water Bridge @ M 25	59.7 (96.1)

Travel North on M 25/Lake Shore Park Dr.

Travelers Note

For the next 30 mi. (48 km.) there are limited facilities along M 25. This is rural America. The Michigan DOT describes this section of M 25 as heavily trafficked. It isn't except on the weekends. Use care.

PORT HURON

Info.: Blue Water CVB, 520 Thomas Edison Pkwy., Port Huron MI 48060, 810 987-1441, www.bluewater.org; Downtown Port Huron, 985-8843. Area code: 810. Zip code: 48060.

Port Huron is across the St. Clair River from Sarnia. Sarnia Listings are in the *Grand Bend to Sarnia Segment.*

Services: All. Bike shop.

Transportation: Blue Water Bridge Authority, 519 336-2720, www.bwba.org. The Authority or the Michigan DOT (313 984-3131) will provide transportation across the Bridge. The rules for having the Authority help you cross the Bridge are: 1. You must be a *bona fide* tourist. 2. You must show a picture identification of your residence. The Blue Water Bridge suggests you use the Ferry between Marine City, MI and Sombra, ON which is ~32 km. (~20mi.) South of where you are standing. No joke!

My usual way of crossing a bridge who's operating Authority have failed to make arrangements for bicyclists and pedestrians is to stand at entrance to the highway leading to the Bridge and try to hitch a ride. It usually works.

Attractions: Port Huron Mus. 1116 6th St., 982-0891; Knowlton's Ice Mus., 1665 Yeager St., 987-7100; U. S. Coast Guard Cutter *Bramble*, Pine Grove Pk., 982-2684; Huron Lighthouse, Garfield St., 385-7387; Thomas Edison Depot, 500 Thomas Edison Pkwy., 987-8687; International Symphony Orchestra, 984-8857. Charter and tour boats. Lightship. Port Huron to Mackinaw Sail Boat Race.

Lodging: If you are planning to be in either Pt. Huron or Sarnia during Race weekend, usually the 2nd weekend in July, book accommodations at least 4 months in advance. This applies to Mackinaw City and Mackinac Island too.

Motels. B&Bs: Davidson House, 1707 Military, 987-3922; Hill Estate, 602 Lakeview, 982-8187; Victorian Inn, 1229 7th St., 984-1437. Camping: Lakeport St. Pk., M 25, 327-6224.

8.7 (14.0) Burtch Rd. @ M 25/Lake Shore Park Rd. 51.0 (82.1)

Continue traveling on M 25.
LAKEPORT: Lakeport St. Pk., M 25, 810 327-6224.

19.5 (31.4) M 90 @ M 25/Lake Shore Rd. 40.2 (64.7)

Continue traveling on M 25.
Turn East on to M 90 to go to Croswell, 4.5 mi. (7.2 km.)

LEXINGTON - CROSWELL

Info.: Lexington-Croswell CofC, PO Box 142, Lexington MI 48450, 810 359-2262, www.cros-lex-chamber.com. City of Croswell, 100 N. Howard St., Croswell MI 48422, 810 679-2299, www.croswell-mich.com. Area Code: 810. Zip codes: Lexington, 48450; Croswell, 48422.
Services: Groceries, restaurants, retail shops.
Lodging: Lexington: Motels. B&Bs: Governor's Inn, 7277 Simons St., 359-5770; Inn the Garden, 7156 Huron Ave., 359-8966; Powell House, 5076 Lakeshore Rd., 359-5533; Primrose Manor, 6740 Peck Rd., 359-2686. Camping: Lakeport St. Pk., 11 mi. (17.7 km.) S. of Lexington, 327-6224; Sanilac Co. Pk. Lexington, 3 mi. (5 km.) N. of town, 359-7473. **Croswell:** Motels.

30.6 (49.3) M 46 @ M 25 29.1 (46.9)

Continue traveling on M 25.
PORT SANILAC: B&B: The Raymond House Inn, 111 S Ridge St., 810 622-8800. Camping: Sanilac Co. Pk., 6.5 mi. (10.5 km.) N. of Pt. Sanilac, 810 622-8715.

46.7 (75.2) Bay City-Forestville Rd. @ M 25 13.0 (20.9)

Continue traveling on M 25.
FORESTVILLE
See the *Cross the Thumb Route* after the Harbor Beach entries.

59.7 (96.1) Section Line Rd. @ M 25/Lake Shore Rd. 0.0 (0.0)

Continue traveling on M 25/Lake Shore Rd.

HARBOR BEACH

Info.: Harbor Beach CofC, PO Box 113, Harbor Beach MI 48441, 800 426-4245/517 479-6477.
www.harborbeachchamber.com.
Area code: 517. Zip code: 48441.

Janis Kellogg

Attractions: Grice House Mus.; Murals, State St. & Huron Ave.; Murphy House Mus.

Lodging: Motels. B&Bs: Deborah's Wellock Inn, 404 S Huron Ave.; Jill's International, 203 State St.; State Street Inn, 646 State St. Camping: North Pk., 836 N. Huron Ave. (M 25), 479-9554; Wagener Co. Pk., 2761 S. Lakeshore Rd. (M 35, 5 mi. (8 km.) N. of Town), 479-9131.

Clockwise ↓ Read mi. (km.)	**Port Huron to Harbor Beach**	Counterclockwise mi. (km.) Read ↑

Clockwise ↓ Read mi. (km.)	**Cross the Thumb Route** **Harbor Beach to Caseville**	Counterclockwise mi. (km.) Read ↑

Travelers Note

$a^2 + b^2 = c^2$, Pythagagoras was right! The *thumb* of the *mitten* (Lower Peninsula of Michigan) can be crossed several ways.
You could turn West here in Harbor Beach, using M 142 and to go to Bay Port; continue North along the eastern shore to Port Hope, turn West there on to Kinde Rd. and go to Caseville; or use the *Cross the Thumb Route.*
You will save ~50 mi. (80 km.) following this route.
You will miss beautiful lakeshore sights and interesting villages by cutting across the peninsula.

0.0 (0.0)	M 25/Lake Shore Rd. @ Bay City - Forestville Rd.	43.2 (69.6)

Turn East on to Bay City - Forestville Rd.

3.8 (6.1)	Charleston Rd. @ Bay City - Forestville Rd.	39.4 (63.4)

Bay City - Forestville Rd. makes a Northwest turn here. Follow the road!

5.0 (8.1)	Potts Rd. @ Bay City - Forestville Rd.	38.2 (61.5)

Turn West, following Bay City - Forestville Rd.

43.2 (69.6)	M 25 @ Bay City - Forestville Rd.	0.0 (0.0)

Continue traveling West on M 25.
Counterclockwise travelers can use this peninsula to cross the thumb's tip!
The main *Port Huron to Harbor Beach Segment* is before the *Cross theThumb Route.*

Clockwise ↓ Read mi. (km.)	**Cross the Thumb Route** **Caseville to Harbor Beach**	Counterclockwise mi. (km.) Read ↑

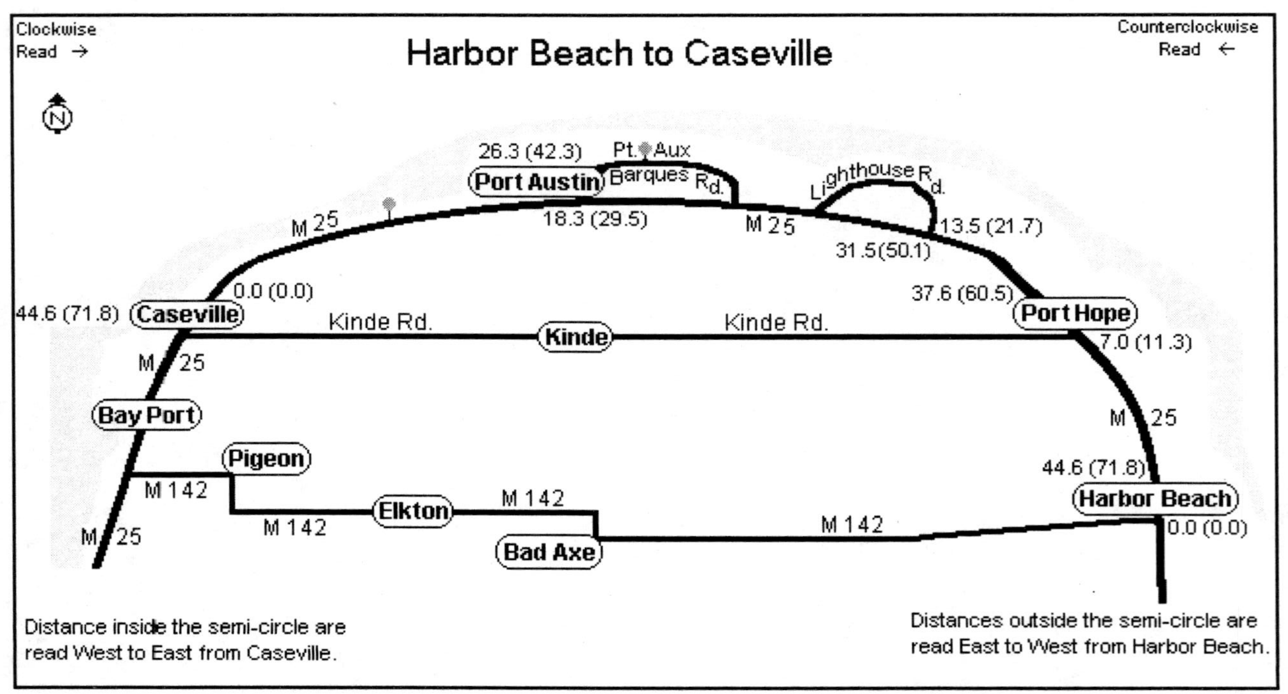

Clockwise Read →
Harbor Beach to Caseville
Counterclockwise Read ←
26.3 (42.3)
Pt. Aux Barques Rd.
Port Austin
Lighthouse Rd.
M 25
18.3 (29.5)
M 25
13.5 (21.7)
31.5(50.1)
0.0 (0.0)
37.6 (60.5)
44.6 (71.8)
Caseville
Kinde Rd.
Kinde
Kinde Rd.
Port Hope
7.0 (11.3)
M 25
Bay Port
M 25
Pigeon
44.6 (71.8)
M 142
Harbor Beach
M 142
Elkton
M 142
M 142
0.0 (0.0)
M 25
Bad Axe
Distance inside the semi-circle are read West to East from Caseville.
Distances outside the semi-circle are read East to West from Harbor Beach.

HARBOR BEACH TO CASEVILLE

Clockwise ↓ Read mi. (km.)	**Harbor Beach to Caseville**	Counterclockwise mi. (km.) Read ↑

0.0 (0.0) Section Line Rd. @ M 25/Lake Shore Rd. 44.6 (71.8)

Travel North on M 25/Lakeshore Rd.
HARBOR BEACH information is in the *Port Huron to Harbor Beach* segment.

7.0 (11.3) Hope Rd. @ M 25 37.6 (60.5)

Continue traveling on M 25.
If you want to skip rounding the top of the thumb's peninsula, turn West on to Kinde Rd., .5 mi. (.8 km.) North of this intersection.

PORT HOPE

Info.: 800 358-4862/517 428-4882.
Area code: 517. Zip code: 48468.
Lodging: Motels. B&B: Stafford House, 4489 Main St., 428-4554. Camping: Stafford Co. Pk., 4451 Huron St. (M 25), 428-4213; Lighthouse Co. Pk., 7320 Lighthouse Rd., 428-4749.

13.5 (21.7) Lighthouse Rd. @ M 25/Lake Shore Rd. 31.1 (50.1)

Continue traveling on M 25.
Or turn Northeast on to Lighthouse Rd. to circle around past the Lighthouse.

16.8 (27.0) Lighthouse Rd. (N.) @ M 25/Grindstone Rd. 27.8 (44.8)

Continue traveling on M 25.
Counterclockwise cyclotourists can turn on to Lighthouse Rd. to circle around the lighthouse.

19.5 (31.4) Pearson Rd. @ M 25/Grindstone Rd. 25.1 (40.4)

Turn North on to Pearson Rd. to go to the very top of peninsula. Hey! Since you're here, you might as well go to Pt. Aux Boes. The distance is about the same as traveling on M 25.
Or continue traveling West on M 25.

20.0 (32.2) Pt. Aux Barques Rd. @ Pearson Rd. 24.6 (39.6)
Turn West on to Pt. Aux Barques Rd.

23.2 (37.4) Point Rd. @ Pt. Aux Barques Rd. 21.4 (34.5)
Turn North and round the Point. Lighthouse.

24.1 (38.8) Pt. Aux Barques Rd. @ Point Rd. 20.5 (33.0)
Turn West on to Pt. Aux Barques Rd.

26.3 (42.3) M 25/Pt. Austin Rd. @ Pt. Aux Barques Rd. 18.3 (29.5)
Continue traveling West on to M 25/Port Austin Rd.

PORT AUSTIN & HURON CITY

Info.: Greater Port Austin CofC, PO Box 274, Port Austin MI 48467, 517 738-7600. Area code: 517. Zip: 48467.
Services: Grocery, restaurants and other retail stores.
Attractions: Huron City Mus., 7930 Huron City Rd., 428-4123. Lighthouse. Pt. Austin Community Playhouse, 738-5217. Charter boats. Fishing.
Lodging: Motels. B&Bs: Lake Street Manor, 8569 Lake St., 738-7720; Garfield Inn, 8544 Lake St., 373-5254; Whalens, 3373 Pte. Aux Barques Rd., Grindstone City MI 48467, 738-7664. Camping: Pt. Austin KOA, 8195 N. Van Dyke, 738-2267; Pt. Crescent St. Pk., 1775 Pt. Austin Rd., 5 mi. (8 km.) SW, 738-8663; Oak Beach Co. Pk., 3356 Pt. Austin Rd., 5 mi. (8 km.) SW, 856-2344.

39.2 (63.1) Albert E. Sleeper St. Pk. @ M 25 5.4 (8.7)
Continue traveling on M 25/Pt. Austin Rd. Albert E. Sleeper St. Pk., 6573 St. Pk. Rd., Caseville 48725, 517 856-4411.

43.8 (70.5) Sand Rd. @ M 25 0.8 (1.3)
Continue traveling on M 25.

44.6 (71.8) Kinde Rd. @ M 25/Port Austin Rd. 0.0 (0.0)
We'll take a break here. If you're hearty then continue cycling into the next chapter.
Counterclockwise travelers: If you want to cut off some distance you can travel due East on Kinde Rd. to Port Hope. You really will not save much distance and you'll miss the top of the peninsula!

CASEVILLE

Info.: Caseville CofC, PO Box 122, Caseville MI 48725, 800 606-1347/517 856-3818, www.tourmichigan.com/~chamber. Area code: 517. Zip: 48725,

Services: Grocery, restaurants and other retail stores.
Attractions: Charity Island Light via North Star Ferry, 846-4992. Fishing.
Lodging: Motels and resorts. B&Bs: Farmstead Inn, 5048 Conkey Rd., 856-3110; Bella Vista Inn, 6024 Port Austin Rd., 856-2650; Country Charm Farm, Conkey Rd., 856-2170. Camping: Caseville Co. Pk., 6400 Main St., 856-2080; Sleeper St. Pk., 6573 St. Pk. Rd., 856-4411.

Clockwise ↓ Read mi. (km.)	**Caseville to Harbor Beach**	Counterclockwise mi. (km.) Read ↓

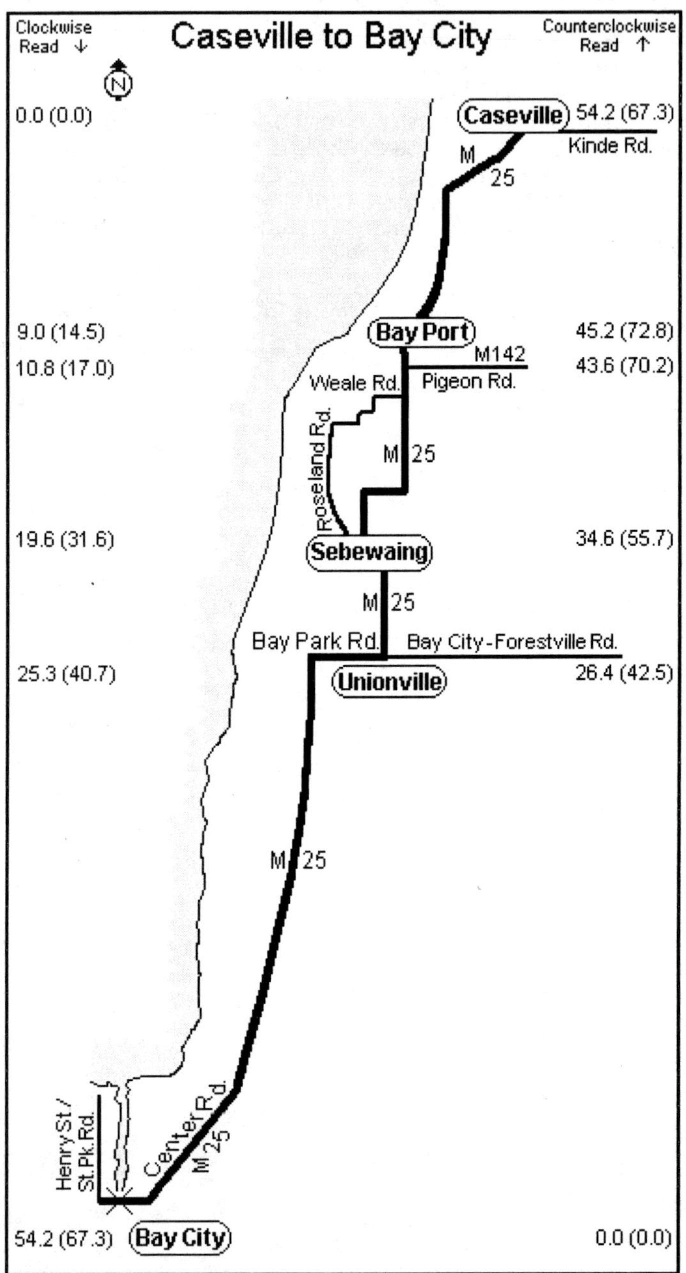

Clockwise Read ↓
Caseville to Bay City
Counterclockwise Read ↑
N
0.0 (0.0)
Caseville
54.2 (67.3)
Kinde Rd.
M 25
9.0 (14.5)
Bay Port
45.2 (72.8)
10.8 (17.0)
M142
Pigeon Rd.
43.6 (70.2)
Weale Rd.
Roseland Rd.
M 25
19.6 (31.6)
Sebewaing
34.6 (55.7)
M 25
Bay Park Rd.
Bay City-Forestville Rd.
25.3 (40.7)
Unionville
26.4 (42.5)
M 25
Center Rd.
M 25
Henry St / St.Pk.Rd.
54.2 (67.3)
Bay City
0.0 (0.0)

CASEVILLE TO BAY CITY

Clockwise ↓ Read mi. (km.)	**Caseville to Bay City**	Counterclockwise mi. (km.) Read ↑

0.0 (0.0) Kinde Rd. @ M 25/Port Austin Rd. 54.2 (87.3)

Travel South on M 25/Port Austin Rd.

CASEVILLE information is in the *Harbor Beach to Caseville* segment.

Counterclockwise travelers can cross the *Thumb* by riding due East on Kinde Rd. You'll emerge on the East side of the peninsula in Port Hope on M 25.

3.0 (4.8) Crescent Beach Rd. @ M 25 51.2 (82.4)

Continue traveling on M 25.

Or turn West on to Crescent Beach Rd. to go to Sand Point. It's a 7.6 mi. (12 km.) round trip to the Point.

9.0 (14.5) M 25/Unionville Rd. @ M 25/Port Austin Rd. 45.2 (72.8)

Continue traveling on M 25. Just a road name change.

BAY PORT

Info.: Bay Port CofC, P.O. Box 188, Bay Port MI 48720, 517 453-0109. Area code: 517. Zip: 48720.

Lodging: Motels. B&B: Bayview Country Inn, 9695 Cedar St., 656-9952.

10.6 (17.0) M 142/Pigeon Rd. @ M 25 43.6 (70.2)

Continue cycling on M 25.

M 142 goes East across the *Thumb* through the Villages of PIGEON & BAD AXE: Pigeon CofC, PO Box 618, Pigeon MI, 517 453-2733; Bad Axe CofC, 517 269-7661.

11.4 (18.4) Weale Rd. @ M 25/Unionville Rd. 42.8 (68.9)

Continue traveling on M 25.

Or take the scenic route close to the Lake's shore by turning West here and then at the shore line, follow a zig zag pattern: West on Weale to South on Kuhl Rd. to West on Geiger Rd. to South on Rose Ridge Rd. to West on Haist Rd. to South on Rose Land Rd. finally re-emerging on M 25 in Sebewaing. The distance is about the same as the direct route.

14.4 (23.2) M 25/Dotcher Rd. @ M 25/Unionville Rd. 39.8 (64.1)

Continue traveling on M 25 no matter what it is called.

18.9 (30.4) Rose Land Rd. @ M 25/Canboro Rd. 35.3 (56.8)

Continue on M 25.

Counterclockwise travelers can use the on the waterfront route via Rose Land Rd. to Weale Rd.

19.1 (30.8) M 25/Unionville Rd. @ M 25 35.1 (56.5)

Follow M 25 into Sebewaing.

19.6 (31.6) Gremel Rd. @ M 25/Unionville Rd. 34.6 (55.7)

Continue on M 25.

SEBEWAING

Info.: Sebewaing CofC, 4 N. Center St., Sebewaing MI 48759. Area code: 517. Zip: 48759

Services: Grocery, restaurants and other shops.

Attractions: Museums: Great Lakes Lore Maritime Mus.; Sebewaing Hist. Soc. Mus.; Immanuel Mission; The Mast one-room school; Heidleberg Art Gallery. Fishing.

Lodging: Motels. B&B: Antique Inn, 4 N. Center St., 883-9424, www.antiqueinn.com; Tree Haven, 883-2450.

25.3 (40.7) M 25/Bay Park Rd. @ M 25/Unionville Rd. 28.9 (46.5)

Continue on M 25.

Cyclists who crossed the *Thumb* via Bay City - Forestville Rd. join us here.

Counterclockwise travelers can cross the *Thumb* by traveling due East on Bay City - Forestville Rd. They'll emerge on the East side of the *Thumb* at *Forestville* on M 25/Lakeshore Rd..

UNIONVILLE

27.8 (44.8) M 25 @ M 25/Bay Park Rd. 26.4 (42.5)

M 25 turns Southwest at this point.

42.4 (68.3) M 25 @ M 25/Center Ave. 11.8 (19.0)

Follow the M 25 signs into Bay City.

48.3 (77.8) M 25/Center Ave. @ Madison St. 5.9 (9.5)
Turn South on to Madison Ave. You are in the center of Bay City, the directions continue for a few more miles to Bay City State Park.

BAY CITY

Info.: Bay Area CofC, 517 893-4567, 901 Saginaw St., 893-3586/893-3573, www.baycityarea.com; Downtown Bay City, www.downtownbaycity.com.
Area code: 517. Zip: 48708.
Services: All. Bike shop.
Attractions: Appledore Tall Ship, 5th St. & Saginaw River, 893-1222; Bay Co. Hist. Mus., 321 Washington Ave., 893-5733; Bay City Arts Center, 901 Water St., 894-2323; Bay City Players, 1214 Columbus Ave., 893-5555; Delta College Planetarium, 100 Center Ave., 667-2260.
Lodging: Motels. B&Bs: Clements Inn, 1712 Center Ave., 894-4600; Keswick Manor, 1800 Center Ave., 893-6598; Stonehedge Inn, 924 Center Ave., 864-4342.
Camping: Bay City St. Rec. Area, M 247, 5 mi. N of Town, 231 864-3814.

48.7 (78.4) 7th St. @ Madison Ave.. 5.5 (8.9)
Turn West on to 7th St.
Cross the Saginaw River via the Bridge.

49.3 (79.4) Henry Rd. @ M 25 Brdg. West side 4.9 (7.9)
Turn North on to Henry St.

51.2 (82.4) Wilder Ave. @ Henry Rd./State Park Rd. 3.0 (4.8)
Continue traveling on State Park Rd./Henry St. It's the same street just the name changes North of Wilder Ave.

54.2 (87.3) Beaver Rd. @ State Park Rd. Bay City St. Pk. @ Lake Huron 0.0 (0.0)

Clockwise ↓ Read mi. (km.)	**Bay City to Caseville**	Counterclockwise mi. (km.) Read ↑

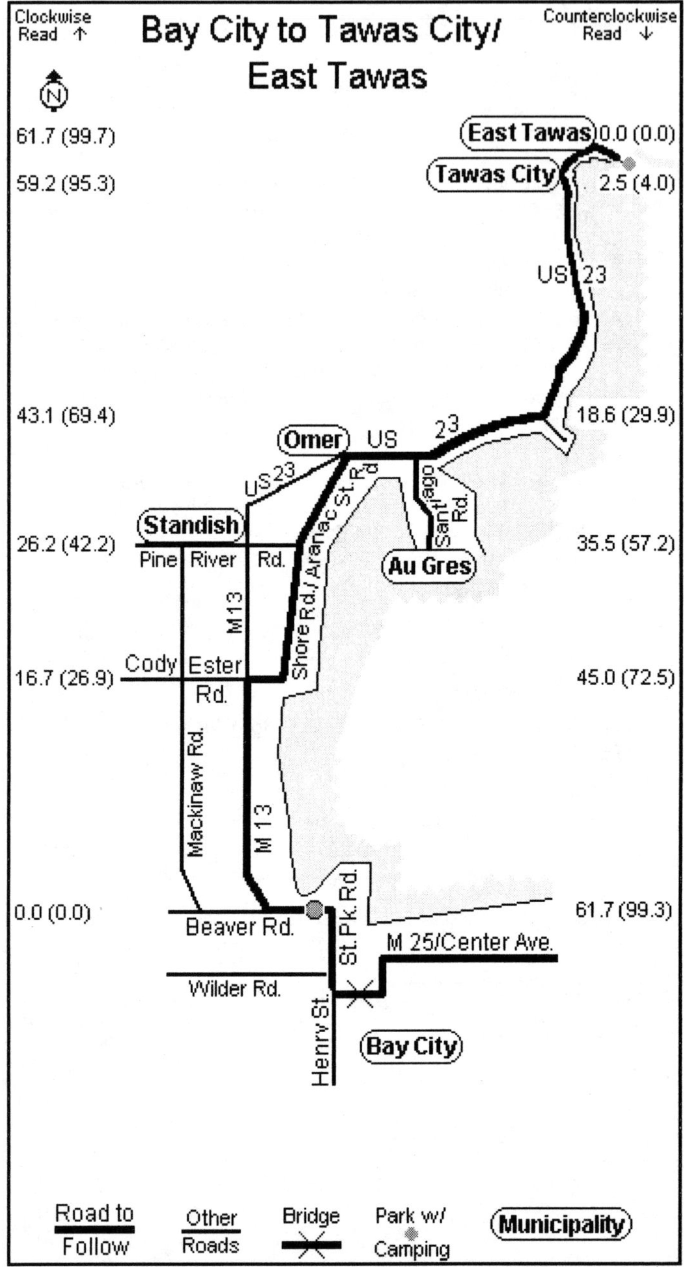
Clockwise Read ↑
Bay City to Tawas City/ East Tawas
Counterclockwise Read ↓
N
61.7 (99.7)
East Tawas
0.0 (0.0)
59.2 (95.3)
Tawas City
2.5 (4.0)
US 23
43.1 (69.4)
18.6 (29.9)
Omer
US 23
US 23
Shore Rd./ Aranac St. Rd
Santiago Rd.
Standish
26.2 (42.2)
Pine River Rd.
35.5 (57.2)
Au Gres
M13
Cody Ester Rd.
16.7 (26.9)
45.0 (72.5)
Mackinaw Rd.
M 13
0.0 (0.0)
St. Pk. Rd.
61.7 (99.3)
Beaver Rd.
M 25/Center Ave.
Wilder Rd.
Henry St.
Bay City
Road to Follow
Other Roads
Bridge
Park w/ Camping
Municipality

BAY CITY TO TAWAS CITY & EAST TAWAS

Clockwise ↓ Read mi. (km.)	**Bay City to Tawas City & East Tawas**	Counterclockwise mi. (km.) Read ↑
0.0 (0.0)	Beaver Rd. @ State Park Rd.	61.7 (99.3)

Travel West along Beaver Rd.
BAY CITY information is in the *Caseville to Bay City* segment.

2.7 (4.3)	M 13 @ Beaver Rd.	59.0 (95.0)

Turn North on to M 13. M 13 is more heavily trafficked than Mackinaw Rd. which is 2 mi. (3.2 km.) further West along Beaver Rd. Mackinaw Rd. runs parallel to M 13. If you use Mackinaw Rd. turn East on to Cody Ester Rd. to rejoin the main route.

16.7 (26.9)	Cody Ester Rd. @ M 13	45.0 (72.5)

Turn East on to Cody Ester Rd.
PINCONNING

17.7 (28.5)	Shore Rd./Arenac St. Rd. @ Cody Ester Rd.	44.0 (70.8)

Turn North on to Shore Rd.

26.2 (42.2)	Pine River Rd. @ Arenac St. Rd.	35.5 (57.2)

Continue traveling NE on Arenac St. Rd.
Or turn East on to Pine River Rd. to go into Standish, 3.4 mi. (5.5 km.)

STANDISH & STERLING

Info.: Standish CofC, P.O. Box 458, Standish MI 48658, 989 846-7867, www.sunrisesidemi.com/standish.
Area code: 989. Zip code: 48658.
Lodging: Motels. B&B: Rifle River, 653-2543. Camping: Big Bend, 513 Conrad Rd., 653-2484; H & R, 4738 Foco, 846-6443; Plantation, 3555 US 23, 846-9991; River View Cpgd. & Canoe, 5755 W. Townline Rd., 654-2447.

30.9 (49.7)	US 23 @ Arenac St. Rd./Shore Rd.	30.8 (49.6)

Turn East on to US 23.
OMER: **Lodging**: Camping: Crystal Creek, Grove Rd., 6 mi. (10 km.) from US 23, 800 552-4928; Russell Canoes, 146 Carrington St., 989 653-2644.

37.9 (61.0) Santiago Rd. @ US 23 23.8 (38.3)
Continue traveling on US 23.
Or turn South on to Santiago Rd. to go to Au Gres.

AU GRES

Info.: AuGres Area TVB, PO Box 586, AuGres MI 48703, 876-8131; AuGres CofC, P.O. Box 455, AuGres MI, 876-6688. Area code: 989. Zip code: 48703.
Lodging: Motels. B&B: AuGres Guest House, US 23, 876-7010. Camping: AuGres City Pk., 522 Park, 876-8310; Pt. Au Gres Cpgd., Green Rd., 876-7314.

43.1 (69.4) Pt. Lookout Rd. @ US 23 18.6 (29.9)
Continue traveling on US 23.

59.2 (95.3) M 55/Hemlock Rd. . 2.5 (4.0)
@ US 23/Huron Dr
Continue traveling on US 23/Huron Dr.

TAWAS CITY

Info.: Tawas Area CofC, P.O. Box 608, 989 362-8643; Tawas City, MI 48764, Tawas City, www.tawas.com. Area code: 989. Zip code: 48764.
Services: All.
Lodging: Motels. Brown's Landing RV Pk., 1129 Dyer Rd., 362-3737; Shady Oaks Cpgd., 115 Proctor St., 10 mi. (16 km.) W. of Tawas City, 692-3947; Trails End Ranch Cpgd., 1400 N. Rempert St., 362-3393.
Attraction: Tawas Bay Players, 362-8373; Lighthouse; Huron Nat'l. Forest, 739-0728; www.fs.fed.us/.

61.7 (99.7) Tawas Beach Pt. Rd. 0.0 (0.0)
@ US 23/Huron Dr.
Turn on to Tawas Beach Pt. Rd., Tawas Point St. Pk.

EAST TAWAS

Info.: Tawas Bay CVB, P.O. Box 10, Tawas City MI 48764, 877 868-2927, www.tawasbay.com. Area code: 989. Zip code: 48730.
Lodging: Motels. B&Bs: East Tawas Junction, 514 W Bay, 362-8006. Camping: East Tawas City Pk., US 23, 362-5562; Tawas Point St. Pk., 686 Tawas Beach Rd., 362-5041, 4 mi. (6 km.) from this intersection.
Attraction: Iosco Co. Mus., 405 W. Bay St., 362-8911.

Clockwise ↓ Read mi. (km.)	**East Tawas & East Tawas to Bay City**	Counterclockwise mi. (km.) Read ↑

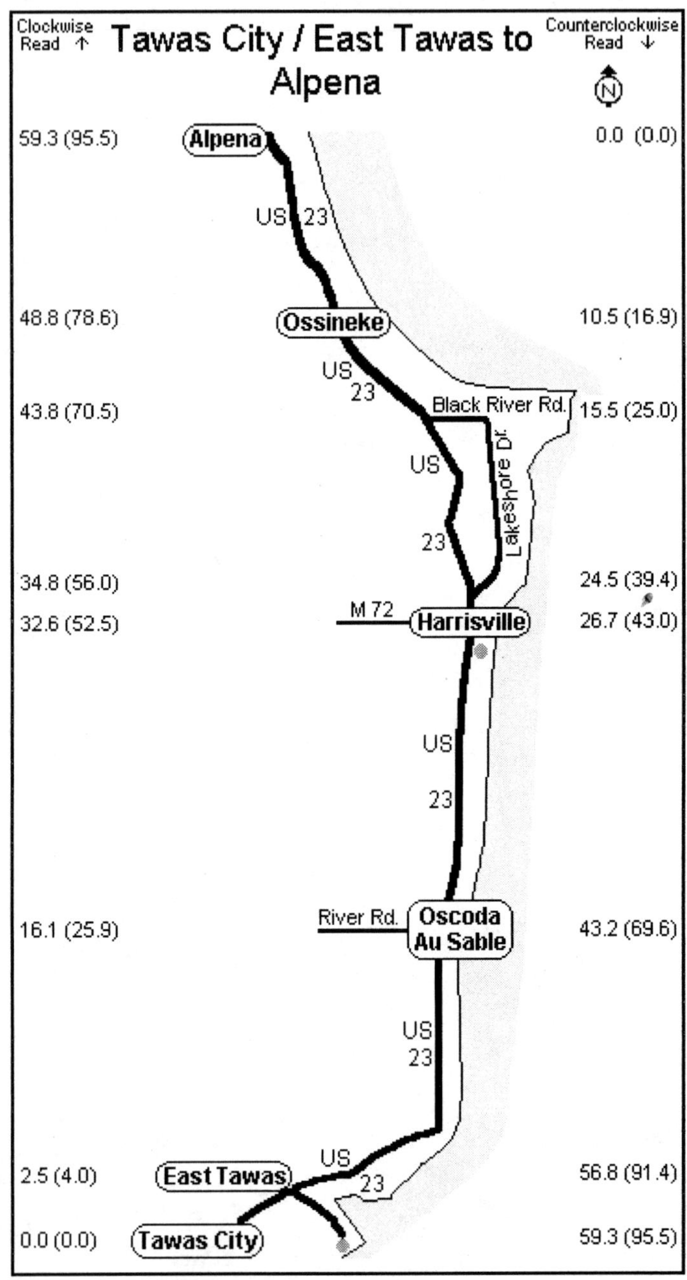
Clockwise Read ↑
Tawas City / East Tawas to Alpena
Counterclockwise Read ↓
N
59.3 (95.5)
Alpena
0.0 (0.0)
US 23
48.8 (78.6)
Ossineke
10.5 (16.9)
US 23
43.8 (70.5)
Black River Rd.
15.5 (25.0)
US
Lakeshore Dr.
23
34.8 (56.0)
24.5 (39.4)
M 72
32.6 (52.5)
Harrisville
26.7 (43.0)
US
23
River Rd.
16.1 (25.9)
Oscoda Au Sable
43.2 (69.6)
US 23
US
2.5 (4.0)
East Tawas
23
56.8 (91.4)
0.0 (0.0)
Tawas City
59.3 (95.5)

EAST TAWAS & TAWAS CITY TO ALPENA

Clockwise ↓ Read mi. (km.)	**East Tawas & Tawas City to Alpena**	Counterclockwise mi. (km.) Read ↑
0.0 (0.0)	M 55/Hemlock Rd. @ US 23/Huron Dr.	59.3 (95.5)

Travel North on US 23/Huron Dr.

TAWAS CITY and EAST TAWAS information is in the *Bay City to Tawas City & East Tawas* segment.

2.5 (4.0)	Tawas Beach Pt. Rd. @ US 23	56.8 (91.4)

Continue traveling on US 23.

Tawas Beach Pt. Rd. takes you, in 3.5 mi. (5.6 km.) to Tawas St. Pk.

16.1 (25.9)	Michigan Ave. @ US 23/Huron Dr.	43.2 (69.6)

Continue traveling on US 23.

OSCODA & AU SABLE

Info: Oscoda-AuSable CVB, 4440 N. US 23, Oscoda MI 48750, 800 235-4625/989 739-7322, www.oscoda.com. Area code: 989. Zip code: 48750.

Attractions: Lumberman's Monument Visitors Ctr., Huron Shores Nat'l. Forest, 14 mi. (22 km.) W. of Oscoda, 362-4477; Au Sable St. Forest, US 23 & CR F41, 5 mi. (8 km.) NW of Oscoda, 826-3211. Charter boats. Yankee Air Force, Wurtsmith Airport, 362-5740.

Lodging: Motels. B&B: Huron House, 3124 N. US 23, 739-9255. Camping: Old Orchard Co. Pk., 883 East River Rd., 8 mi. (13 km.) from US 23, 739-7814; KOA Acres & Trails, 3591 Forest Rd., 739-5115; Golden Arrow Stables, 1679 Kings Corner Rd., 739-7800; Van Ettan Lake MI DNR Cpgd., off US 23, 4 mi. (6 km.) NW of Oscoda, 736-8336; Huron Nat'l. Forest Cpgds., Loud Dam to Oscoda along Au Sable River Trl., 739-0728.

32.6 (52.5)	M 72 @ US 23	26.7 (43.0)

Continue traveling on US 23.

HARRISVILLE

Info.: Huron Shores CofC, PO Box 151, Harrisville MI 48740, 800 432-2823. Area code: 989. Zip code: 48740.

Attraction: Negwegon St. Pk. (undeveloped, no camping), 248 State Park Rd., 739-7407.

Lodging: Motels. B&Bs: Red Geranium, Harrisville Harbor. 724-6153; Widow's Watch, 401 Lake St., 724-5465. Camping: Harrisville St. Pk., US 23, 724-5126; Paul Bunyan, 6969 N. Huron Dr., (US 23 between Harrisville & Alpena), 471-2921; J&J Cpgd., 724-5012.

34.8 (56.0) Lakeshore Dr. @ US 23 24.5 (39.4)

Continue traveling on US 23.

Or turn on to Lakeshore Dr. If you use Lakeshore Dr. you'll add about 1.5 mi. (2.4 km.) to your distance but its more scenic. Follow Lakeshore Dr. to Black River Hamlet, 9 mi. (14.4 km.) from this intersection. Then turn West on to Black River Rd. to return to US 23. It is 2.8 mi. (4.5 km.) from Black River Village to US 23.

43.8 (70.5) Black River Rd. @ US 23 15.5 (25.0)

Continue traveling on US 23.

Clockwise travelers who used Lakeshore Dr. rejoin us here.

Counterclockwise travelers who want a diversion from US 23 can turn East on to Black River Rd. At the Lake, turn South on to Lakeshore Dr.

48.8 (78.6) Piper Rd. @ US 23 10.5 (16.9)

Continue traveling on US 23.

Take Piper Rd. into Ossineke.

OSSINEKE

Info.: Ossineke CofC, PO Box 164, Ossineke MI 49766. Area code: 989. Zip code: 49766.

Attraction: Dinosaur Gardens Prehistorical Zoo, 11160 US 23 S, 471-5477.

Lodging: Motels. B&Bs: Cranberry Creek Cottage, 8123 US-23 S., 471-5196; Fernwood, 10189 Old Ossineke Rd., 471-5176. Camping: Paul Bunyan-Alpena S. Cpgd., US 23, 3 mi. (5 km.) S. of Ossineke, 471-2921; Mackinaw St. Forest-Ossineke, US 23, 1 mi. E. of Ossineke, 732-3541; Ossineke St. Forest Cpgd., 354-2209.

59.3 (95.5) M 32 @ M23 0.0 (0.0)

ALPENA

Info.: Alpena Area CVB, 235 W. Chisolm St., PO Box 65, Alpena MI 49707, 800 425-7362/989 354-4181, www.oweb.com/upnorth/cvb/home.html; Downtown Alpena Bus. Assoc., PO Box 144, 356-6422. Area code: 989. Zip code: 49707.

Services: All. Alpena Bi-Path, 800 425-7362; Borrow A Bike!,

Thunder Bay Shores Marine & around town, 354-4181.

Attractions: Jesse Besser Mus., 491 Johnson St., 356-2202; Alpena Civic Theatre, 401 River St., 354-3624; Granum Theatre, Alpena Comm. Coll., 354-4181; Thunder Bay Theatre, 400 N. Second Ave., 354-2267; Alpena Flour Mills, 633 Campbell St., 356-0438; Farmer's Mkt., City Hall; Island Pk. & Alpena Wildfowl Sanct., US 23 N & Long Rapids Rd., Besser Natural Area, 14 mi. (22 km.) N. of Alpena; Norway Ridge Hiking Trails, 5 mi. (8 km.) S. of Alpena, Thunder Bay Underwater Preserve, Off Shore, 734 741-2270; Great Lakes Lighthouse Fest., 354-4181; Michigan Brown Trout Fest., 800 425-7362.

Lodging: Motels. B&B: Besser House, 232 S. 1st Ave., 356-0592. Camping: Alpena Co. Fairgrounds, 625 S. 11th Ave., 356-1847; Camper's Cove, 5005 Long Rapids Rd. (Johnson St.), 6 mi. W. of Alpena, 356-3708; Long Lake Co. Pk., US 23, 10 mi. (16 km.) N. of Alpena, 595-2401; Paul Bunyan, 6969 N. Huron Dr., (US 23 between Harrisville & Alpena), 471-2921; Thunder Bay River St. Forest, Indian Reserve Rd., 9 mi. (14 km.) SW of Alpena, 785-4251; Thunder Bay RV Park, 4250 US 23 S., 4 mi. (7 km.) S of Alpena, 354-2528.

Clockwise ↓ Read mi. (km.)	**Alpena to East Tawas & Tawas City**	Counterclockwise mi. (km.) Read ↑

Janis Kellogg

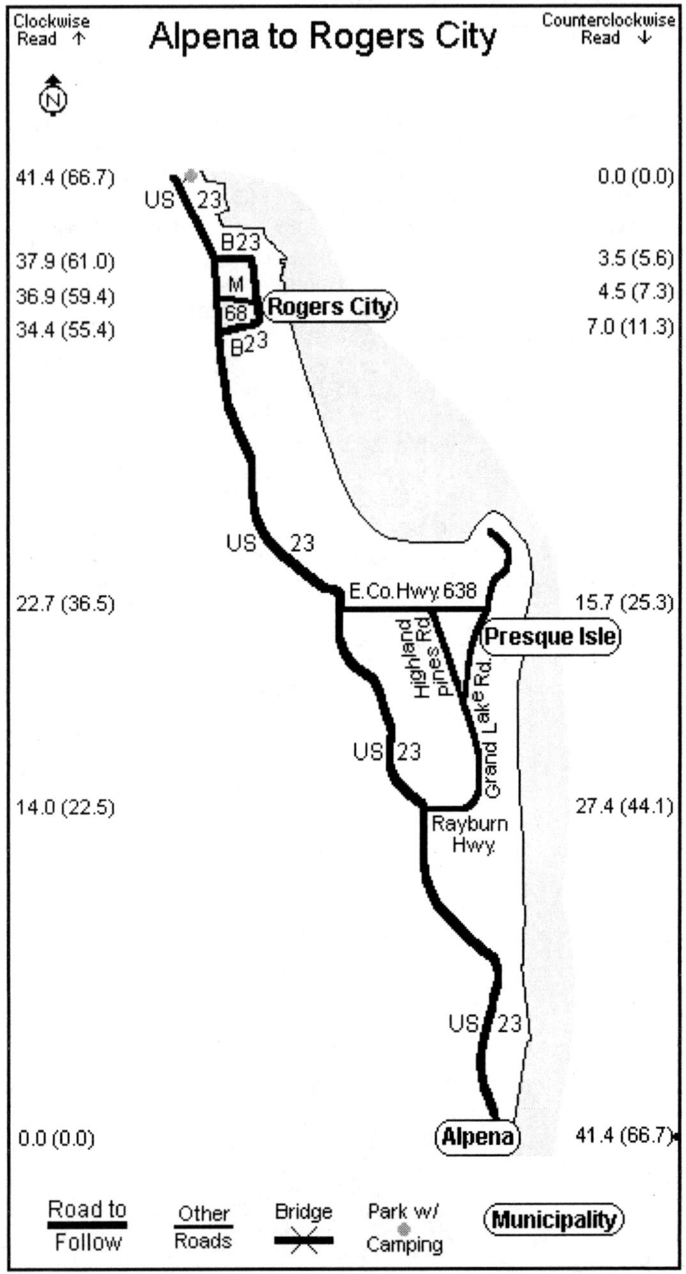
Clockwise Read ↑
Alpena to Rogers City
Counterclockwise Read ↓
N
41.4 (66.7)
0.0 (0.0)
US 23
B23
37.9 (61.0)
3.5 (5.6)
M
36.9 (59.4)
4.5 (7.3)
68
Rogers City
34.4 (55.4)
7.0 (11.3)
B23
US 23
E.Co.Hwy 638
22.7 (36.5)
15.7 (25.3)
Presque Isle
Highland Rd
pines
Grand Lake Rd.
US 23
14.0 (22.5)
27.4 (44.1)
Rayburn Hwy.
US 23
0.0 (0.0)
Alpena
41.4 (66.7)
Road to Follow
Other Roads
Bridge
Park w/ Camping
Municipality

ALPENA TO ROGERS CITY

Clockwise ↓ Read mi. (km.)	**Alpena to Rogers City**	Counterclockwise mi. (km.) Read ↑

0.0 (0.0) Water St. @ US 23 41.4 (66.7)

Travel North on US 23/Huron Dr.

ALPENA information is in the *East Tawas & Tawas City to Alpena* segment.

14.0 (22.5) Rayburn Hwy. @ US 23 27.4 (44.1)

Continue traveling on US 23.

Turn East on to Rayburn Hwy. for a diversionary *Loop* to Presque Isle Harbor.

Counterclockwise folks who diverted to go to Presque Isle Harbor rejoin us here.

Travelers Note

The main *Alpena to Rogers City* route continues after the *Presque Isle Harbor Loop.*

Clockwise ↓ Read mi. (km.)	**Rogers City to Alpena**	Counterclockwise mi. (km.) Read ↑

Clockwise ↓ Read mi. (km.)	**Presque Isle Harbor Loop**	Counterclockwise mi. (km.) Read ↑
0.0 (0.0)	Rayburn Hwy. @ US 23	14.5 (23.3)

Turn East on to Rayburn Hwy.

2.8 (4.5)	Grand Lake Rd. @ Rayburn Hwy.	11.7 (18.8)

Turn North (the only way to go) on to Grand Lake Rd.

10.5 (16.9)	E. Co. Hwy. 638 @ Grand Lake Rd.	4.0 (6.4)

To return to US 23, turn West on to E. Co. Hwy. 638.
To view the Old Lighthouse & North Point Lighthouse continue traveling North on Grand Lake Rd.

PRESQUE ISLE HARBOR

Info.: Presque Isle Area CofC, PO Box 74, Presque Isle MI 49777, 989 595-5095, www.presqueilemi.com.
Area code: 989. Zip code: 49777.
Attractions: Presque Isle Lighthouses, 595-9917; Huron Greenways, NEMCOG, PO Box 457, Gaylord, MI 49735, 989 732-3551, www.nemcog.org.
Lodging: Motels. B&Bs: North Bay, 17266 Bay View Dr., 595-5289; Presque Isle Lodge, 8211 Grand Lake Rd., 595-6970.

12.1 (19.5)	Highland Pines Rd. @ E. Co. Hwy. 638	2.4 (3.9)

Continue traveling due West on E. Co. Hwy. 638.

12.2 (19.6)	Old State Rd. @ E. Co. Hwy. 638	2.3 (3.7)

Continue traveling on E. Co. Hwy. 638.

14.5 (23.3)	US 23 @ E. Co. Hwy. 638	0.0 (0.0)

Clockwise travelers turn North on US 23.
Counterclockwise travelers turn East on to E. Co. Hwy. 638 to go to Presque Isle Harbor and the lighthouses.

Clockwise ↓ Read mi. (km.)	**Presque Isle Harbor Loop**	Counterclockwise mi. (km.) Read ↑

Clockwise ↓ Read mi. (km.)	**Alpena to Rogers City**	Counterclockwise mi. (km.) Read ↑

22.7 (36.5) E. Co. Hwy. 638 @ US 23 15.7 (25.3)

Continue traveling on US 23.
Counterclockwise: turn East on to E. Co. Hwy 638 to go to Presque Isle Harbor and the lighthouses.
The main *Alpena to Rogers City* route continues after the *Presque Isle Harbor Loop.*

34.4 (55.4) Bus. US 23 @ US 23 7.0 (11.3)

Either turn on to Bus. US 23
Or continue traveling on US 23.
Either way you go you're on the way to Rogers City.

36.9 (59.4) M 68 @ US 23 4.5 (7.2)

Turn Northeast on to M 68 to go into Rogers City.

ROGERS CITY

Info.: Rogers City CofC, 292 S. Bradley Hwy., Rogers City MI 49779, 800 622-4148/989 734-2535, http://george.lhi.net/chamber. Area code: 989. Zip : 49779.

Attractions: Lakeshore Trail, paved trail along the lakeshore; 40 Mile Point Lighthouse Soc., PO Box 205, Presque Isle Co. Hist. Mus., 4th & Michigan; Hammond Bay Biological Station; Quarry View; Nautical Fest,; Salmon Tournament; Thompson's Harbor St. Pk. (day use, MTB trls.), US 23 N., 734-2543.

Lodging: Motels. B&B: Roger's Ranch & Lodge, 2132 W Heythaler Hwy. Camping: P H Hoeft St. Pk., US. 23, 5 mi. (8 km.) N of Rogers City, 734-2543.

37.9 (61.0) Bus. US 23 @ US 23 3.5 (5.6)

Continue traveling on US 23.
Counterclockwise travelers should turn East here to go into Rogers City. Continue traveling South on Bus. US 23 to return to US 23.

41.4 (66.7) P. H. Hoeft St. Pk. @ US 23 0.0 (0.0)

Continue traveling on US 23.
Stop for a swim or the night. 734-2543.

Clockwise ↓ Read mi. (km.)	**Rogers City to Alpena**	Counterclockwise mi. (km.) Read ↑

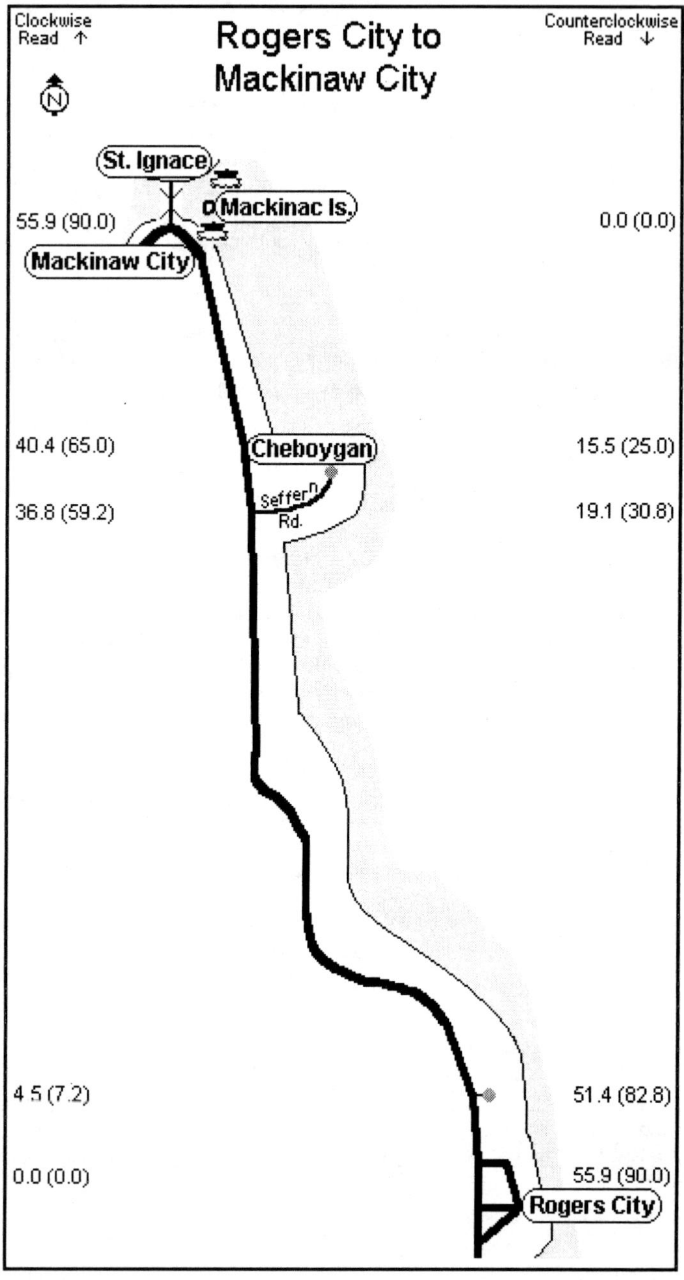
Clockwise
Read ↑
Rogers City to
Mackinaw City
Counterclockwise
Read ↓
N
St. Ignace
Mackinac Is.
55.9 (90.0)
0.0 (0.0)
Mackinaw City
40.4 (65.0)
Cheboygan
15.5 (25.0)
Seffern
Rd.
36.8 (59.2)
19.1 (30.8)
4.5 (7.2)
51.4 (82.8)
0.0 (0.0)
55.9 (90.0)
Rogers City

ROGERS CITY TO MACKINAW CITY

Clockwise ↓ mi. (km.)	**Rogers City to Mackinaw City**	Counterclockwise mi. (km.) Read ↑

0.0 (0.0) M 68 @ US 23 55.9 (90.0)
Travel North on US 23.
Turn East on M 68 to go to Rogers City.
ROGERS CITY information is in the *Alpena to Rogers City* segment.

4.5 (7.2) P. H. Hoeft St. Pk. @ US 23 51.4 (82.8)
Continue traveling on US 23.

40.4 (65.0) Main St./M 27 @ State St./US 23 15.5 (25.0)
Continue traveling on US 23. As US 23 crosses Main St. it becomes Mackinaw Ave.

CHEBOYGAN

Info.: Cheboygan Area CVB, 847 S. Main St., Cheboygan MI 49721, 800 968-3302/231 627-7183, www.cheboygan.com.
Area code: 231. Zip code: 49721.
Services: All. Bike shop. Bike path, Cheboygan to Mackinaw City, US 23 West side. Local bus service w/bike racks.
Attractions: Hist. Soc. Mus., Huron & Court Sts.; Cheboygan Opera House, 403 N. Huron Ave., 627-5841; Coast Guard Cutter Mackinaw, Turning Basin, 627-3181; Inland Waterway; Huron Greenways, 989 732-3551.
Lodging: Motels. B&Bs: Gables, 314 S. Main St., 627-5079; North Country Inn, 1355 Mackinaw Ave., 627-3129; Northwinds Lodge, 2390 S. Straits Hwy., 238-7729; Rohn House, 10950 Rogers Rd. 548-3652. Camping: Cheboygan St. Pk., 4490 Beach Rd., 627-2811; Roberts Landing, 5992 W. US 23, 627-2285; Sunset Bluff, 1095 Highbluff Rd., 625-9230; Spring Lake, 561 N. Straits Hwy., 238-7733; Aloha St. Pk., 4347 3rd St. (Rt. 212), 10 mi. (16 km.) S. of Cheboygan off Rt. 33, 625-2522; Waterways, Rt. 33, 3 mi. (5 km.) S. of Cheboygan, 888 882-7066.

55.9 (90.0) Central Ave. @ Huron Ave./ US 23 0.0 (0.0)
If you continue traveling on US 23 you'll end up in the water! US 23/Mackinaw Ave. (in Cheboygan) becomes Huron Ave. in Mackinaw City. The ferries to Mackinac Island and St. Ignace are at your wheel!

MACKINAW CITY

Info.: Greater Mackinaw Area CVB, 708 S. Huron Ave., Mackinaw City MI 49701, 800 666-0160/231 436-5664, www.mackinawcity.com.

Area code: 231. Zip code: 49701.

Services: All. Bike shop. Bike path Mackinaw City to Cheboygan, US 23, West side. Local buses w/bike racks.

Transportation: Ferries to St. Ignace on the Upper Peninsula & Mackinac Island.: All are at the docks on Huron St. Shepler's Mackinac Is. Ferry, 436-5023; Arnold Line, 436-5542; Star Line, 436-5954. The ferry is the preferred transportation medium across the Straits of Mackinaw.

Mackinaw Bridge: To cross the Straits using the Bridge call 906 643-7600 for the pick-up truck. Small fee.

Attractions: Big Mac Bike Tour. Mackinaw Bridge. Center Stage Theater, Mackinaw Crossings, 436-2200. Charter Fishing. Mackinac Island. Pt. Huron to Mackinac Is. & Chicago to Mackinac Is. yacht races (on race weekends, book lodging 1 month in advance).

Lodging: Motels. B&Bs: Brigadoon, 207 Langlade St., 436-8882; Deer Head Lodge, 109 Henry St., 436-3337. Camping: Mackinaw Municipal, Nicolet St., 436-5219; Mackinaw Mill Creek, 1284 US 23, 436-5584; Tee Pee, 1365 S. Huron St., 436-5391; Mackinaw City KOA, 566 Trails End, 436-5643; Wilderness St. Pk., Wilderness Pk. Rd., 11 mi. (18 km.) W. of Mackinaw City, 436-5381.

MACKINAC ISLAND

Mackinac Island's CofC, PO Box 451, Mackinac Island MI 49757, 800 454-5227, www.mackinacisland.org.

Area code: 906. Zip code: 49757.

Services: Restaurants and boutique style shops.

Transportation: Ferries to/from St. Ignace and Mackinaw City: Shepler's Mackinac Is. Ferry, 643-9440; Arnold Line, 643-8275; Star Line, 800 638-6562.

Attractions: No automobile traffic on the Island. Bicycling is encouraged. Mackinac St. Hist. Pks., Colonial Michilimackinac, Historic Mill Creek, & Fort Mackinac, 231 436-4100.

Lodging: Hotel. No camping on the Island. See Mackinaw City or St. Ignace for camping information. B&Bs: This is a very desirable tourist destination. Book lodging at least 1 week in advance. Many of the B&Bs listed only provide a *continental* breakfast. Bay View, 847-3295; Bogan Lane Inn, 847-3439; Chateau Lorraine, 847-8888; Cloghaun, 888 442-5929; Cottage Inn, 847-4000; Hann's 1830 Inn, 847-6244; Hart's Haven, 847-3854; Hillside Inn, 847-6557; Inn on Mackinac, 800 462-2546; LaChance Cottage, 847-3526; Lilac House, 847-3708; Market St. Inn, 888 899-3811; McNally Cottage, 847-3565; Metivier Inn, 888 695-6562; Pine Cottage, 847-3820; Small Point, 847-3758.

Clockwise	**Mackinaw City**	Counterclockwise
↓ Read mi. (km.)	**to Rogers City**	mi. (km.) Read ↑

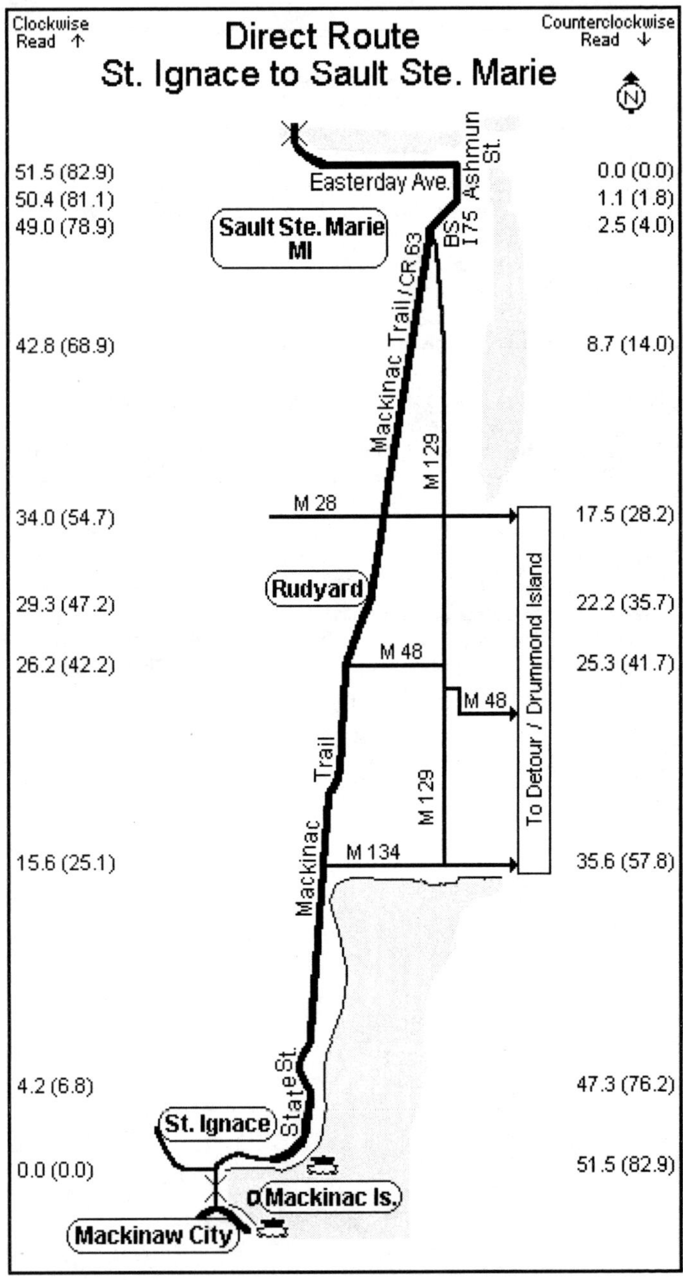
Clockwise Read ↑
Direct Route
St. Ignace to Sault Ste. Marie
Counterclockwise Read ↓
N
51.5 (82.9)
50.4 (81.1)
49.0 (78.9)
42.8 (68.9)
34.0 (54.7)
29.3 (47.2)
26.2 (42.2)
15.6 (25.1)
4.2 (6.8)
0.0 (0.0)
0.0 (0.0)
1.1 (1.8)
2.5 (4.0)
8.7 (14.0)
17.5 (28.2)
22.2 (35.7)
25.3 (41.7)
35.6 (57.8)
47.3 (76.2)
51.5 (82.9)
Easterday Ave.
Ashmun St.
BS I75
Sault Ste. Marie MI
Mackinac Trail / CR 63
M 129
M 28
Rudyard
M 48
M 48
To Detour / Drummond Island
Mackinac Trail
M 129
M 134
State St.
St. Ignace
Mackinac Is.
Mackinaw City

ST. IGNACE TO SAULT STE. MARIE

Clockwise ↓ Read mi. (km.)	**Direct Route**	Counterclockwise mi. (km.) Read ↑
	St. Ignace to Sault Ste. Marie	

0.0 (0.0) State St. @ Ferry Docks 51.5 (82.9)

Travel Northeast on State St.

ST. IGNACE

Info.: St. Ignace CVB, 560 N. State St., St. Ignace MI 49781, 800 338-6660, www.stignace.com.
Area code: 906. Zip code: 49781.

Services: All.
Transportation: Ferry to Mackinaw City and Mackinac Island: Arnold Line, 643-8275; Shepler's Ferry, 643-9440; Star Line, 643-7635.
Mackinaw Bridge: to cross the Straits using the Bridge pick-up truck, call 643-7600. Small fee.

Attractions: Fort deBaude Indian Mus., 643-6622; Fr. Marquette Nat'l. Mem. & New France Disc. Ctr., 643-9394; Marquette Mission Pk. & Mus. of Ojibwa Culture, 643-9161. Kewadin Casinos, 3039 Mackinac Trl. 643-7071. Hiawatha Nat'l Forest, St. Ignace Ranger Dist. Off., 1798 West US 2, 643-7900.

Lodging: Motels. B&Bs: Colonial House, 90 N. State St., 643-6900; Boardwalk Inn (not a b&b), 316 N. State, 643-7500. Camping: Along the route: Castle Rock Mackinac Trail, 2811 Mackinac Trl. (M 48), 643-9222; Tiki Travel Pk., 200 S. Airport Rd., 888 859-4258. Cpgds. not on the 'round Lake Huron route (all are West of St. Ignace): KOA St. Ignace, 1242 US 2 W, 2 mi. W. of St. Ignace, 643-9303; Lake Shore, 416 Pt. La Barbe Rd. (CR 405), 4 mi. NW off US 2, 643-9522; Straits St. Pk., 720 Church St., (at the Bridge) 643-8620.

4.2 (6.8) Mackinac Trl. Jct. State St. 47.3 (76.2)

Continue traveling on Mackinac Trail/State St. The road's the same the name's different. This is not an off road *bikeway*, its a road!

15.6 (25.1) M 134 @ Mackinaw Trl. 35.9 (57.8)

Continue traveling on the Mackinaw Trail.
M 134 takes the cyclist to the eastern most point on the Upper Peninsula, Drummond Island. Going to Drummond Island will double the distance between St. Ignace and Sault Ste. Marie. It is a scenic ride along the

shore line and then inland through the State and National Forests.

There is no official connection between Drummond Island or Detour Village, MI, USA and Manitoulin Island or Meldrum Bay, ON, Canada. However, you do not have to double back to this intersection if you use the Drummond Island Route. The route from Drummond Is. to Sault Ste. Marie is in the *Drummond Island Route* segment, which is presented after this *Direct Route*.

26.2 (42.2) M 48 @ Mackinaw Trl. 25.3 (40.7)

Continue traveling on M 129.

Cyclotourists who rode to Drummond Island join the *Direct Route: St. Ignace to Sault Ste. Marie* here.

Counterclockwise travelers who want to go to Drummond Island turn East on to M 48 here. Follow the Drummond Island Route from counterclockwise mi. 25.0 (40.3) reading upwards from Detour village.

29.3 (47.2) CR 63 @ M 48/Mackinaw Trl. 22.2 (35.7)

Bear Northeast on to CR 63.

M 48 goes East to I 75/US 2. Going due North on Tilson Rd. will bring you into the forest.

RUDYARD

34.0 (54.7) Kinross Rd. @ CR 63 17.5 (28.2)

Continue traveling on CR 63.

KINROSS: Kinross Cpgd., PO Box 175, Fair Rd. off Tone Rd. off SR 48, 906 495-5350/7207.

42.8 (68.9) 9 Mi. Rd./M 28 @ CR 63/Bus. Spur I 75 8.7 (14.0)

Continue traveling on CR 63/Bus. Spur I 75.

M 28 is the main East<-->West Upper Peninsula road.

49.0 (78.9) 3 Mile Rd. @ CR 63/Bus. Spur. I 75 2.5 (4.0)

Continue traveling on CR 63/Bus. Spur (BS) I 75.

50.4 (81.1) M 129 Jct. Bus. Spur I 75 1.1 (1.8)

Continue traveling on M 129/BS I 75.

51.5 (82.9) Easter Day Ave. @ CR 63/Bus. Spur I 75 0.0 (0.0)

Turn West on to Easter Day Ave. to bike on the International Bridge across the river.

Continue traveling North to see the Soo Locks.

Sault Ste. Marie, Ontario information is in the *Sault Ste. Marie to Espanola* segment.

SAULT STE. MARIE, MICHIGAN

Info.: Sault Ste. Marie CVB, 2581 I-75 Business Spur, Sault Ste. Marie MI 49783, 800 647-2858/906 632-3301, www.saultstemarie.com. Area code: 906. Zip code 49783.

Services: All. Bike shop. International Bridge, 906 635-5255, toll for bicyclists.

Attractions: Le Sault Hist. Mus. 501 E. Water St., 632-3658; Steamship Valley Camp Maritime Mus., Docks; Great Lakes Shipwreck Mus., Paradise (on L. Superior), 635-1742.

Lodging: Motels. Camping: Aune-Osborn Trl. Pk., 1225 Riverside Dr., 632-3268; Chippewa, 412 W. 3 Mile Rd., 632-8581; Kewadin Village, 825 W. 3 Mile Rd., 632-1952; Sherman City Pk., 635-5875; Soo Locks, 1001 E. Portage Ave., 632-3191; Hiawatha Nat'l Forest, Sault Ste. Marie Ranger Dist. Off., 4000 I-75 Business Spur, 635-5311.

Clockwise ↓ Read mi. (km.)	**Direct Route**	Counterclockwise mi. (km.) Read ↑

Sault Ste. Marie to St. Ignace

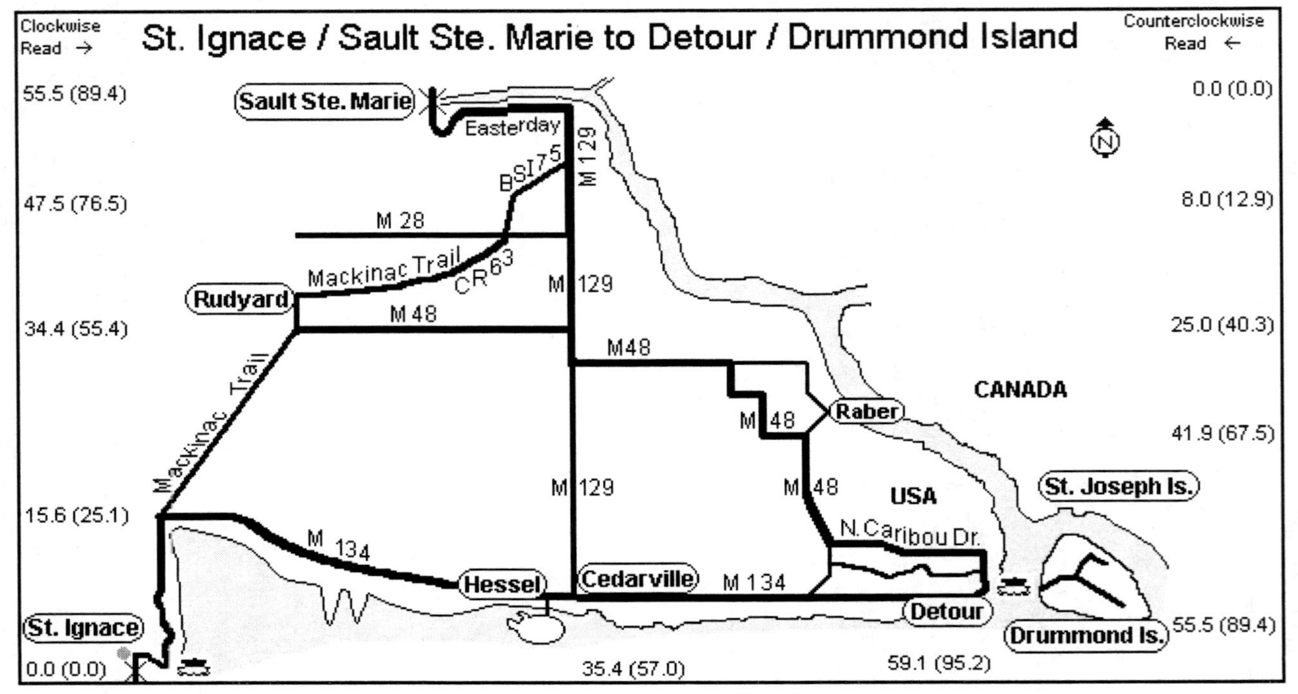
St. Ignace / Sault Ste. Marie to Detour / Drummond Island
Clockwise Read →
55.5 (89.4)
47.5 (76.5)
34.4 (55.4)
15.6 (25.1)
0.0 (0.0)
Counterclockwise Read ←
0.0 (0.0)
8.0 (12.9)
25.0 (40.3)
41.9 (67.5)
55.5 (89.4)
Sault Ste. Marie
Easterday
M 129
BS I 75
CR 63
M 28
Mackinac Trail
M 48
Rudyard
Mackinac Trail
M 129
M48
M 48
M 48
Raber
CANADA
USA
N. Caribou Dr.
M 134
Cedarville
Hessel
M 134
Detour
St. Joseph Is.
Drummond Is.
St. Ignace
35.4 (57.0)
59.1 (95.2)

Clockwise ↓ Read mi. (km.)	**Drummond Island Route**	Counterclockwise mi. (km.) Read ↑

St. Ignace to Detour / Drummond Island

Travelers Note

The *Drummond Island Route* is divided into two sections, St. Ignace to Drummond Island/Detour and Detour/ Drummond Island to Sault Ste. Marie.

The *Direct Route, St. Ignace to Sault Ste. Marie* is in the previous segment.

0.0 (0.0) M 134 @ Mackinaw Trl. 59.1 (95.2)

Turn East on to M 134.

31.3 (50.4) 3 Mile Rd. @ M 134 27.8 (44.8)

Continue traveling East on M 134 to go to Drummond Is.
Turn North on 3 Mile Rd. to go to Sault Ste. Marie.
HESSEL: Grocery and other stores. Resorts.

35.4 (57.0) M 129 @ M 134 23.7 (38.2)

Continue traveling East on M 134 to go to Drummond Is.
Turn North on M 129 to go to Sault Ste. Marie.

CEDARVILLE

Info.: Les Cheneaux Islands Area TA., PO Box 422, Cedarville MI 49719, 888 364-7526/906 484-3935; http://home.northernway.net/~lescheneaux/.
Area code: 906. Zip: 49719.
Services: Grocery and other stores.
Attractions: Arts Council of Les Cheneaux, 484-3398; Les Cheneaux Maritime Hist. Mus., M 134 & Lake St.; Les Cheneaux Hist. Mus., Meridian Rd., 484-2821.
Lodging: Motels. B&B: Les Cheneaux Inn, Hodeck & Beach Sts., 484-2007. Camping: Cedarville, Lake St., 484-3351; Lazy Days, 266 Mary L, 484-4088; Lonns Pt., 1332 E. M 134, from Cedarville, 484-2881.

49.4 (79.5) M 48 @ M 134 9.7 (15.6)

Continue traveling East on M 134 to go to Detour.
M 48 takes you North to Sault Ste. Marie.

59.1 (95.2) Drummond Is. Ferry @ M 134 0.0 (0.0)

You're at the tip!
Take the ferry to Drummond Island or stay in Detour.

DETOUR

Info.: Detour CofC, 414 St. Mary's St., Detour MI 49725, 906 297-5987.

Services: Drummond Island Ferry.
Lodging: Motel. Camping: Lake Superior St. Forest, 5 mi. (8 km.) W. of Detour off M 134.

0.0 (0.0) Ferry Dock @ Cove Pt. Rd. 14.8 (23.8)
Travel East on Lakewood Rd.

Travelers Note

There is no road which circumnavigates Drummond Island. Good thing! Let's keep it that way. The forest has a right to remain a bit isolated. Do not forget that you must double your distance when touring the Island.

DRUMMOND ISLAND

Info.: Drummond Island Tourism Assoc., PO Box 200, Drummond Island MI 49726, 800 737-8666/906 493-5245, www.drummond-island.com.
Area code: 906. Zip code: 49726.
Lodging: Motel. B&Bs: Annie's Attic, Whitney Bay, 493-5378; Tree Top's, Between Whitney Bay & Parrish Lake, 493-5894. Camping: Four Seasons Resort, Tourist Rd., 800 865-2916; Johnson Resort, Scott Bay, 493-5550; Papke's Last Resort, 5 mi. (8 km.) fr. ferry, 493-5550.

7.8 (12.6) Drummond Rd. @ Cove Pt. Rd./Lakewood Rd. 7.0 (11.3)
Turn North on to Drummond Rd. to go to Drummond Village in 1.8 mi. (2.9 km.)
Or continue traveling East on Cove Pt. Rd. which becomes Lakewood Rd.
Turning South on to the dirt surfaced Bailey Lake Rd. brings you to Lake Huron's shoreline.

14.8 (23.8) Glen Cove Rd. @ Lakewood Rd. 0.0 (0.0)
End of paved surfaced roads.
You'll have to double back the way you came.
Johnswood Hamlet.

Clockwise **Drummond Island Route** Counterclockwise
↓ Read mi. (km.) mi. (km.) Read ↑

Detour / Drummond Island to St. Ignace

Clockwise ↓ Read mi. (km.)	**Drummond Island Route**	Counterclockwise mi. (km.) Read ↑

Detour / Drummond Island to Sault Ste. Marie

0.0 (0.0) M 134 @ Drummond Is. Ferry 55.5 (89.4)
Turn North on to M 134.
You could turn South and then West on to South Caribou Dr. The distance is about the same using either North or South Caribou Dr.

0.8 (1.3) N. Caribou Dr. @ M 134 54.7 (88.1)
You don't have much choice, it's a westward turn or a dip in the Lake.

9.3 (15.0) M 48 @ N. Caribou Dr. 46.2 (74.4)
Turn North on to M 48.

13.6 (21.9) Raber Rd. @ M 48 41.9 (67.5)
Turn West continuing to follow M 48.
M 48 zig zags West and North through Lake Superior National Forest. The road N. of Raber is gravel/dirt.

30.5 (49.1) M 129 Jct. M 48 25.0 (40.3)
Turn North on to M 129/M 48.
Counterclockwise travelers going directly to Drummond Island turn East here and follow M 48 to North Caribou Rd. At N. Caribou Rd. they turn East again.
Counterclockwise travelers going to St. Ignace and the Lower Peninsula should travel South on M 129.

34.4 (55.4) Riverside Dr./M 48 @ M 129/M 48 21.1 (34.0)
Continue traveling North on M 129.
M 48 turns West here and goes to the Mackinaw Trail where you can join the *Direct Route: St. Ignace to Sault Ste. Marie.* There are few services along M 48.
Turning East on to Riverside Dr. and traveling through

Sterlingville will bring you to the Munuscong River Cpgd. in Lake Superior St. Forest, 906 635-5281.

41.4 (66.7) 15 Mile Rd. @ M 129 14.1 (22.7)

Continue traveling North on M 129.
You can turn East on 15 Mile Rd. to go to West Neebish Channel; you'll have to back track unless you like gravel/ dirt roads.

47.5 (76.5) 9 Mile Rd. @ M 129 8.0 (12.9)

Continue traveling North on M 129.
9 Mile Rd. is a gravel/dirt road going East<—>West. If you go West for 2.5 mi. (4 km.) then 9 Mile Rd. becomes M 28 the main road going East<-->West on the Upper Peninsula. At that point you'll encounter I 75 and CR H 63. CR H 63 goes North into Sault Ste. Marie and is used as part of the *Direct Route* from St. Ignace to Sault Ste. Marie.
Traveling East on 9 Mile Rd. you can turn North on Riverside Rd. and make your way North to Sault Ste. Marie. Parts of Riverside Rd. are gravel/dirt.

54.4 (87.6) Bus. Spur I 75 Jct. M 129 1.1 (1.8)

Continue North on BS I 75/M 129/Ashmun Ave.
Yeah, all three names/numbers are used.

55.5 (89.4) Easter Day Ave. @ BS I 75/M 129 0.0 (0.0)

Turn West on Easter Day Ave. to go to the Bridge.
Continue North to go to the US Soo Locks area.
Sault Ste. Marie MI information is in the *Direct Route: St. Ignace to Sault Ste. Marie, Michigan.*

Counterclockwise Travelers Note

This *Drummond Island Route* is divided into two sections, St. Ignace to Drummond Island/Detour and Detour/Drummond Island to Sault Ste. Marie.
The *Direct Route: St. Ignace to Sault Ste. Marie* is in the previous segment.

Clockwise **Drummond Island Route** Counterclockwise
↓ Read mi. (km.) mi. (km.) Read ↑

Sault Ste. Marie to **Drummond Island / Detour**

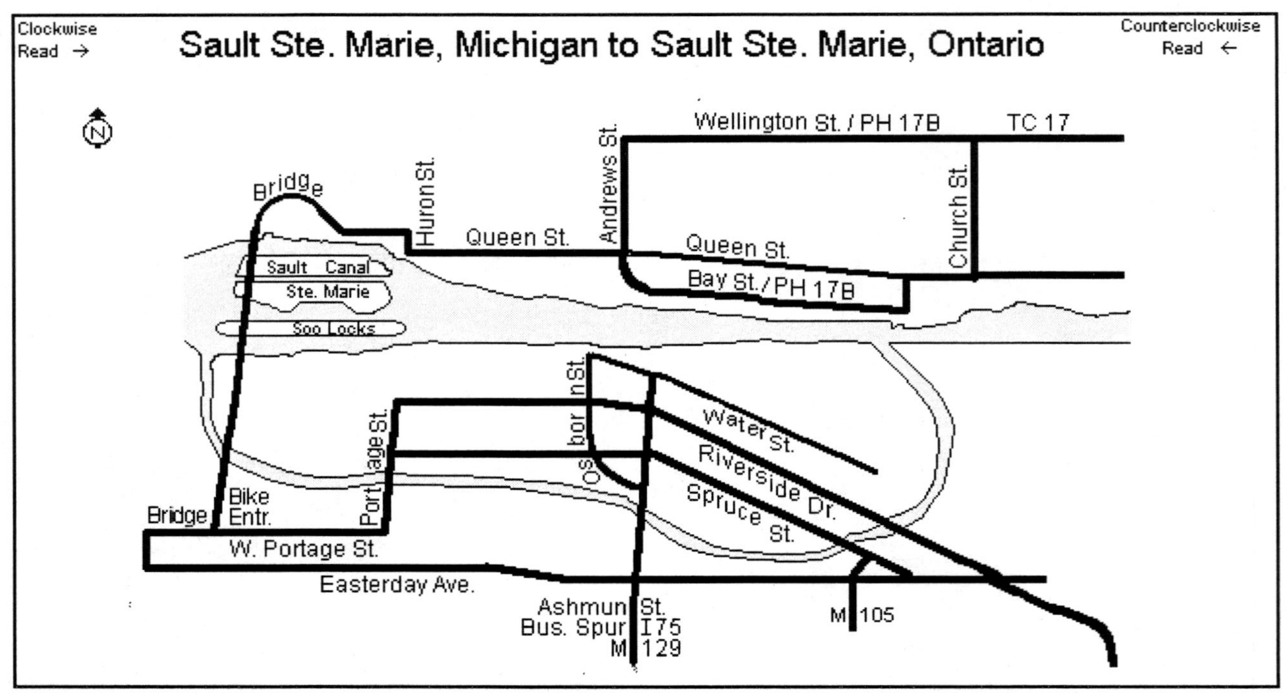
Clockwise
Read →
Sault Ste. Marie, Michigan to Sault Ste. Marie, Ontario
Counterclockwise
Read ←
N
Wellington St. / PH 17B
TC 17
Andrews St.
Church St.
Huron St.
Bridge
Queen St.
Queen St.
Bay St. / PH 17B
Sault Canal
Ste. Marie
Soo Locks
Osborn St.
Portage St.
Water St.
Riverside Dr.
Spruce St.
Bridge
Bike
Entr.
W. Portage St.
Easterday Ave.
Ashmun St.
Bus. Spur I75
M 129
M 105

SAULT STE. MARIE, ONTARIO TO ESPANOLA

Travelers notes

Trans Continental Highway 17, abbreviated TC 17 in the text, is the main East<—>West highway across Canada. TC 17 has a very heavily trafficked, narrow, shoulderless roadway. Use extreme caution. TC 17 is being improved as you are pedaling but bear these roadway conditions in mind as you are planning your tour.

When you see a truck or other wide bodied motor vehicle (RV, bus) in the opposing lane and a truck or other wide bodied vehicle behind you, move off the roadway! Truck and bus drivers are very experienced but other motorists may be *freaked* encountering bicyclist on this highway.

When the sun is low in the sky motorists have a difficult time discerning a bicyclist on the roadway, choose your traveling times accordingly. Under no circumstances should you bicycle on TC 17 at night.

This section of the route will take you much longer to traverse due to these road conditions. The entire route along TC 17 is provided as one *Segment* in order for bicycle tourists to make logical stopping decisions based on their physical condition and with a regard for safety.

It is strongly recommended that you hitch a ride or use the bus to traverse this section of the route. See Sault Ste. Marie ON & Espanola *Services* for bus company telephone numbers.

This is a long section of the route on a very heavily trafficked dangerous road. Use extreme care.

Highway designation conventions in Ontario:

TC means Trans-Continental Highway. A major highway but not usually a limited access road. The designation signs have the highway number superimposed on a maple leaf.

PH means Provincial Highway which is the new name for the Kings Highway system. The designation signs look like a shield with a crown on top. Most Provincial/Kings Highways are not limited access roads.

Hwy means a major or secondary road.

CR means county road.

Expwy means a limited access highway. Bicycles are not permitted on these roads or on the shoulder of these roads.

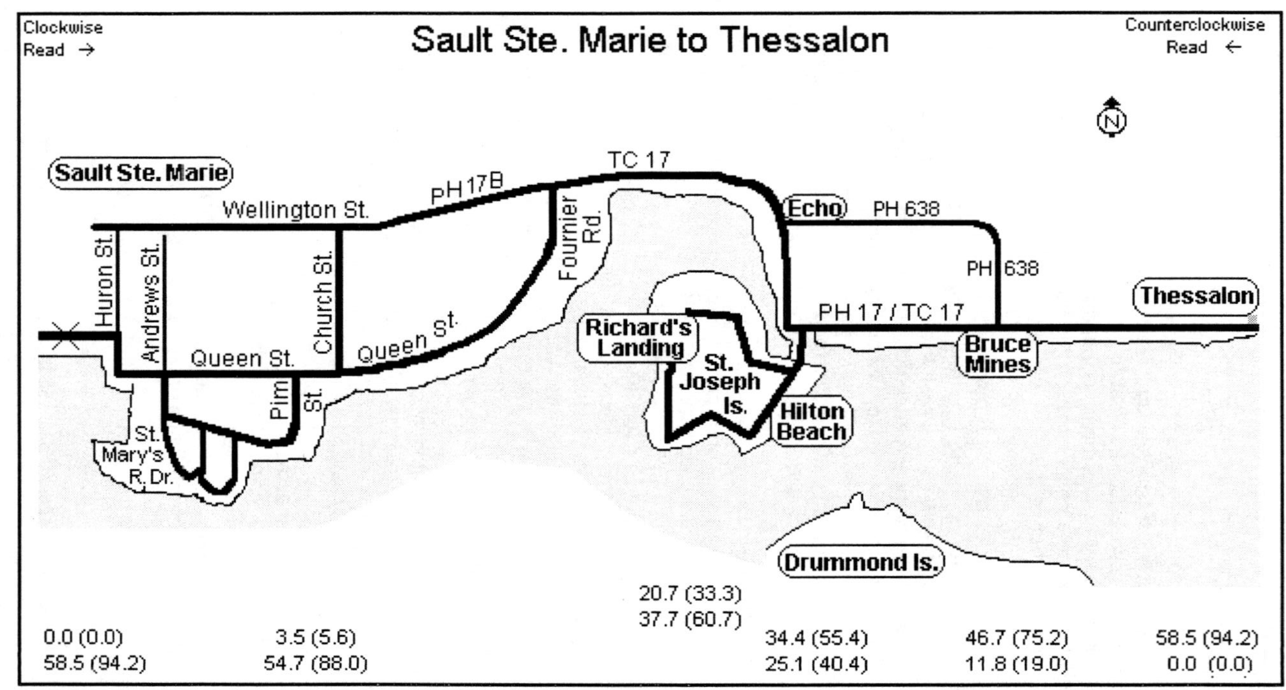
Clockwise
Read →
Sault Ste. Marie to Thessalon
Counterclockwise
Read ←
Sault Ste. Marie
Wellington St.
PH17B
TC 17
Echo
PH 638
PH 638
Thessalon
Huron St.
Andrews St.
Church St.
Fournier Rd.
Queen St.
Queen St.
PH 17 / TC 17
Richard's Landing
St. Joseph Is.
Bruce Mines
Pim St.
St. Mary's R. Dr.
Hilton Beach
Drummond Is.
20.7 (33.3)
37.7 (60.7)
0.0 (0.0)
58.5 (94.2)
3.5 (5.6)
54.7 (88.0)
34.4 (55.4)
25.1 (40.4)
46.7 (75.2)
11.8 (19.0)
58.5 (94.2)
0.0 (0.0)

Clockwise ↓ Read mi. (km.)	**Sault Ste. Marie, ON to Espanola**	Counterclockwise mi. (km.) Read ↑
0.0 (0.0)	Bridge Exit @ Huron St.	154.3 (248.4)

Turn South on to Huron St.

Counterclockwise travelers: Bicyclists can use the roadway on the International Bridge.

Sault Ste. Marie, Michigan information is in the *Direct Route: St. Ignace to Sault Ste. Marie* segment.

SAULT STE. MARIE, ONTARIO

Info.: Sault Ste. Marie Ontario Travel, 261 Queens St. W., Sault Ste. Marie ON P6A 1A3, 705 945-6941/800 668-2746; www.ontariotravel.net; Algoma Kinniwabi Travel Assoc., 485 Queen St. E., Ste. 204, Sault Ste. Marie ON P6A 1Z9, 800 263-2546, www.algomacountry.com; Queenstown Area, 540 Queen St. E., 705 942-2919. Area code: 705. PC: various.

Services: All. Bike shops.

International Bridge: Bikes ride on the bridge roadway.

Greyhound-Canada, 73 Brock St., 949-4711. There are two buses a day in each direction between Sault Ste. Marie and Espanola. Your bicycle must be boxed or bagged to be transported on the bus. The Greyhound station may not have bike boxes/bags. Telephone 2 to 3 days ahead of your departure day to make certain that the bus terminal has bike boxes or bike bags.

Attractions: Algoma Central Railway, 129 Bay St., 946-7300; Sault Canal Nat'l Hist. Site, 1 Canal Dr., 941-6205; Canadian Bushplane Heritage Ctr., 50 Pim St., 945-6242; Art Gallery of Algoma, 10 East St., 949-9067; Great Lakes Forestry Ctr., 1219 Queen St. E., 949-9461; Sault Ste. Marie Mus., 690 Queen St. E., 759-7278; St. Mary's River Marine Ctr., Mus. Ship Norgoma, Foster Dr., 256-7447; Lock Tour Boats, 253-9850. Fort Creek & Shore Ridges Cons. Areas, both day use, 946-8530. Voyageur Hiking Trail.

Lodging: Motels. B&Bs: Brockwell Chambers, 183 Brock St., 949-1076; Churchill, 63 Harten St., 942-0659; Hiawatha House, 972 Fifth Line E., 888-848-9889; Hillsview, 406 Old Garden River Rd., 759-8819; Knight Home, 61 Lansdowne Ave., 949-4874; St. Christopher's Inn, 923 Queen St. E., 759-0870; Top O' the Hill, 40 Broos Rd., 253-9041; Twin Oaks Beach Front, 57 Nokomis Beach Rd., 779-3817.

Camping: Bell's Pt. Beach, TC 17, 6 km. (4 mi.) E. of town, 759-1561. The following cpgds. are North of the City: Glenview, 2611 Great Northern Rd., 759-3436; KOA Sault Ste. Marie, 5th Line Rd. nr. TC 17 N., 6 km. (4 mi.), 759-

2344; Point Des Chenes, Airport Rd., 779-2696.

0.1 (0.2) Queen St. E. @ Huron St. 154.2 (248.3)
Travel East on Queen St.
The tourist info. office is in front of your wheel, stop in.

0.4 (0.6) Andrews St. @ Queen St. E. 153.9 (247.8)
Gore St. @ Queen St. E.
Clockwise travelers: Turn South on to Andrews St. Travel all the way to the Lake shore.
Counterclockwise Turn West on to Queen St.

1.7 (2.7) St. Mary's River Dr. @ Andrews St. 152.6 (245.7)
Gore St. @ St. Mary's River Dr.
Clockwise tourists: Turn East East on St. Mary's R. Dr.
Counterclockwise travelers: Turn North on to Gore St.
Bay St. & Queen St. E. run parallel to St. Mary's River Dr. but they are heavily trafficked and are one way streets.

2.2 (3.5) Elgin St. @ St. Mary's River Dr. 152.1 (244.8)
Turn North on to Elgin St.
You'll be making a quick East turn on to Foster Dr.

2.3 (3.7) Foster Dr. @ Elgin St. 152.0 (244.6)
Turn East on to Foster Dr.

2.8 (4.5) Brock St. @ Foster Dr. 151.5 (243.8)
Turn North on to Brock St.

3.0 (4.8) Bay St. @ Brock St. 151.3 (243.5)
Queen St. @ Brock St.
Clockwise cyclists: Turn East on to Bay St.
Counterclockwise tourists: Turn South on to Brock St.

3.5 (5.6) Pim St. @ Bay St. 150.8 (242.7)
Clockwise tourists: Turn North on to Pim St.
Counterclockwise cyclists: Continue West on Queen St.

3.8 (6.1) Queen St. E. @ Pim St. 150.5 (242.2)
Clockwise travelers: Turn East on to Queen St. E.
Counterclockwise travelers: Continue traveling West to Brock St.

7.2 (11.6) Fournier Rd. @ Queen St. E. 147.1 (236.8)
Turn North on to Fournier Rd.

7.5 (12.1) TC 17/Trunk Rd. @ Fournier Rd. 146.8 (236.3)
Turn East on to TC 17/Trunk Rd.

Counterclockwise travelers will have to watch for this street as they enter Sault Ste. Marie. If you miss Fournier, continue West on TC 17 until you reach Boundary Rd. then turn South to Queen St. E.

14.7 (23.7) Garden River Village @ TC 17 139.6 (224.8)
Continue traveling on TC 17.

20.7 (33.3) Hwy. 638 @ TC 17 133.6 (215.1)
Continue traveling on TC 17, it makes a southward turn. TC 17 becomes a divided roadway at this point but the heavy traffic is still at your back.
Turn on to Hwy. 638 if you don't want to use TC 17 for the next 41 km. (25 mi.). Hwy. 638 loops inland and rejoins TC 17 at Bruce Mines. The distance is about the same but Hwy. 638 is hillier than TC 17, which goes along the Lake shore. If you are planning to go to St. Joseph's Island then you must use TC 17. ECHO BAY

34.4 (55.4) Hwy. 548 @ TC 17 120.9 (194.6)
Continue traveling on TC 17.
Or turn South on to Hwy. 548 and visit St. Joseph Island.

ST. JOSEPH ISLAND

Info.: St. Joseph Is. CofC, Box 251, Richards Landing ON P0R 1J0, 705 246-1780, www.stjosephisland.net; Hilton Beach Tourist Info., Gen. Del., Hilton Beach ON P0R 1G0, 705 246-2242.
There are 2 major villages on St. Joseph Island, Hilton Beach and Richards Landing. Area code: 705.
Lodging: Hilton Beach: Motels. B&Bs: Anchorage, RR 1, 246-2221; Rainbow Ridge Farm, RR 1, 246-2683; Rains Homestead Century Farm, RR 1, 246-2556; Sunset Bay, RR 1, 246-2177. Camping: All Tribes Tourist Pk., RR 1, 246-1700; Busy Beaver Cpgd., RR 1, 246-2636; Hilton Beach Tourist Pk., 246-2586; Whiskey Bay Resort & Cpgd., RR 1, 246-2463.
Richards Landing: Motels. B&Bs: Outlook B&B, 246-3468; Puddingstone Place, 246-2501. Camping: Fred's Trailer Pk., 246-2543.
Attraction: Fort St. Joseph Nat'l. Hist. Site, Richards Landing, 246-1796.

46.7 (75.2) Hwy. 638 @ TC 17 107.6 (173.2)
Continue traveling on TC 17.
Counterclockwise travelers can turn North on Hwy. 638 and follow it to Echo. The distance is about the same but Hwy. 638 is hillier.

BRUCE MINES

Info.: Bruce Mines CofC, PO Box 220, Bruce Mines ON
Lodging: Motels and resorts.

58.5 (94.2) Hwy. 129 @ TC 17 95.8 (154.2)
Yeah, keep goin' on TC 17.

THESSALON

Info.: Thessalon CofC, Gen. Del., Thessalon ON P0R 1L0, 705 842-3237; Tsp. of Day & Bright Additional, RR 2, Thessalon ON P0R 1L0, 705 842-5102. AC: 705.
Lodging: Motel. Camping: Lakeside Pk. Municipal Cpgd., TC 17B, Stanley St., 842-2523; Pine Crest, TC 17, 3 km. (2 mi.) fr. Hwy 129, 842-2635.

76.5 (123.2) Hwy. 546 @ TC 17 77.8 (125.3)
You know the routine.

IRON BRIDGE

Lodging: Motels. Camping: Delmar Drive In & Cpgd., TC 17, 3 km. (2 mi.) W. of Iron Bridge, 705 843-2098; Viking TT Pk., P.O. Box 310, TC 17, 2 km. (1 mi.) W of Iron Bridge, 705 843-2834.

92.7 (149.2) Hwy. 555/Woodward Ave. @ TC 17/Causley St. 61.6 (99.2)
Continue traveling on TC 17.

BLIND RIVER

Info.: Blind River/North Channel MEDA, PO Box 998, Blind River ON P0R 1B0, 800 563-8719, www.inorth.on.ca/~missdev.
Lodging: Resorts, cottages. B&B: A Taste Of Home, 29 Fullerton St., 705 356-7165.

99.6 (160.4) Algoma Mills Village @ TC 17 54.7 (88.1)
Continue traveling on TC 17.

ALGOMA MILLS & SPRAGGE

Info.: Tsp. of the North Shore, PO Box 108, Algoma Mills ON P0R 1A0, 800 461-7285/705 849-2213.
Services: Spragge: Greyhound scheduled stop
Lodging: Algoma Mills: Motels. **Spragge**: Motels. Camping: KOA Spragge, TC 17, 2 km. (1 mi.) W of Rt. 108, 705 849-2210.

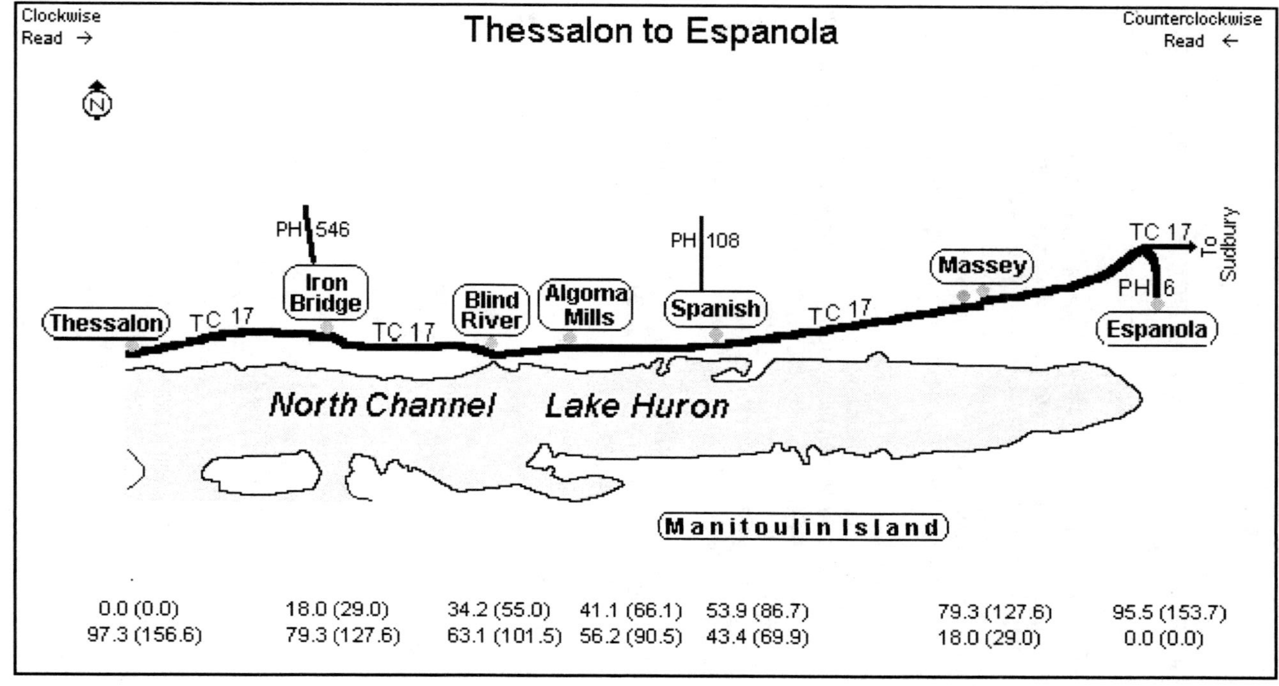
Clockwise Read →
Thessalon to Espanola
Counterclockwise Read ←
Thessalon
TC 17
PH 546
Iron Bridge
TC 17
Blind River
Algoma Mills
PH 108
Spanish
TC 17
Massey
TC 17
To Sudbury
PH 6
Espanola
North Channel
Lake Huron
Manitoulin Island
0.0 (0.0)
97.3 (156.6)
18.0 (29.0)
79.3 (127.6)
34.2 (55.0)
63.1 (101.5)
41.1 (66.1)
56.2 (90.5)
53.9 (86.7)
43.4 (69.9)
79.3 (127.6)
18.0 (29.0)
95.5 (153.7)
0.0 (0.0)

112.4 (181.0) Hwy. 108 @ TC 17 41.9 (67.5)

Continue traveling on TC 17.

SERPENT RIVER: Motels & resorts on TC 17.

ELLIOT LAKE: turn North on to Hwy. 108 & cycle for 26 mi. (42 km.) Further North on Hwy. 108 is Mississagi Prov. Pk., 7.5 mi. (12 km.) from Elliot Lake.

SPANISH

Info.: North Channel Tourism Council, Tsp. of Shedden, PO Box 70, Spanish, ON P0P 2A0, 705 844-2522. Spanish is between Serpent River and Massey.

Lodging: Motel. B&B: Le Bel Abri B&B, 3 Garnier St., 844-2545. Camping: Mitchells' at the Spanish River, 844-2202; Vance's, Trunk Rd. (TC 17), 844-2442.

137.8 (221.9) Hwy. 553 @ TC 17 16.5 (26.6)

Continue traveling on TC 17.

MASSEY

Attraction: Massey Mus., 160 Sauble St., 705 865-2266.

Lodging: Motels. B&B: Pinecrest Farm, 106 Woolsey Rd., 705 865-2249. Camping: Chutes Prov. Pk., Hwy 553, 3 km. (2 mi.) N of TC 17, 705 865-2021.

154.3 (248.4) PH 6 @ TC 17 0.0 (0.0)

Espanola information is in the *Espanola to South Baymouth* segment.

Clockwise Lake Huron 'rounders: Turn South on to PH 6. Espanola is 2.4 km. (1.5 mi.) South of this intersection. PH 6 goes South to Manitoulin Island and the Bruce Peninsula It is 53 km. (33 mi.) to Little Current at the North edge of Manitoulin Island from this intersection.

Clockwise Georgian Bay 'rounders: Turn East on to TC 17 to go to Sudbury. It is 84 km. (52 mi.) from this intersection to Sudbury.

Counterclockwise Lake Huron travelers: Turn West on to TC 17. Chutes Prov. Pk., at Massey, is 26.6 km. (16.5 mi.) West of this intersection.

Counterclockwise Lake Huron 'Rounders and Georgian Bay cyclotourists must read the *Travelers Note* at the beginning of this *segment* before proceeding beyond Espanola.

Clockwise ↓ Read mi. (km.)	**Espanola to Sault Ste. Marie**	Counterclockwise mi. (km.) Read ↑

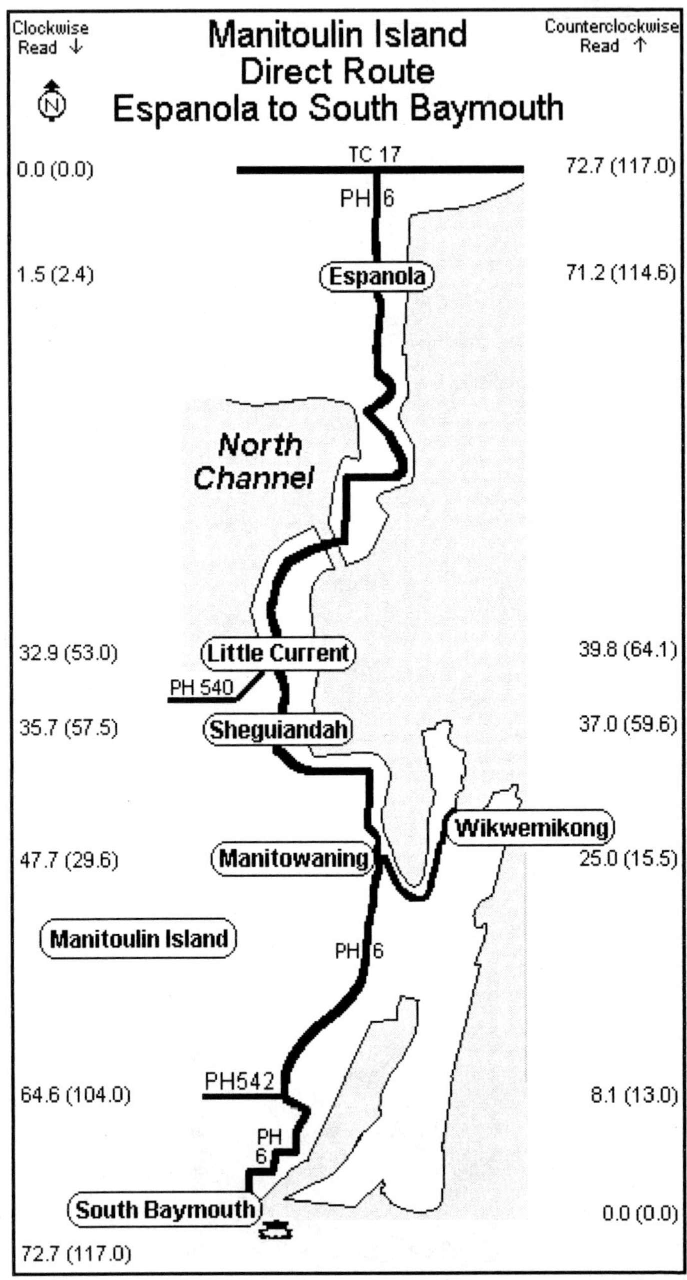
Clockwise
Read ↓
Manitoulin Island
Direct Route
Espanola to South Baymouth
Counterclockwise
Read ↑
N
0.0 (0.0)
TC 17
72.7 (117.0)
PH 6
1.5 (2.4)
Espanola
71.2 (114.6)
North
Channel
32.9 (53.0)
Little Current
39.8 (64.1)
PH 540
35.7 (57.5)
Sheguiandah
37.0 (59.6)
Wikwemikong
47.7 (29.6)
Manitowaning
25.0 (15.5)
Manitoulin Island
PH 6
64.6 (104.0)
PH542
8.1 (13.0)
PH
6
South Baymouth
0.0 (0.0)
72.7 (117.0)

ESPANOLA TO SOUTH BAYMOUTH

Clockwise ↓ Read mi. (km.)	**Manitoulin Island Direct Route** **Espanola to** **South Baymouth**	Counterclockwise mi. (km.) Read ↑

0.0 (0.0) TC 17 @ PH 6 72.7 (117.0)

Turn South on to PH 6.
Counterclockwise cyclotourists turn West on to TC 17.
Georgian Bay cyclists turn East on to TC 17.

Counterclockwise & Georgian Bay Travelers Note

TC 17 is a very heavily trafficked road. Large wide bodied trucks, RVs and buses use this road at high speeds. There is a gravel shoulder.

Use extreme caution. When two wide bodied vehicles pass each other in opposite directions or the same direction there is not enough room on the roadway for a bicycle. Go off the roadway!

It is recommended that you take the bus or hitch a ride to either Sault Ste. Marie or Sudbury from Espanola.

1.5 (2.4) Barber St. @ Centre St./PH 6 71.2 (114.6)

Continue traveling on PH 6 through Espanola.

ESPANOLA

Services: Grocery and other retail stores.

Transportation: Scheduled Greyhound bus stop, 134 Barber St., 705 869-2242. There are 2 buses a day, in each direction, between Espanola and Sault Ste. Marie. Call at least 1 day in advance to make certain that the Espanola Greyhound station has bicycle boxes/bags. If they say that boxes or bags are not available, ask the agent to have a driver bring bike boxes/bags from the Ontario-Northland office in Sudbury to the Greyhound agent in Espanola.

Scheduled Ontario-Northland bus stop. There are 3 buses a day between Espanola and Sudbury.

Many bicyclists do cycle on TC 17 and many wished they took the bus.

Lodging: Motels.

32.9 (53.0) Hwy. 540 @ PH 6 39.8 (64.1)

If you're rounding Lake Huron via the *Direct Route* continue traveling on PH 6.

The *Direct Route* across Manitoulin Island, continues after the *Manitoulin Island Scenic Loop.*

If you're touring with time to spare, stop at here for supplies and wander around Manitoulin Island using the *Loop*.

Counterclockwise Lake Huron cyclists & Georgian Bay clockwise 'rounders who took the *Manitoulin Island Scenic Loop* rejoin the *Main Route* here, and continue on their respective tours by turning North on to PH 6.

MANITOULIN ISLAND

Info.: Manitoulin CofC, PO Box 289, Gore Bay ON P0P 1H0 800 698-6681/705 282-0713 www.manitoulin-island/chamber; www.manitoulin.com. Area code: 705.

Services: Little Current, Gore Bay and South Baymouth have grocery and other retail stores.

Attractions: Bicycling. Bike shop someplace on the Island; Bike Manitoulin Tour Co., 377-4272. Birding. Fishing.

Lodging: Listed under the villages on the Island.

LITTLE CURRENT

Attractions: Gordon's Outdoor Wildlife Mus. Trail; Cup & Saucer Trail.

Lodging: B&Bs: Ruth's, Box 102, 368-3891; Wedgewood Inn, 31 Worthington St., 368-3876; Nancy's, 368-1253. Camping: At Sheguiandah, 12 km. (10 mi.) S. of Little Current, on PH 6.

Clockwise ↓ Read mi. (km.)	**Manitoulin Island Direct Route, continued** **South Baymouth** **to Espanola**	Counterclockwise mi. (km.) Read ↑

The *Direct Route* across Manitoulin Island continues after the *Manitoulin Island Scenic Loop.*

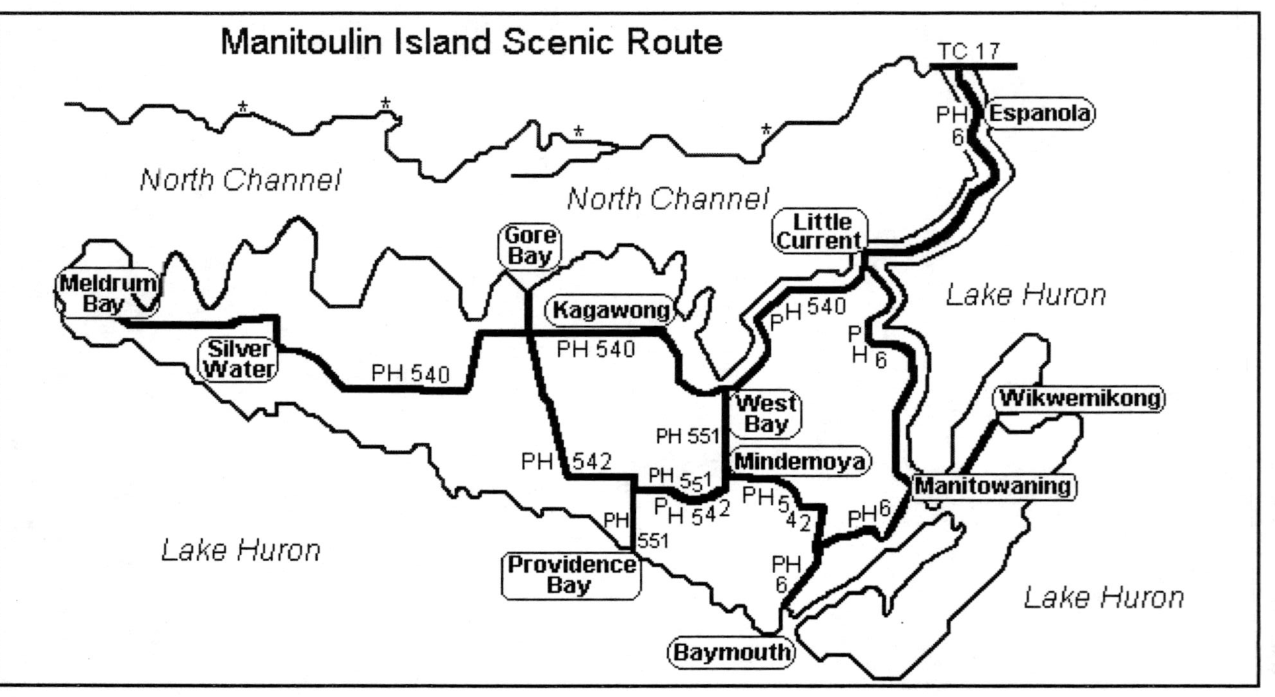
Manitoulin Island Scenic Route
TC 17
PH 6
Espanola
North Channel
North Channel
Little Current
Gore Bay
Meldrum Bay
Kagawong
PH 540
Lake Huron
PH 540
P H 6
Silver Water
PH 540
PH 540
West Bay
Wikwemikong
PH 551
Mindemoya
PH 542
PH 551
Manitowaning
PH 542
PH 542
PH 6
PH 551
Lake Huron
Providence Bay
PH 6
Lake Huron
Baymouth

MANITOULIN ISLAND SCENIC LOOP

Clockwise ↓ Read mi. (km.)	**Manitoulin Island Scenic Loop** **Little Current to** **South Baymouth**	Counterclockwise mi. (km.) Read ↑

Travelers Note

It is 83 mi. (133 km.) from Little Current to Meldrum Bay at the western end of Manitoulin Is. You will have to return to PH 6 to continue traveling around the Lake or Bay.

There is a possibility of hiring a local boat or cruising yacht to take you from either Meldrum Bay or Gore Bay to Drummond Is., Michigan, USA or Blind River, Ontario, Canada. It will be expensive, entail a good deal of convincing and will most likely be a rough crossing on a small boat.

The roads on Manitoulin Is. are almost devoid of traffic. There are a limited number of lodgings and campers have a distinct advantage. It's a wonderful place to pedal around.

0.0 (0.0) Hwy. 540 @ PH 6 180.0 (289.8)

Turn West on to Hwy. 540.

LITTLE CURRENT: Refer to the *Manitoulin Island Direct Route* for Little Current information.

18.6 (29.9) Hwy. 551 @ Hwy. 540 161.4 (259.9)

Continue traveling West on Hwy. 540.

Turning South on Hwy. 551 will bring you to Hwy. 542 in 12 km. (7.5 mi.) From the intersection of Hwys. 551 & 542 you can travel East on Hwy. 542 to return to PH 6 not far from South Baymouth and the Ferry to Tobermory. See clockwise intersection, Hwy. 551 @ Hwy. 542, 149.6 (240.9).

KAGAWONG

Info.: Kagawong is about 10 km. (16 mi.) further West along Hwy. 540.

Attractions: Post Office Mus.; Obijwe Cultural Ctr.; Bridal Veil Falls Trl.; M'Chigeeng Trl.

Lodging: B&Bs: Bridal Veil, Main St., 282-3300; Bayview, 282-0741. Camping: Mike's Pk., 817 Piete St., 2 km. (1 mi.) W. of Hwy. 548, 282-2745.

37.3 (60.1) Hwy. 542/Hwy. 540B @ Hwy. 540 142.7 (229.7)

Continue traveling West on Hwy. 540 to go to the

western end of the Island.
Turning South on to Hwy. 542 will sweep you inland and then East back to PH 6 near South Baymouth.
Hwy. 540B will bring you into Gore Bay.

GORE BAY

Info: Town of Gore Bay, 15 Water St., Postal Bag 298, Gore Bay ON POP 1HO, 705 282-2420, www.manitoulin.com.
Services: You may be able to hire a boat to take you across the North Channel to Blind River or another village on the mainland. Ask around at the marinas.
Attractions: Western Manitoulin Hist. Soc. Mus., 282-2040; Gore Bay Trl., Janet Head Lighthouse Trl.
Lodging: B&B: Burt Farm, RR 1, 282-0328; Bluff Hill, 282-2474, Thorburn House, 282-2253. Camping: Janet Head Pk., Lighthouse Rd., 282-3044.
BIRCH ISLAND: **Lodging:** Camping: Birch Island TT Pk., 285-4335.

41.7 (67.1) Hwy. 540A @ Hwy. 540 138.3 (222.7)
Continue westward on Hwy. 540 by turning South on 540.
Hwy. 540A goes to Barrie Island.

64.8 (104.3) Silver Water @ Hwy. 540 115.2 (185.5)
Just a stopping point on the way to the western end.
SILVER WATER: **Lodging:** Camping: Zhiibaahaasing, 283-3963; Pirie Haven, 283-3330.

82.9 (133.5) Meldrum Bay @ Hwy. 540 97.1 (156.3)
Hey! You're here! Pop a wheelie and spin around 180°. Turn East!

MELDRUM BAY

Attractions: Net Shed Mus., 283-3324; Mississagi Lighthouse Herit. Pk., 866-2682; Lighthouse Trl.
Lodging: Camping: Mississagi Lighthouse Mus. Cpgd., Off Hwy. 548, 11 km. (7 mi.) on Lighthouse Rd., 282-7258; Point Pk., PO Box 29, 283-4133.

101.0 (162.6) Silver Water Hamlet @ Hwy. 540 79.0 (127.2)
Continue traveling East.
You can follow your front wheel along a few dirt roads for adventure. You'll end up at the Lake. The water's real clean but cool.

124.1 (199.8) Hwy. 540A @ Hwy. 540 55.9 (90.0)

Continue East to Gore Bay.

128.5 (206.9) Hwy. 542/Hwy. 540B 51.5 (82.9)
@ Hwy. 540

Clockwise loop travelers turn South on to Hwy. 542.
Or take a break and visit Gore Bay via Hwy. 540B.
Counterclockwise cyclotourists who are returning from Meldrum Bay should continue their 'round the Lake trek by traveling East on Hwy. 540 to PH 6.

149.6 (240.9) Hwy. 551 @ Hwy. 542 30.4 (48.9)

Clockwise loopers continue traveling on Hwy. 542.
Turn South on to Hwy. 551 fpr Providence Bay.
Hwy. 551 jcts. with Hwy. 542 and goes East here.
Counterclockwise loopers continue West on Hwy. 542.
PROVIDENCE BAY: **Lodging:** Camping: Providence Bay TT Pk., 377-4650.

SPRING BAY

Info: Spring Bay is ~6 km. (4 mi.) West of here.
Lodging: Camping: Red Rock-Glow At Night, Perivale Rd., 6 km. (4 mi.) N. of Spring Bay, 377-4512; Oake's, 377-4638; Santa Maria Trailer Pk., 377-5870.

155.8 (250.8) Hwy. 551 @ Hwy. 542 24.2 (39.0)

Clockwise: continue their westward trek on Hwy. 542.
Hwy. 551 goes North here to Hwy. 540, 12 km. (7.5 mi.).
Hwy. 540 traverses the North shore of the Island and brings the counterclockwise cyclist to Little Current at the Northeast end of Manitoulin Is.
Counterclockwise travelers: To take a shorter *Loop*, see intersection Hwy. 551 @ Hwy. 540.

MINDEMOYA

Attractions: Agricultural Mus., 377-4754; Pioneer Mus., Hwy. 551; Carnavon-Billings Line Trl., Lake Mindemoya; Wagg's Woods Trl., Hwy. 542.
Lodging: B&B: Mindemoya Lake View Farm, RR 1, 377-5714; MacDougall, Box 16, 377-4739; On The Beach, 377-5182, Rockville Inn, 377 4923. Camping: Idyll-Glen Resort, 2 km. (1 mi.) N. on Hwy 551 fr. PH 6, 377-4095; Stanley Park, 5 km. (3 mi.) N. of 5th Side Rd., 377-4661; Mindemoya Court, 377-5778.

SANDFIELD: Sandfield is ~20 km. (12 km.) East of this intersection. **Lodging:** Camping: Watson's Cpgd., 859-3347.

171.9 (276.8) PH 6 @ Hwy. 542 8.1 (13.0)

Clockwise looping cyclotourists turn South on to PH 6. Counterclockwise loopers turn West on to Hwy. 542.
TEHKUMMAH: **Info.:** Tehkummah is ~4 km. (2.5 mi.) SW of this intersection via Hwy. 542A.
Lodging: B&B: Happy Acres, 19680A PH 6, 859-3453.

180.0 (289.8) Ferry Terminal @ PH 6 0.0 (0.0)
The ferry will be here soon!
SOUTH BAYMOUTH Info. is in the *Manitoulin Direct Route* segment.
Counterclockwise Lake Huron and clockwise Georgian Bay cyclotourists travel North on PH 6.

Travelers Notes

The *Direct Route* across Manitoulin Island continues after the *Manitoulin Island Scenic Loop* route.
It is 143 km. (89 mi.) from this intersection to Meldrum Bay at the western end of Manitoulin Is. You will have to backtrack to PH 6 to continue traveling North or South. There is a possibility of hiring a local boat or cruising yacht to take you from either Meldrum Bay or Gore Bay to Drummond Is., Michigan, USA or Blind River, Ontario, Canada. It will be expensive, entail a good deal of convincing and will most likely be a rough crossing on a small boat. The roads on Manitoulin Is. are almost devoid of traffic. There are a limited number of lodgings and campers have a distinct advantage. It's a wonderful place to pedal around.

Manitoulin Island Scenic Loop

Clockwise ↓ Read mi. (km.)	**South Baymouth to Little Current**	Counterclockwise mi. (km.) Read ↑

Clockwise ↓ Read mi. (km.)	**Manitoulin Island Direct Route, continued** **Espanola to South Baymouth**	Counterclockwise mi. (km.) Read ↑

Counterclockwise Travelers Note

The *Direct Route* across Manitoulin Island continues after the *Manitoulin Island Scenic Loop.*

32.9 (53.0) Hwy. 540 @ PH 6 39.8 (64.1)

Clockwise

If you're in a rush to round Lake Huron continue traveling South on PH 6.

If you're touring with time to spare, wander around Manitoulin Island using the *Manitoulin Island Scenic Loop* route. Little Current: Information after the *Scenic Loop.*

Counterclockwise Lake Huron and Georgian Bay

Cyclists who pedaled the *Scenic Loop* route rejoin the *Direct Route* across Manitoulin Island here and turn North here.

35.7 (57.5) Sheguiandah @ PH 6 37.0 (59.6)

Continue traveling on PH 6.

SHEGUIANDAH

Attractions: Howland Centennial Mus., 368-2367; Orr's Mountain, Orr's Rd.; Lewis Twin Peaks Trl.

Lodging: B&B: Lakeview Garden, Gen. Del., 859-2042; Whitehaven Resort, 368-2554. Camping: Green Acres TT Pk., PH 6, 368-2428; Batman's Cottages TT Pk., PH 6, 368-2180.

47.7 (29.6) Manitowaning Village @ PH 6 25.0 (15.5)

Continue traveling on PH 6.

Turn East here to go to Wikwemikong.

MANITOWANING & WIKWEMIKONG

Attractions: The Assiginack Mus., 859-3905; S.S. Norisle Herit. Pk.; McLean Pk. Trl., New England Rd.

Lodging: Camping: Camp Bray More, RR 1, 859-3488; Holiday Haven Resort, 152 Holiday Haven Rd., 859-3550; L & J TT Pk. RR 2, 859-3154; Black Rock Resort, 859-3347.

WIKWEMIKONG

Attraction: Wikwemikong Bay Marina Mus., 859-2850.

Lodging: B&B: Baywatch, Murray Hill Rd., 859-2955. Camping: Peltier's TT Pk. 61A61B Cape Smith Rd., 859-

3657.

64.6 (104.0) Hwy. 542 @ PH 6 8.1 (13.0)

Clockwise circumnavigators continue traveling South on PH 6.

Counterclockwise 'rounders who want a bit of change turn West on to Hwy. 542 and then follow the *Manitoulin Island Scenic Loop* route.

72.7 (117.0) Ferry Terminal @ PH 6 0.0 (0.0)

The ferry will be here soon!

Counterclockwise 'round the Lake & clockwise Georgian Bay cyclotourists travel North on PH 6.

SOUTH BAYMOUTH

Info.: Area code: 705.

Services: Grocery and other stores.

Transportation: Chi-Cheemaun Ferry, call to check the current schedule, South Baymouth ferry terminal, 859-3161. Four departures from South Baymouth each day during the main tourist season.

Attraction: Little School House & Mus.

Lodging: B&Bs: Gramsi's, 68 Church St., 859-2333; Southbay Guesthouse, 1802 South Bay Rd, 859-2363. Camping: John Budd Mem. Pk., First St., 859-3293; South Bay Resort TT Pk., 21214 PH 6, 859-3106.

MANITOULIN ISLAND

Info.: Manitoulin CofC, PO Box 289, Gore Bay ON P0P 1H0 800 698-6681/705 282-0713 www.manitoulin-island/chamber; Look at: www.manitoulin.com.

Area code: 705, for all phones on the Island.

Services: Little Current, Gore Bay and South Baymouth have grocery and other retail stores.

Attractions: Bicycling. Bike shop someplace on the Island; Bike Manitoulin Tour Co. (commercial tours), 377-4272. Birding. Fishing.

Lodging: Listed under the villages on the Island.

Clockwise ↓ Read mi. (km.)	**Manitoulin Island Direct Route South Baymouth to Espanola**	Counterclockwise mi. (km.) Read ↑

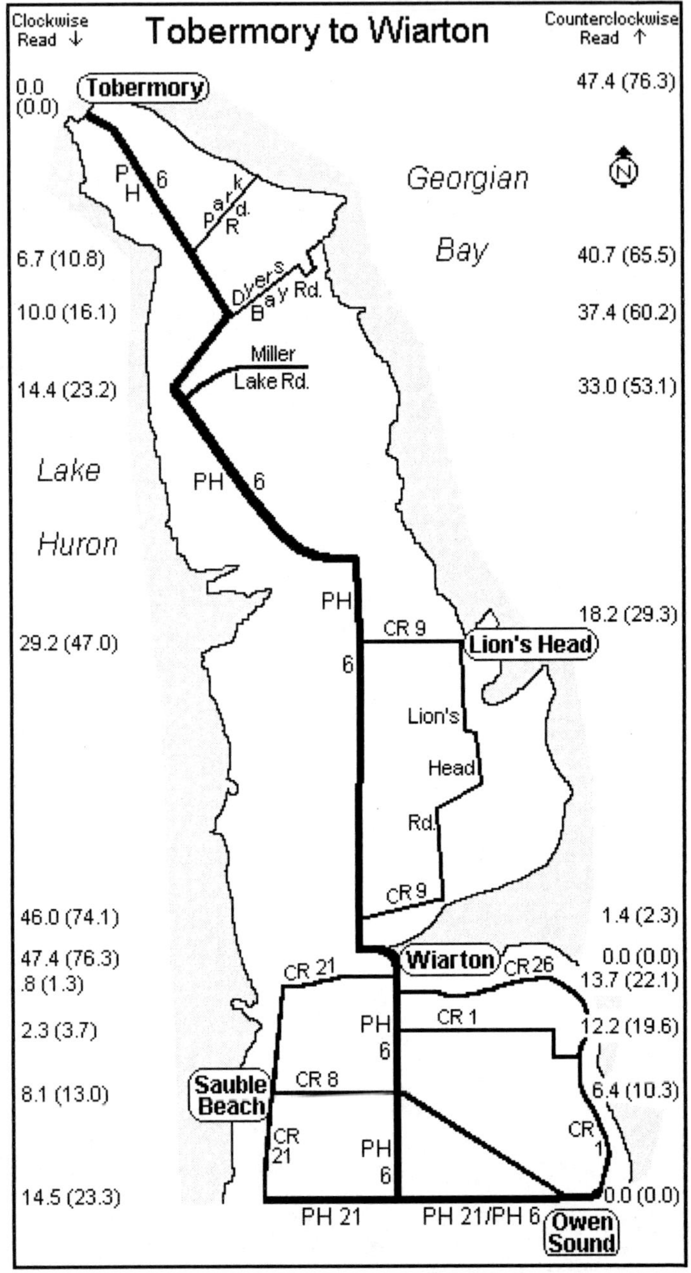
Tobermory to Wiarton
Clockwise Read ↓
Counterclockwise Read ↑
0.0 (0.0)
Tobermory
47.4 (76.3)
PH 6
Park Rd.
Georgian
Bay
6.7 (10.8)
40.7 (65.5)
Dyers Bay Rd.
10.0 (16.1)
37.4 (60.2)
Miller Lake Rd.
14.4 (23.2)
33.0 (53.1)
Lake
Huron
PH 6
PH 6
18.2 (29.3)
CR 9
29.2 (47.0)
Lion's Head
Lion's Head Rd.
CR 9
46.0 (74.1)
1.4 (2.3)
47.4 (76.3)
.8 (1.3)
Wiarton
0.0 (0.0)
CR 21
CR 26
13.7 (22.1)
CR 1
2.3 (3.7)
12.2 (19.6)
PH 6
CR 8
8.1 (13.0)
Sauble Beach
6.4 (10.3)
CR 21
PH 6
CR 1
14.5 (23.3)
0.0 (0.0)
PH 21
PH 21/PH 6
Owen Sound

TOBERMORY TO WIARTON

Clockwise ↓ Read mi. (km.)	**Tobermory to Wiarton**	Counterclockwise mi. (km.) Read ↑
0.0 (0.0)	Tobermory Ferry @ PH 6	47.4 (76.3)

Turn South on to PH 6.

TOBERMORY

Info.: Tobermory CofC, PO Box 250, Tobermory, ON N0H 2R0, 800 265-3163/519 596-2510, www.tobermory.com. Area code: 519. Postal code: various.

Services: Groceries and other retail stores.
Local bike route maps on the CofC web site.
Transportation: Chi-Cheemaun Ferry, 4 departures from Tobermory each day during the primary tourist season. Call to check the current schedule, Tobermory terminal, 596-2510.

Attractions: Fathom Five Nat'l. Pk, PH 6, 596-2263; Bruce Peninsula Nat'l. Pk., PH 6, 596-2263. St. Edmund's Mus., PH 6, 596-2452. Diving around ship wrecks; sailing; canoeing. Bruce Hiking Trail, Bruce Trail Assoc., PO Box 857, Hamilton ON L8N 3N9, 800 665-4453, www.brucetrail.org

Lodging: Motels. B&Bs: Bayside, Eagle Rd., 596-2712; Casa Verano, RR 1, 596-2471; Christine's, Elgin St., 596-8014; Cedars & Birches, Water St., 596-2100; Dogwood Point, 97 Eagle Rd. E., 596-2671; Guesthouse, Carlton St., 596-2350; Innisfree, Bay St., 596-8190; Our Nest, Maple Grove Cres., 596-2936; Paddling Gourmet, Bay St., 596-8343; Setting Sails, Eagle Rd., 596-2038; Sunset Bay, 432 Eagle Rd. W., 596-2286; Tobermory Shores, 7 Grant Watson Dr., 596-2010; Vista Hermosa, 119 Eagle Rd., 596-8065.

Camping: Bruce Peninsula Nat'l. Pk., Cyprus Lk., PH 6, 596-2263; Cha Nao Zah TeePee, PH 6, 596-2708; Happy Hearts TT Pk., RR 1, 596-2455; Harmony Acres, RR 1, 596-2735; Land's End Pk., Hay Bay Rd., Box 28, 596-2523; Tobermory Village, RR 1, 596-2689. Also see entries below for Miller Lake Rd. & Dyer's Bay Rd.

6.7 (10.8)	Bruce Peninsula Nat'l Pk. @ PH 6	40.7 (65.5)

Bruce Peninsula Nat'l Pk., camping.

10.0 (16.1)	Dyer's Bay Rd. @ PH 6	37.4 (60.2)

Continue traveling on PH 6.
If you decide to go to Dyer's Bay, turn East on Dyer's

Bay Rd. Note that this is a dead end road ~9.7 km. (6 mi.).

Lodging: B&Bs: Applewood Inn, 878 Dyers Bay Rd., 795-7552; Moeke's Ankerstee, 479 Dyers Bay Rd., 795-7769.

14.4 (23.2) Miller Lake Rd. @ PH 6 33.0 (53.1)

B&B: Plumica, RR 1, 795-7499.

29.2 (47.0) Lion's Head Rd./CR 9 @ PH 6 18.2 (29.3)

PH 6 is the direct route to Wiarton. It is not as pleasant a cycling experience as using Lion's Head Rd./CR 9.

Turn East on to Lion's Head Rd./CR 9 to go to Lion's Head. You will be following CR 9 South for ~24 km. (15 mi.) to where it once again joins PH 6. However, there may be a 8 km. (5 mi.) section of dirt road which you'll have to traverse.

Or continue traveling on PH 6.

Counterclockwise travelers who took the Lion's Head route from Wiarton join the Main Route here.

LION'S HEAD

Info: Area Code: 519. Postal code: NOH 1W0

Attractions: Bruce Trail (hiking). Rock formations.

Lodging: Motels. B&Bs: 45th Parallel, 21 Main St., 793-3529; Cape Chin Connection, Cape Chin Rd N., 888 999-6254; Cat's Pajamas, 64 Main St., 793-3767; Harvest Moon, PH 6, 592-5742; Northwinds, RR 1, 793-4590; Spirit of the Bruce, 672 East Rd., 795-7200; Taylor's, 31 Byron St., 793-4853.

Camping: Heron Point Trailer Pk., Box 275, 592-5871; Lakeside Pk., RR 2, 800 463-5514; Lion's Head Beach Pk., Box 310, 793-4090; Rockshore Trailer Pk., Isthmus Bay Rd., Box 197, 793-3326; Whispering Cedars, RR 2, 793-3219. Also see the entries above for Miller Lake Rd. & Dyer's Bay Rd.

46.0 (74.1) Lion's Head Rd./CR 9 @ PH 6 1.4 (2.3)

Clockwise travelers: Turn South on to PH 6.

Continue on PH 6.

Counterclockwise travelers: Turn East on to CR 9. Travel North on CR 9 to Lion's Head and then West to PH 6. Note that there is a ~5 mi. (8 km.) section of dirt road on CR 9. PH 6 is the direct way to Tobermory but it is a heavily trafficked, narrow road.

47.4 (76.3) CR 21 @ PH 6 0.0 (0.0)

Clockwise 'round Lake Huron cyclotourists turn West on to CR 21. Sign states, *To Oliphant.*

Clockwise bicyclists could continue traveling South on PH 6 to PH 21 using the *Wiarton Extension Route.*

Counterclockwise Lake Huron cyclists turn North on to PH 6.

Georgian Bay travelers continue traveling North on PH 6.

WIARTON

Info.: Bruce Peninsula Tourism, PO Box 269, Wiarton ON N0H 2T0, 519 534-2502.

Area code: 519. Postal code: various.

Lodging: A number of the lodgings listed are not actually in Wiarton Telephone for the B&Bs' location and directions to it. Motels. B&Bs: Grey Bruce B&B Assoc., PO Box 916, 534-1210; Bayview, RR 6, Box 903, 534-5013; Bruce Gables, 410 Berford St., 534-0429; Cedarholme, RR 6, 534-3705; Gadd-About, 501 Frank St., 800 354-9078; Hillcrest, 394 Gould St., 534-2262; Maplehurst, 277 Frank St., 534-1210; McIvor House, RR 4, 534-1769; Rosecliffe, 502435 Island View Dr., 534-2776; Sally & Leighton's, Box 298, RR 4, 534-3504; The Green Door, 376 Berford St., 534-4710; The Parke House, 220 Bruce Rd. 9, 534-0922; Thomas, 270 William St., 534-5432.

Clockwise ↓ Read mi. (km.)	**Wiarton to Tobermory**	Counterclockwise mi. (km.) Read ↑

Clockwise	**Wiarton Extension Route**	Counterclockwise
↓ Read mi. (km.)	**PH 6/Wiarton to PH 21/Southampton/Owen Sound**	mi. (km.) Read ↑

This extension is for folks who are going to Owen Sound. If you're stopping in Wiarton, it is suggested that you return to this intersection and then use CR 21 to 'round the Lake.

0.0 (0.0) CR 21 @ PH 6 14.5 (23.3)
Travel South on PH 6.

0.8 (1.3) CR 26 @ PH 6 13.7 (22.1)
Continue traveling on PH 6.
Turn East on CR 26 to visit Bruce Caves Cons. Area, ~8 km. (5 mi.); the Bruce (hiking) Trail; and Coploy Lookout.

2.3 (3.7) CR 1 @ PH 6 12.2 (19.6)
Continue traveling on PH 6.
Turn East on CR 1 to go to Owen Sound. At Kemble turn South, continuing to follow CR 1 and you'll be in Owen Sound without any hastle. See *Georgian Bay* route.

8.1 (13.0) CR 8/PH 70 @ PH 6 6.4 (10.3)
Turn West on to CR 8 to go to the lakeshore. Sauble Beach is 10.6 km. (6.6 mi.) from this intersection.
Turn Southeast on to PH 70, travel for 22 km. (14 mi.) and you'll be in Owen Sound.
HEPWORTH: **Lodging:** Eldridge Terrace B&B, RR 1, Hepworth ON N0H 1P0, 519 935-2863.

14.5 (23.3) PH 21 @ PH 6 0.0 (0.0)
Turn West on to PH 21 to go to Southampton and Lake Huron's shore.
Turn East on to PH 21/PH 6 to go to Owen Sound.

Clockwise	**Wiarton Extension Route**	Counterclockwise
↓ Read mi. (km.)	**PH 21/Southampton/Owen Sound to Wiarton**	mi. (km.) Read ↑

Counter Clockwise Travelers Notes

The Wiarton Extension Route is provided for folks who traveled to the intersection of PH 21 and PH 6 from either Owen Sound or Southamption.

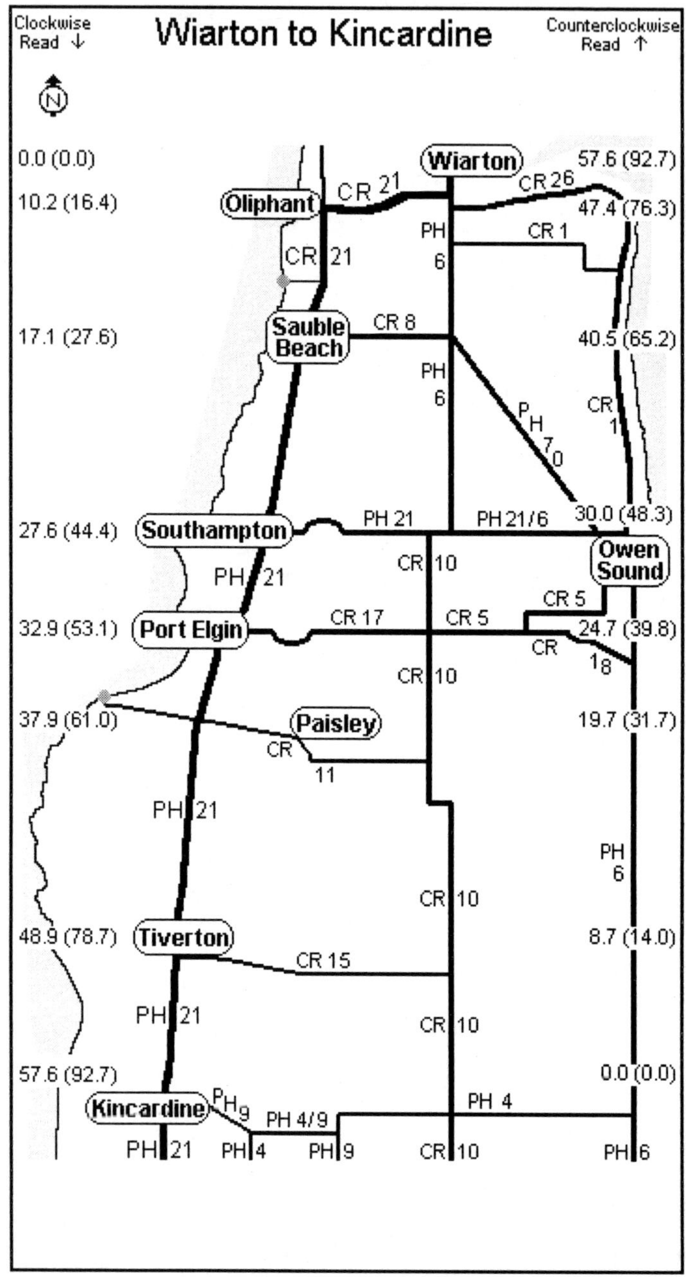
Clockwise
Read ↓
Wiarton to Kincardine
Counterclockwise
Read ↑
N
0.0 (0.0)
10.2 (16.4)
17.1 (27.6)
27.6 (44.4)
32.9 (53.1)
37.9 (61.0)
48.9 (78.7)
57.6 (92.7)
57.6 (92.7)
47.4 (76.3)
40.5 (65.2)
30.0 (48.3)
24.7 (39.8)
19.7 (31.7)
8.7 (14.0)
0.0 (0.0)
Wiarton
Oliphant
Sauble Beach
Southampton
Port Elgin
Paisley
Owen Sound
Tiverton
Kincardine
CR 21
CR 26
CR 1
CR 8
PH 6
PH 70
PH 21
PH 21/6
CR 10
CR 5
CR 17
CR 18
CR 11
CR 15
PH 4
PH 4/9
PH 9
PH 6

WIARTON TO KINCARDINE

Clockwise ↓ Read mi. (km.)	**Wiarton to Kincardine**	Counterclockwise mi. (km.) Read ↑
0.0 (0.0)	CR 21 @ PH 6	57.6 (92.7)

Turn East on to CR 21.

WIARTON information is in the *Tobermory to Wiarton* segment.

10.2 (16.4)	Oliphant @ CR 21	47.4 (76.3)

CR 21 turns southward before Oliphant. Follow CR 21 rather than going into Oliphant.

OLIPHANT, PIKE BAY & RED BAY

Info.: Area code: 519.

Lodging: Oliphant B&Bs: Bienvenue Bay, 9 Devil's Glen Rd. 793-3278; Down A Country Lane, RR 3, 534-3170. Camping: Fiddlehead Resort, RR 3, 534-0405; Spry Lake, RR 3, 534-0192; Trillium Woods, RR 3, 534-2555. Red Bay: B&B: Haven On The Bay, RR 1, 534-4002. Camping: By The Bay, RR 1, 793-3317. Crystal Springs, RR 1, 793-3714; Red Bay TT Pk., RR 1, 877 901-2098.

13.8 (22.2)	Sable Falls Prov. Pk. @ CR 21	43.8 (70.5)

Continue traveling on CR 21.

Sauble Falls Prov. Pk., 422-1952, camping.

17.1 (27.5)	CR 8 @ CR 21	40.5 (65.2)

Continue traveling on CR 21.

CR 8 goes East to PH 6, the main highway to Tobermory at the pinnacle of the Bruce Peninsula.

CR 8 becomes PH 70 at PH 6 and continues eastward to Owen Sound.

SAUBLE BEACH

Info.: Sauble Beach Info. Ctr., RR 1, Sauble Beach, ON N0H 2G0, 519 422-1262. Area code: 519.

Services: Grocery, convenience store.

Lodging: Motels. B&B: Sauble Falls, 6 Rankin Bridge Rd., 422-3304. Camping: Carson's, Southampton Pkwy., 422-1143; Sauble Beach Hideaway, RR 3, 534-2555; Sauble Beach Resort, RR 1, 422-1101; Sauble Falls Prov. Pk., RR 3, 422-1952; Sauble Falls TT Pk., RR 3, 422-1322; Sauble River Family Camp, 1341 Sauble Falls Pkwy., 422-1891; White Sands, 1425 Sauble Falls

Pkwy., 534-2781; Winding River., 94 Fedy Dr., 422-1509; Woodland Pk., 47 Sauble Falls Pkwy, 422-1161.

27.6 (44.4) CR 21/Turner St. @ PH 21/Albert St. 30.0 (48.3)

Clockwise travelers continue traveling South on PH 21/ Albert St.
Counterclockwise travelers continue traveling North on CR 21/Turner St.
Use PH 21 eastward to go to Owen Sound.

SOUTHAMPTON

Info: Southampton Info. Ctr., 204 High St., Southampton ON N0H 2L0, 519 797-2215.
Area code: 519. Postal code: N0H 2L0.
Services: Grocery and other retail stores.
Attraction: Bruce Co. Mus., 55 Victoria St., 797-3644.
Lodging: Motels. Burrows House, 44 Grey St. N., 797-3046; Chantry Breezes, 107 High St., Box 1576, 797-1818; Chinaman's Hat, 122 Miramichi Bay Rd., 389-4530; Country Comfort Acres, RR 2, 934-2384; Crescent Manor, 48 Albert St. N., 797-5637; Hollingborne House, Box 324, 48 Grey St. N, 797-3202; McGregor House, 123 Leeder Ln., 797-1702; Solomon Knechtel House, 106 Victoria St. S., 797-2585; The Old Manse, 349 High St, 797-3691; The Second Tee, 270 Tyendinaga, 797-3976. Camping: Dreamaker Family, PH 21 N., 797-9956; Holiday Pk. RR 1, High St., 797-2328; Southampton Municipal, 277 Lake St., Box 340, 797-3648.

32.9 (53.0) CR 17/Bustavus St. @ PH 21/Goderich St. 24.7 (39.8)

Continue traveling on PH 21/Goderich St.

PORT ELGIN

Info.: Port Elgin CofC, 515 Goderich St., Port Elgin ON N0H 2C0, 800 387-3456/519 832-2332.
Area code: 519. Postal code: N0H 2C0.
Services: Grocery, retail stores.
Attractions: Bruce Nuclear Power Develop., PH 21, 361-7777; Brucedale Cons. Area (Day), Hwy. 210, (S. of Port Elgin), 389-4516; MacGregor Point Prov. Pk. (Day), PH. 21 S., 888 668-7275.
Lodging: Motels. B&Bs: Bluebell Lane, 858 Goderich St., 832-3633; Franklin House, 273 Mill St., 389-5555; George House, 657 Mills St., 389-4896; Gowanlock

Country, Cons. Rd. 2, 389-5256; Sprucehall, 824 Goderich St., 832-9835; Windspire Inn, 276 Mill St., 389-3898. Camping: Kenorus "Quiet" Resort, PH 21, 832-5183; MacGregor Point Prov. Pk., PH 21, 389-9056; New Fairway Pk., PH 21, 389-9800; Port Elgin Tourist Camp, 584 Bruce St., 832-2512.

37.9 (61.0) CR 11 @ PH 21 19.7 (31.7)

Continue traveling on PH 21.

Taking CR 11 westward for 11 km. (7 mi.) will bring you to Paisley.

PAISLEY

Info.: Paisley Village, PO Box 460, Paisley ON N0G 2N0, 519 353-5609. Area code: 519. Postal code: N0G 2N0.

Attraction: Saugeen Bluffs Cons. Area, RR 1, 353-1255.

Lodging: Motel. B&Bs: Gar-Ham Hall, 538 Queen St., 353-7243; Lovat, RR 2, 353-5534. Camping: Paisley Rotary, on the Saugeen River, 353-5575.

47.8 (77.0) CR 15 Jct. PH 21 9.8 (15.8)

Continue traveling on PH 21/CR 15 into Tiverton.

48.9 (78.7) PH 21 Jct. CR 15 8.7 (14.0)

Travel West on to CR 15.

PH 21 goes due South from Tiverton and then hugs the Lake Huron shore. You can use PH 21 instead of CR 15/CR 23 shore route. The distance is about the same since we'll be rejoining PH 21 further South.

TIVERTON

Info.: Bruce Tsp., PO Box 1540, Tiverton ON N0G 2T0, 519 361-7777.

Lodging: Camping: Bigelow Pine Tree Pk., Box 190, 368-7951.

50.1 (80.7) CR 23 @ CR 15 7.5 (12.1)
Turn South on to CR 23.
Continuing West on CR 15 will bring you to Inverhuron Prov. Pk.

57.6 (92.7) Broadway St. @ Queen St./CR 23 0.0 (0.0)
Turn East on to Broadway St./PH 9.
It is 1.6 km. (1 mi.) East of this intersection to PH 21.
After visiting Kincardine you'll be rejoining the PH 21 riders at the intersection of Broadway St./PH 9 & PH 21.

KINCARDINE

Services: Grocery, retail stores.
Info.: Kincardine CofC, PO Box 315, Kincardine ON N2Z 2Y6, 519 396-2731. Area code: 519.
Lodging: Motels. B&Bs: Abide In, 869 McKendrick Dr., 396-3912; Bellfree, 854 Princes St., 396-4822; Belvedere House, 715 PH 21 S., 395-2873; Cedarbrook, 361 River (Pt. Clark), 395-0640; Glory, 376 Nelson St., 396-7518; Hanks' Heritage House, 776 Princes St., 396-7991; Highfield House, 5872 PH 9, RR 4, 395-0217; Lake Front, 328 Goderich St., 396-4345; Lakeside Trail, 655 Lakeside Trl., RR 1 (Pt. Clark), 395-0541; Lambton Lakeview, 216 Lambton St. 396-2073; Lucerne, 215 Mechanics Ave., 396-9895; Saugeen Lake View, 885 Saugeen St, Box 471, 396-2036; Victoria, 685 Victoria St., 396-4423; Wedgewood, 105 Miniwmini Rd, RR 1 (Pt. Clark), 395-3423; Wickens House, 779 Princes St., 396-3163; Woods Haven Homestead, RR 1, 368-7651. Camping: Fisherman's Cove, 13 Southline Ave, 395-2757; Green Acres, PH 21, 395-2808.

Clockwise ↓ Read mi. (km.)	**Kincardine to Wiarton**	Counterclockwise mi. (km.) Read ↑

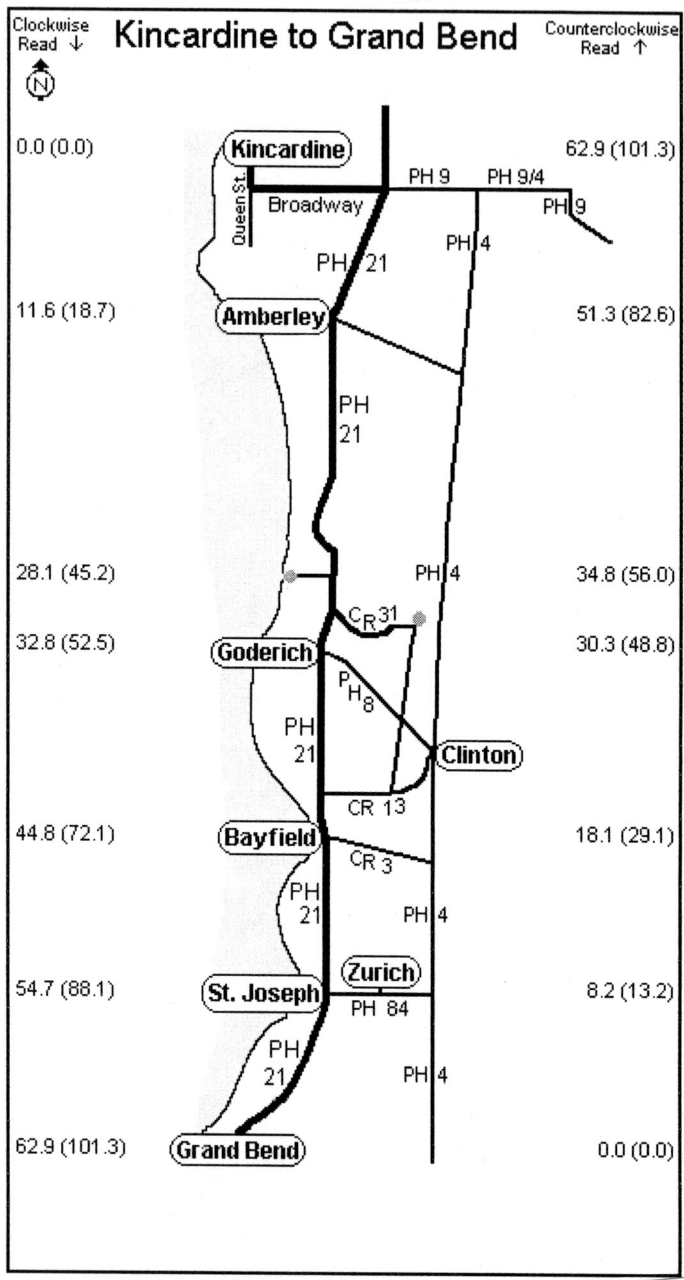

Clockwise Read ↓
Kincardine to Grand Bend
Counterclockwise Read ↑
N
0.0 (0.0)
Kincardine
62.9 (101.3)
Queen St.
Broadway
PH 9
PH 9/4
PH 9
PH 4
PH 21
11.6 (18.7)
Amberley
51.3 (82.6)
PH 21
28.1 (45.2)
PH 4
34.8 (56.0)
CR 31
32.8 (52.5)
Goderich
30.3 (48.8)
PH 8
PH 21
Clinton
CR 13
44.8 (72.1)
Bayfield
18.1 (29.1)
CR 3
PH 21
PH 4
Zurich
54.7 (88.1)
St. Joseph
8.2 (13.2)
PH 84
PH 21
PH 4
62.9 (101.3)
Grand Bend
0.0 (0.0)

KINCARDINE TO GRAND BEND

Clockwise ↓ Read mi. (km.)	**Kincardine to Grand Bend**	Counterclockwise mi. (km.) Read ↑
0.0 (0.0)	Broadway St. St./CR 23 @ Queen St.	62.9 (101.3)

Clockwise travelers turn East on to Broadway St.
Counterclockwise riders travel North on Queen St./CR 23.
KINCARDINE information is in the *Wiarton to Kincardine* segment.

1.0 (1.6)	PH 21 @ Broadway St./PH 9	61.9 (99.7)

Clockwise tourists turn South on PH 21.
Counterclockwise travelers turn West on Broadway St. to go into Kincardine.

11.6 (18.7)	PH 86 @ PH 21	51.3 (82.6)

Continue traveling on PH 21.
PH 86 takes you to Waterloo and Kitchener.
AMBERLEY: White Birches Cpgd., 117 Lake Range Rd., 519 395-5472.

28.1 (45.2)	Pt. Farms Prov. Pk. @ PH 21	34.8 (56.0)

Continue traveling on PH 21.
Or stop for the night.

32.6 (52.5)	Huron Rd./PH 8 @ PH 21/Victoria St.	30.3 (48.8)

Continue traveling on Victoria St./Bayfield St./PH 21.
At this intersection PH 21/Victoria takes a new name going South, Bayfield St. The road's the same the name's different.
PH 8/Huron Rd. goes Southeast towards Waterloo & Kitchener. You can travel to London and then to Lake Erie by using PH 8 then PH 4.
On the northern edge of Goderich is CR 31 which leads to Falls Reserve Cons. Area, 9 km. (5.6 mi.)

GODERICH

Info.: Tourism Goderich, 57 West St., Goderich ON N7A 2K5, 800 280-7637/519 524-6600. Area code: 519.

Attractions: Huron County Mus., 110 North St., 524-2686; Huron Goal, 181 Victoria St., 524-6971; Marine Mus., 110 North St., 524-2686.

Services: All. Bike shop.

Lodging: Motels. Goderich Int'nat'l. Hostel, Black's Pt. Rd., RR 2, 524-8428. B&Bs: Argyle House, 92 Britannia Rd. E., 524-5741; Brunk's, 8 Elgin Ave. E., 524-8805; Finnigan, 164 Brock St., 524-6986; Galt House, 35 Nelson St. E., 524-2963; Hibbert's, 242 Bennett St., 524-8478; In Lee of the Pines, RR 2, 524-7184; In The Garden, RR 3, 529-3256; Kathi's Guesthouse, RR 4, 524-8587; Kenfran Jersey, RR 4, 524-9724; La Brassine, RR 2, 524-6300; Maison Tanguay, 40 Nelson St. W., 524-1930; Pillars, 95 Toronto St., 524-5201; Quidi Vidi Manor, RR 2, 524-9481; Stadelmann's, RR 4, 524-6380; Sunset View, 128 Warren St., 524-7855; The Beauchemins, 88 Andrew Cres., RR 2, 524-2897; The Loft, 276 Mill Rd., 524-4912; The Maddens, 11 Britannia Rd. W., 524-5128; The Parsonage, 40 Victoria St. S., 524-6927; Twin Porches, 55 Nelson St. E., 524-5505; Windswept, 244 Picton St. W., 524-4438.

Camping: Gardiner's, 400 Bayfield Rd., 524-7302; Happy Hollow, Drury Ln., RR 3, Port Albert, 529-7632; Kitchigami, PH 21, 524-9596; Lake Huron Resort, PH 21, 524-5343; Mackenzie's TT Pk., PH 21, RR 3, 529-7536; Point Farms Prov. Pk., PH 21, RR 3, 524-7124; Riverside Pk., PH 21, RR 3, 529-7424.

44.8 (72.1) CR 3 @ PH 21 18.1 (29.1)

Continue traveling on PH 21.

BAYFIELD

Info.: Area code 519.

Lodging: Motel. B&Bs: Folmar Windmill, Frank & Mary de Jong Rd., RR 2, 482-7559; Camborne House, 23 Main St., 565-5563; Clair on the Square, 12 The Square, 565-2135; Millside House, CR 13, 482-5058. Camping: Bluewater, PH 21, 482-7197; Old Homestead, Bayfield Concession Line, RR 2, 482-9256; Paul Bunyan, PH 21, 565-5355; Pinelake, PH 21, 482-3380.

54.7 (88.1) PH 84 @ PH 21 8.2 (13.2)

Continue traveling on PH 21.

Turning East on PH 84 and traveling for 7 km. (4.5 mi.) brings you to Zurich and Zurich Cons. Area.

ST. JOSEPH'S SHORES & ZURICH: **Lodging:** Lilacs & Lace Tower, PH 21, Zurich ON N0M 2T0, 519 236-7640.

62.9 (101.3) PH 81 @PH 21 0.0 (0.0)

Traveling on PH 21 for 9.6 km. (6 mi.) will bring you to Pinery Prov. Pk.

GRAND BEND

Info.: Grand Bend & Area CofC, 4 Ontario St. N., Grand Bend ON N0M 1T0, www.grandbend.com, 519 238-2001. Area code: 519. Postal Code: various.

Attractions: Huron County Playhouse, RR 1, 238-6000; Lambton Heritage Mus., PH 21, 243-2600. Beaches.

Lodging: Motels. B&Bs: Black's, 21 Lake Rd., 238-6348; By the Old River, 10128 John St., 238-1499; Grand Bend's, 56 Ontario St. N., 238-8638; Green Acres, 16 Green Acres, 631-8987; Hearth & Home B&Bs, various homes, 238-6586; Magnolia Plantation, 9873 Leonard St., 238-8700; The Pines, 10300 Pines Pkwy., 238-5256. Camping: Birch Bark TT Pk., PH 21/CR 83, 238-8256; Carolinian Forest., 9589 Ipperwash Rd., 243-2258; Dunes Oakridge Pk., 9910 Northville Cres. 243-2500; Green Haven Pk., 52 Ontario St. N., 238-7275; Klondyke Trailer Pk., PH 21, 238-8348; Pinery Prov. Pk. (book 2+ days in advance), PH 21, 888 668-7275; Rock Glen Family Resort, Rock Glen Rd., 828-3456; Rus-Ton Family Cpgd., PH 21, 243-2424. Note: Ipperwash Prov. Pk., is closed.

Clockwise ↓ Read mi. (km.)	**Grand Bend to Kincardine**	Counterclockwise mi. (km.) Read ↑

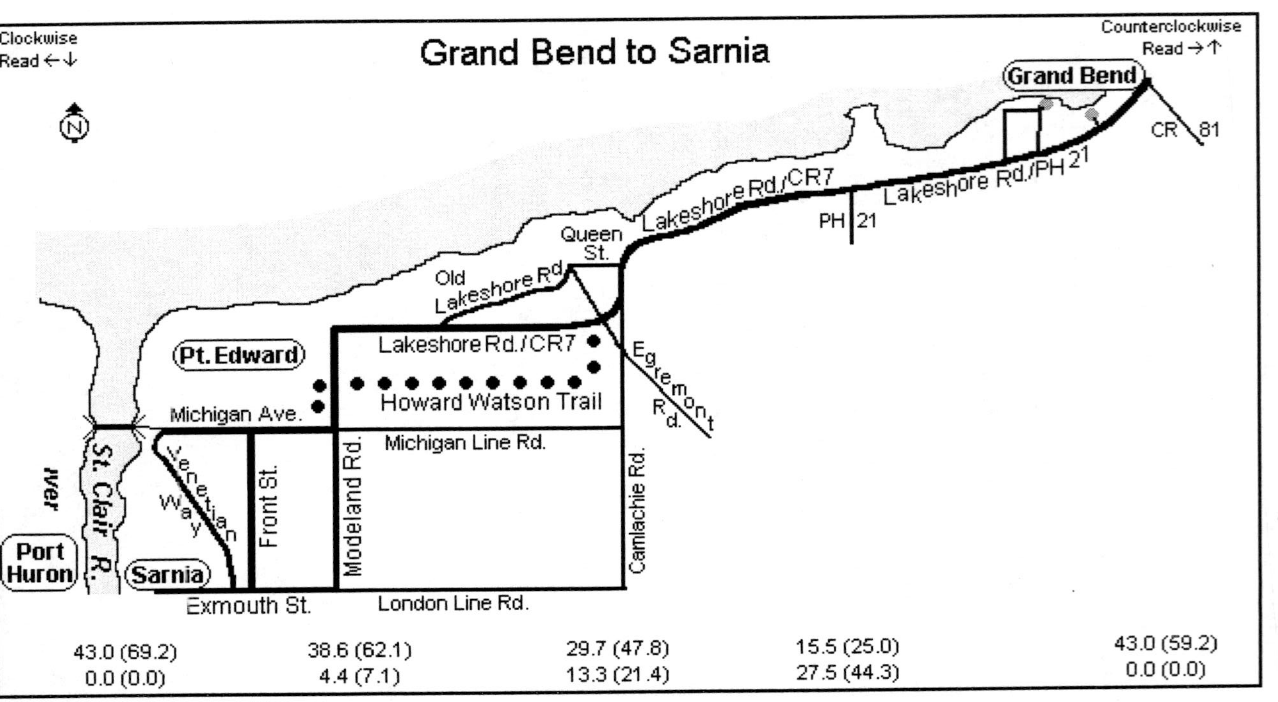
Clockwise Read ← ↓
Grand Bend to Sarnia
Counterclockwise Read → ↑
N
Grand Bend
CR 81
Lakeshore Rd./PH 21
PH 21
Lakeshore Rd./CR7
Queen St.
Old Lakeshore Rd.
Pt. Edward
Lakeshore Rd./CR7
Howard Watson Trail
Egremont Rd.
Michigan Ave.
Michigan Line Rd.
Venetian Way
Front St.
Modeland Rd.
Camlachie Rd.
iver
St. Clair R.
Port Huron
Sarnia
Exmouth St.
London Line Rd.
43.0 (69.2)
0.0 (0.0)
38.6 (62.1)
4.4 (7.1)
29.7 (47.8)
13.3 (21.4)
15.5 (25.0)
27.5 (44.3)
43.0 (59.2)
0.0 (0.0)

GRAND BEND TO SARNIA

Clockwise ↓ Read mi. (km.)	**Grand Bend to Sarnia**	Counterclockwise mi. (km.) Read ↑

0.0 (0.0) Main St./PH 81 @ PH 21/Ontario St. 43.0 (69.2)

Travel South on PH 21/Ontario St./Lakeshore Rd.
GRAND BEND information is in the *Kincardine to Grand Bend* segment.

6.0 (9.7) Pinery Prov. Pk. @ PH 21/Lakeshore Rd. 37.0 (59.6)

Continue traveling on PH 21/Lakeshore Rd.

8.7 (14.0) Outer Dr. @ PH 21 34.3 (55.2)

Continue traveling on PH 21.
Outer Dr. leads to Port Franks & Thedford Cons. Areas.
PORT FRANKS & IPPERWASH BEACH: **Lodging:** Motels. B&Bs: Cherry Lodge, 9938 Superior St., 243-2932; Gillespie Gardens, 7608 Gillespie St., 243-1515; Gilley's, 6652 Foster Cres., 243-1264; Lavendar House, 8333 Glendale Beach, 899-4372. Camping: Carolinian Forest, 9589 Ipperwash Rd., 786-4289; Our Ponderosa, 9338 W. Ipperwash Rd., 786-2031; Dunes Oakridge, CR 79 @ PH 21, 243-2500; Sunnyside, Army Camp Rd., 243-2952; Silver Birches, 9537 Army Camp Rd., 243-2480

15.5 (25.0) Rawlings Rd./ CR 7/Lakeshore Rd. @ PH 21/Lakeshore Rd. 27.5 (44.3)

Travel straight on to CR 7/Lakeshore Rd.
PH 21 turns South here.
Lodging: Camping between this intersection and Sarnia: Orchard View Pk, CR 7, 786-4700; Paradise Valley, 4895 Lakeshore Rd., 899-4080.

29.7 (47.8) Egremont Rd. @ CR 7/Lakeshore Rd. @ Howard Watson Nature Trail 13.3 (21.4)

Turn on to the Howard Watson Nature Trail.
The Watson Nature Trail has a hard limestone surface and parallels Lakeshore Rd./CR 7 for 14.3 km. (8.9 mi.)
Or continue traveling on CR 7/Lakeshore Rd.

Stephen Kamnitzer

31.7 (51.0) Watson Trail / CR 7/Lakeshore Rd. @ CR 26/ Mandaumin Rd. 10.3 (16.6)

Continue riding on the Watson Trail or Lakeshore Rd.

38.6 (62.1) Modeland Rd./CR 27 @ Howard Watson Trail @ Lakeshore Rd./CR 7 4.4 (7.1)

Watson Trail Route: Continue traveling on The Howard Watson Nature Trail as it swings South to Michigan Ave. Lakeshore Rd. riders: Turn South on to Modeland Rd./ CR 27. Ride 1 block to the Cathcart Blvd. @ Modeland Rd. @ Watson Trail. Travel Southwest on the Trail.

39.9 (64.2) Michigan Ave. @ Howard Watson Trl. 3.1 (5.0)

Turn West on to Michigan Ave. Michigan Ave. is a signed on street bike route.

41.0 (67.3) Front St. @ Michigan Ave. 2.0 (3.2)

Turn South on to Front St.

42.6 (68.6) Exmouth St. @ Front St.. .4 (.7)

Turn West on to Exmouth St.
One block East Exmouth St. at Christina St. is the Sarnia-Lambton CVB.

43.0 (69.2) Venetian Way @ Exmouth St. 0.0 (0.0)

Entrance to the Sarnia-Lambton Tourist Ctr.

SARNIA

Info.: Sarnia-Lambton CVB, 556 Christina St., Sarnia ON N7T 5W6, 800-265-0316/519 336-3232, www.tourism-sarnia-lambton.com; Ontario Tourism, 1499 Venetian Way, Sarnia, 519 344-7403. Area code: 519. Postal code: various.

Services: All.

Transportation: Blue Water Bridge, 519 336-2720. The rules for having the Bluewater Bridge Authority help you cross the Bridge are: 1. You must be a *bona fide* tourist. 2. You must show a picture identification of your residence.

The Authority suggests that you use the Ferry between Sombra, ON and Marine City, MI which is ~32 km. (~20mi.) South of where you are standing. No joke!

We brought you to the Tourist Office because a telephone call from tourist folks always helps.

Attractions: Discovery House Mus., 475 N. Cristina, 332-1556; Environmental Sci. Ctr., 120 Seaway Rd., 383-8472; Imperial Oil Ctr. for the Performing Arts, 160 N. Christina St., 344-7469; Petrolia Discovery, Off Petrolia Street, behind Bridgeview Pk., 882-0897. Horse racing. Casino. Yacht Racing.

Lodging: Motels. B&Bs: Catalpa Tree, 2217 London Line, 800-276-5135/542-5008; Talfourd's Little Inn, 11 Talfourd St., 337-1557; Zoe's, 286 N. Vidal St., 332-0511; Lakeshore, 1576 Mallah Dr., 542-2025; Mac-Beth's, 309 N. Brock St., 336-9697. Camping: East & South of Sarnia. Book accommodations 2 months in advance if you plan to be in Sarnia or Pt. Huron during the Mackinac Is. to Sarnia/Pt. Huron Yacht Race.

Clockwise ↓ Read mi. (km.)	**Sarnia to Grand Bend**	Counterclockwise mi. (km.) Read ↑

Yipes! You've 'rounded Lake Huron!

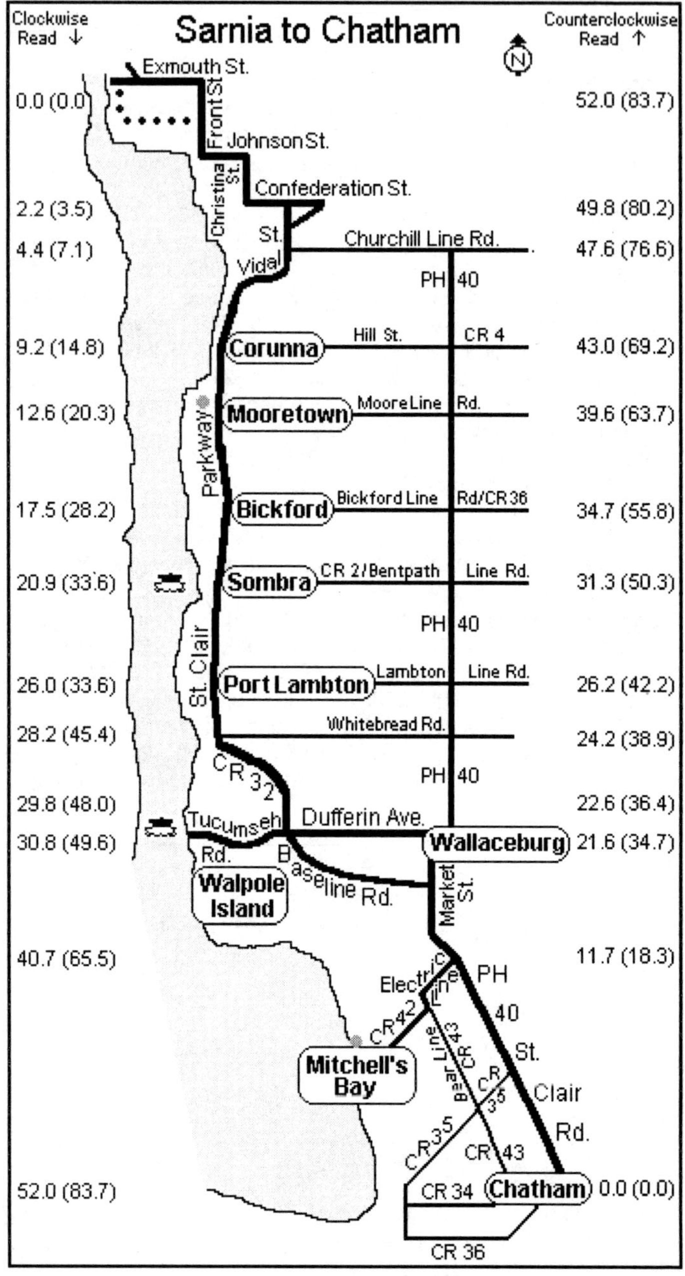

Sarnia to Chatham
Clockwise Read ↓
Counterclockwise Read ↑
N
Exmouth St.
Front St.
Johnson St.
Christina St.
Confederation St.
Vidal St.
Churchill Line Rd.
PH 40
Corunna
Hill St.
CR 4
Mooretown
Moore Line Rd.
Parkway
Bickford
Bickford Line Rd/CR 36
Sombra
CR 2/Bentpath Line Rd.
St. Clair
Port Lambton
Lambton Line Rd.
Whitebread Rd.
CR 32
Tecumseh Rd.
Dufferin Ave.
Wallaceburg
Baseline Rd.
Walpole Island
Market St.
Electric Line
CR 42
Mitchell's Bay
Bear Line CR 43
CR 35
PH 40 St. Clair Rd.
CR 43
CR 34
Chatham
CR 36
0.0 (0.0)
2.2 (3.5)
4.4 (7.1)
9.2 (14.8)
12.6 (20.3)
17.5 (28.2)
20.9 (33.6)
26.0 (33.6)
28.2 (45.4)
29.8 (48.0)
30.8 (49.6)
40.7 (65.5)
52.0 (83.7)
52.0 (83.7)
49.8 (80.2)
47.6 (76.6)
43.0 (69.2)
39.6 (63.7)
34.7 (55.8)
31.3 (50.3)
26.2 (42.2)
24.2 (38.9)
22.6 (36.4)
21.6 (34.7)
11.7 (18.3)
0.0 (0.0)

SARNIA TO WINDSOR

Clockwise ↓ Read mi. (km.) ↑	**Sarnia to Windsor**	Counterclockwise Read mi. (km.)
0.0 (0.0)	Front St. @ Exmouth St.	103.2 (166.2)

Turn West on to Exmouth St.
SARNIA information is in the *Grand Bend to Sarnia* segment.

0.1 (0.2)	Venetian Blvd. @ Exmouth St.	103.1 (166.0)

Continue traveling West on Exmouth St.
The Sarnia Visitors Ctr. is on Venetian Blvd.

0.2 (0.3)	Harbour Rd. @ Exmouth St.	103.0 (165.8)

Turn South on Harbour Rd.

0.4 (0.6)	Waterfront Trail Head @ Harbour Rd.	102.8 (165.5)

Travel South on the Trail.

1.1 (1.8)	Locheil St. @ Waterfront Trail	102.1 (164.4)

Exit the Trail on to Locheil St.

1.2 (1.9)	Front St. @ Locheil St.	102.0 (164.2)

Turn South on to Front St.

1.7 (2.7)	Johnston St. @ Front St.	101.5 (163.4)

Turn East on to Johnston St.

1.8 (2.9)	Christina St. S. @ Johnston St.	101.4 (163.3)

Turn South on to Christina St.

2.2 (3.5)	Confederation St. @ Christina St.	101.1 (162.8)

Turn East on to Confederation St.

2.4 (3.9)	Vidal St./Brock St. @ Confederation St.	100.8 (162.3)

Turn South on to Vidal St.
Northbound cyclists will arrive at the intersection of Brock St. (1 way going N. for a block or two from a Y intersection with Vidal St.)

4.4 (7.1)	St. Clair Pkwy./Churchill Line @ Vidal St.	98.8 (159.1)

Look for the entrance to the St. Clair Pkwy. Trail.

Or begin bicycling on the roadway.

9.2 (14.8) Hill St./CR 4 @ St. Clair Pkwy. 94.0 (151.3)
Continue traveling on the St. Clair Pkwy.
CR 4 goes to PETROLIA.

CORUNNA

Info.: St. Clair Pkwy. Comm., www.stclairparkway.com; 242 St. Clair Pkwy., Corunna ON N0N 1G0, 519 862-2291. St. Clair Cons. Area, 245-3710, www.scrca.on.ca. Area code: 519.
Lodging: B&B: Mohawk, 413 Beresford St., 862-3840.

12.6 (20.3) Moore Line @ St. Clair Pkwy. 90.6 (145.9)
Continue traveling on the St. Clair Pkwy.

MOORETOWN

Attraction: Moore Mus., 94 Moore Line, 867-2020; St. Clair River Trail, 1155 Emily St., Mooretown ON N0M 1M0, 867-3148, www.xcelco.on.ca/~stclair. AC: 519.
Lodging: B&B: Moore Lodge, 1509 Moore Line, 864-1880. Camping: Mooretown, 1094 Emily St., 867-2951.

14.1 (22.7) Courtright Line/CR 80 @ St. Clair Pkwy. 89.1 (143.5)
Continue traveling on the St. Clair Pkwy. COURTRIGHT

17.5 (28.2) Bickford Line/CR 36 @ St. Clair Pkwy. 85.4 (137.5)
Continue traveling on the St. Clair Pkwy. Begin bicycling on the roadway. BICKFORD

20.9 (33.6) Bentpath Line/CR 2 @ St. Clair Pkwy. 82.3 (132.5)
Continue traveling on the St. Clair Pkwy.

SOMBRA

Info.: Transportation: Bluewater Ferry, Sombra ON-Marine City MI, Dock, 888 638-4726.
Attraction: Sombra Township Mus., 3470 St. Clair Pkwy.
Lodging: B&B: Sombra, 160 Smith St., 892-3311.
Camping: Branton-Cundick Pk., CR 33 N., 892-3968; Cathcart Pk., St. Clair Pkwy, 892-3342.

26.0 (41.9) Lambton Line @ St. Clair Pkwy. 77.2 (124.3)
Continue traveling on the St. Clair Pkwy.
PORT LAMBTON: **Lodging:** B&B: Rosie's, 3853 St. Clair Pkwy., 892-3581.

28.2 (45.4) Whitebread Line 75.0 (120.8)
@ St. Clair Pkwy./CR 33

Southbound: The "official" Parkway ends, continue traveling South on the on CR 33.
Northbound: Travel North on the St. Clair Pkwy.

29.8 (48.0) Baseline Rd./CR 33 73.5 (118.3)
@ Payne Rd./CR 33

Continue traveling South on Baseline Rd./CR 33.

30.8 (49.6) Dufferin Rd./CR 32 72.4 (116.6)
@ Baseline Rd./CR 33

Turn East on to Dufferin Rd./CR 32.
Transportation: Turn West on to CR/32/Tucumseh Rd. to go to Walpole Island and the Ferry to Algonac MI via the Ferry. Traveling via this ferry to Detroit & Windsor will cut off ~97 km. (60 mi.) It is ~5 km. (3 mi.) from this intersection to the Ferry.

WALPOLE ISLAND:

Services: Transportation: Algonac - Walpole Is. Ferry, Dock.
Lodging: Camping: Chemalogan, River Rd. S., 627-1558.

32.7 (52.6) PH 40 Jct. Dufferin Rd./CR 32 70.5 (113.5)

Continue traveling East on PH 40.

35.1 (56.5) McNaughton Ave./PH 40 68.1 (109.6)
@ Dufferin Rd. PH 40

Turn South on to McNaughton Ave./PH 40.

WALLACEBURG

Attractions: Wallaceburg Mus., 505 King St., 627-8962; WISH Ctr. Af. Am Hist, 177 King St. E., 354-5248; Uncle Tom's Cabin Mus., 29251 Uncle Tom's Rd., Dresden, 683-2978.
Lodging: Motels

40.7 (65.5) CR 42/Electric Line 62.5 (100.6)
@ PH 40/St. Clair Rd.

Continue traveling on PH 40.
Turn West on to CR 42/Electric Line for Mitchell's Bay.

MITCHELL'S BAY

Lodging: B&B: Dity's at the Bay, 50 Main St., Mitchell's Bay, 519 354-5235; Parkside, RR#1, Dover Centre, (off PH 40 near Mitchells Bay), 352-4935. Camping: St. Clair Pkwy., Mitchell's Bay 354-8423.

A bit further South on PH 40 you can turn Southwest on to CR 35/St. Andrews Rd. and follow it through the countryside to the Thames River at CR 36/River View Rd. where you'll meet the main route to Windsor once again. CR 35/Andrews Rd. is about 11 km. (7 mi.) from this intersection.

52.0 (83.7) Grand Ave. W./PH 2 51.2 (82.4)
@ St. Clair St./PH 40
Turn West on to Grand Ave. W./PH 2.

CHATHAM

Info.: Mun. of Chatham-Kent, 315 King St. W., Chatham, ON N7M 5K8, 800 561-6125/519 360-1998, www.city.chatham-kent.on.ca. Area code: 519.
Attractions: Chatham-Kent Mus., 75 William St. N., 354-8338; Chatham Railroad Mus., McLean St., 352-3097; J & J Doll Mus., 10364 Fairview Line, 351-4389; Milner House, 75 William St. N., 354-8338.
Lodging: Jordan House, 7725 Eighth Line, 436-0839; Teresa's, 137 St.Clair St., 352-8982;

53.5 (86.1) Grand Ave. W./PH 2/CR 34 49.7 (80.0)
@ Kell Rd./PH 2
Either continue traveling on Grand Ave. W./CR 34;
Or turn South on Kell Rd., cross the Thames River, and turn West on to River View Line/CR 36 immediately after crossing the River. The distance is about the same whether you travel North or South of the Thames River on CR 34 or CR 36.

61.0 (98.2) CR 35/Jacob St. 42.2 (67.9)
@ CR 36/River View Line
CR 35/Jacob St.
@ CR 34/Grande River Rd./Grand St. W.
Continue traveling on CR 36/River View Line. If you took CR 35 or CR 34/Grande River Rd./Grand Ave. W. cross the River to the South bank.

61.6 (99.2) CR 7/Merlin Rd. 41.6 (67.0)
@ CR 36/River View Rd./Tecumseh Line
Continue traveling on CR 36 which is now called Tecumseh Line.

69.4 (111.7) CR 2/Tecumseh Rd. 33.8 (54.4)
@ CR 36/Tecumseh Line
Continue traveling on CR 2/Tecumseh Rd. We've crossed a Municipal boundary and the road numbers and name change.

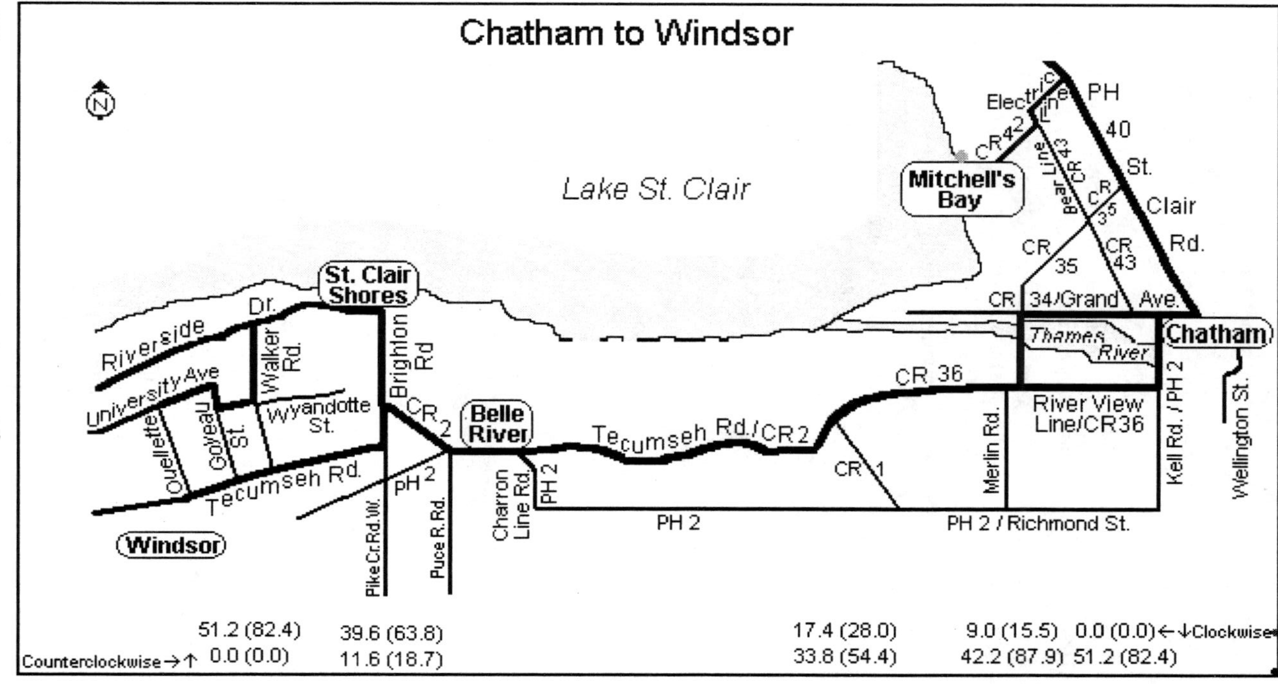
Chatham to Windsor
Lake St. Clair
Mitchell's Bay
St. Clair Shores
Windsor
Belle River
Chatham
Riverside Dr.
University Ave
Ouellette
Goyeau St.
Walker Rd.
Wyandotte St.
Tecumseh Rd.
Pike Cr. Rd. W.
Puce R. Rd.
Brighton Rd
CR 2
PH 2
Charron Line Rd.
PH 2
Tecumseh Rd./CR 2
PH 2
CR 1
CR 36
Merlin Rd.
PH 2 / Richmond St.
River View Line/CR36
Thames River
CR 34/Grand Ave.
CR 35
Bear Line CR 43
CR 43
CR 35
CR 42
Electric Line
PH 40
St. Clair Rd.
Kell Rd. / PH 2
Wellington St.
51.2 (82.4) 39.6 (63.8) 17.4 (28.0) 9.0 (15.5) 0.0 (0.0)←↓Clockwise
Counterclockwise→↑ 0.0 (0.0) 11.6 (18.7) 33.8 (54.4) 42.2 (87.9) 51.2 (82.4)

84.2 (135.6) Notre Dame St. @ Tecumseh Rd. 19.0 (30.6)

Continue traveling on Notre Dame St. which once again becomes Tecumseh Rd. but this time PH 2 after you cross the Belle River. BELLE RIVER

87.8 (141.4) Puce River Rd. @ Tecumseh Rd./PH 2 15.4 (24.8)

Turn North on to Puce River Rd.

88.0 (141.7) Tecumseh Rd./CR 2 @ Puce River Rd. 15.2 (24.5)

Turn West on to Tecumseh Rd./CR 2.

91.6 (147.5) Brighton Rd./Tecumseh Rd. @ Tecumseh Rd./CR 2 11.6 (18.7)

Turn North on to Brighton Rd.
Or Turn South and then West following Tecumseh Rd. Tecumseh Rd./CR 2 cuts diagonally through Windor and its suburbs, saving a few miles/kilometers.
ST. CLAIR BEACH

91.9 (148.0) Riverside Dr. @ Brighton Rd. 11.3 (18.2)

Turn West on to Riverside Dr. As you go closer to the center of Windsor traffic increases.

101.0 (162.6) Walker Rd. @ Riverside Dr. 2.2 (3.5)

Turn on to Walker Rd. VIARail Station.

101.3 (163.1) Wyandotte St. E. @ Walker Rd. 1.9 (3.1)

Turn South (i. e., right) on to Wyandotte St. East.

102.8 (165.5) Goyeau St. @ Wyandotte St. E. 0.4 (0.6)

Turn West on to Goyeau St.
You could continue 2 more blocks to Ouelette St./PH 3B but its a very busy fast moving road. You're at the Windsor-Detroit Tunnel entrance. You want to be 2 blocks West at the bus terminal.

103.1 (166.0) University Ave. W. @ Goyeau St. 0.1 (0.2)

Turn South on to University Ave. W.

103.2 (166.2) Freedom Way @ University Ave. W. 0.0 (0.0)

Windsor Transit Bus Terminal.

WINDSOR

Information: CVB of Windsor, Essex County & Pelee Island, 333 Riverside Dr. W., Ste 103, Windsor ON N9A 5K4, 800 265-3633/ 519 255-6530.
Area code: 519. Postal codes: various

Bicycle Info.: Windsor Transit, 519 944-4111, operates buses between Windsor, ON and Detroit, MI. Supposedly there is a bus which is capable of transporting bicycles through the Tunnel. However, tje Windsor Transit web site states that this bus is not operating at the time of publishing this tour guide (2002).

The Ambassador Bridge (Detroit International Bridge Co.) does not permit bicycles on the roadway or walkway.

The only way to cross the Detroit River with a bicycle is to hitch a ride!

Bike shops, check the telephone book for a shop nearest to your location.

Services: All.

Attractions: Cultural: Art Gallery of Windsor, 3100 Howard Ave. (Devonshire Mall), 969-4494; Coventry Gardens, Riverside Dr. E. at Pillette Rd., 255-6276; François Baby House, 254 Pitt St. W., 263-1812; Serbian Heritage Mus., 6770 Tecumseh Rd. E., 253-1812; Willistead Manor, 1899 Niagara St., 255-6545; Windsor Light Opera Assoc., 2491 Jos. St. Louis, 974-6593.

Sports: Windsor Raceway, Hwy. 18, 969-8311; Casino Windsor, Riverside Dr., 258-7878.

Special: Windsor-Detroit Friendship Festival.

Lodging: Motels & hotels. B&Bs: Branteaney's, 1649 Chaps St., 966-2334; Larry & Marie Rose Neonates B&B, 111 Are PL, 948-1890; Diotte B&B, 427 Elm Ave., 256-3937; Berry Patch, 1521 Wentworth St., 250-0264. Camping: Windsor KOA, 9th Concession Rd. & Rt. 46, 735-3660.

Clockwise ↓ Read mi. (km.)	**Windsor to Sarnia**	Counterclockwise Read mi. (km.) ↑

Picture: Janis Kellogg

GEORGIAN BAY ROUTE

Travelers Notes

Caveat

Before starting to travel 'round Georgian Bay, the cyclotourist must be aware of several difficult sections along the route.

1. **Provincial Highway 6 (PH 6)** is used as little as possible. This is not a particularly pleasant road to cyclotour between Wiarton and Tobermory.
2. **Trans-Canada Highway 17 (TC 17):** The 73.3 km. (45.5 mi.) of Trans-Canada Highway 17 (TC 17) between Espanola and Sudbury is a heavily trafficked road with narrow lanes and a negligible shoulder. It is a dangerous road to bicycle. Consider taking the bus between these two points.
3. **Provincial Highway 69 (PH 69):** From Sudbury to Parry Sound this road is being reclassified as a 400 series limited access expressway. According to Ontario Ministry of Transportation a bicyclist can use PH 69 rom Sudbury to Parry Sound for the next several years (February, 2002 to ?) You are strongly urged to telephone the Ministry to make certain that this is true for the period of time you will be cycling the route.
4. **Provincial Highway 69 (PH 69):** From Parry Sound to Port Severn PH 69 has been reclassified as Expressway 400. This means you will not be able to cycle on this road. This is a significant problem since no other suitable road exists between these two points. Hitch a ride or use the Ontario-Northland bus as an alternative to being given a ticket by the police. Bus information is included in the text.

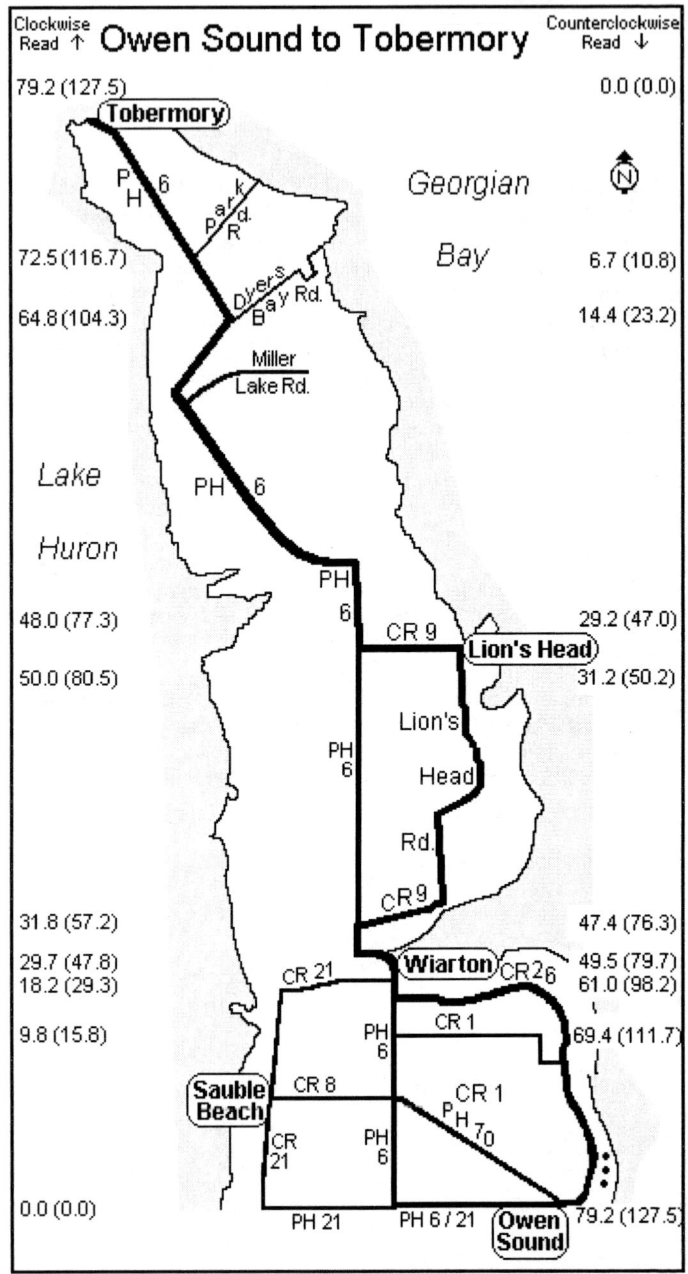
Clockwise Read ↑
Owen Sound to Tobermory
Counterclockwise Read ↓
79.2 (127.5)
0.0 (0.0)
Tobermory
PH 6
Park Rd.
Georgian
Bay
72.5 (116.7)
6.7 (10.8)
Dyers Bay Rd.
64.8 (104.3)
14.4 (23.2)
Miller Lake Rd.
Lake
Huron
PH 6
PH 6
48.0 (77.3)
29.2 (47.0)
CR 9
Lion's Head
50.0 (80.5)
31.2 (50.2)
Lion's Head Rd.
PH 6
CR 9
31.8 (57.2)
47.4 (76.3)
29.7 (47.8)
49.5 (79.7)
18.2 (29.3)
61.0 (98.2)
Wiarton
CR 26
CR 21
CR 1
PH 6
9.8 (15.8)
69.4 (111.7)
Sauble Beach
CR 8
CR 1
PH 70
CR 21
PH 6
0.0 (0.0)
79.2 (127.5)
PH 21
PH 6 / 21
Owen Sound

OWEN SOUND TO TOBERMORY

Clockwise ↓ Read mi. (km.)	**Owen Sound to Tobermory**	Counterclockwise mi. (km.) Read ↑

Travelers notes

You can break this segment into 2 sections, Owen Sound to Wiarton and Wiarton to Tobermory.

0.0 (0.0) Inner Harbor Walkway @ 10th W. St./PH 21/6 79.2 (127.5)

Travel West on W. 10th St./PH 21/6.

OWEN SOUND

Info.: Owen Sound CVB, PO Box 936, 832 2nd Ave. E., Owen Sound, ON N4K 6H6, 519 371-9833; Owen Sound Tourism, 1155 1st Ave. W., Owen Sound, ON N4K 4K8, 800 675-5555/519 371-9833,
http://city.owen-sound.on.ca
Area code: 519. Postal code: various.
Attractions: Niagara Escarpment World Biosphere Res., Owen Sound Pks. Dept., 376-1440; Owen Sound Marine Mus., 1165 1st Ave. W., 371-3333; Owen Sound Mus., 975 6th St. E., 376-3690; Roxy Theatre, 371-2833; Ontario Birding Reports, www.web-nat.com/bic/ont/index.html
Services: All. Bike shop.
Lodging: Motels. B&Bs: Brae Briar, 980 3rd Ave. W., 371-0025; Highland Manor Deluxe Victorian, 867 4th Ave. W., 372-2699; West Winds, RR 3, 376-9003. Camping: Harrison Pk./Kelso Beach, 75 2nd Ave. E., 371-9734; Owen Sound KOA, RR 6, 371-1331.

0.1 (0.2) 2nd Ave. W./ Eddie Sargent Pkwy. @ W. 10th St./PH 6 79.1 (127.4)

Turn North on to 2nd Ave. W./Eddie Sargent Pkwy. This is the scenic route.

Travelers Note

Direct Route North on the Bruce Peninsula

To proceed directly North on the Bruce Peninsula, continue traveling West on PH 21/6. Then cycle North on PH 6 along the Peninsula's spine to Tobermory. This route is described in the *Tobermory to Wiarton* segment as the *Wiarton Extension Route*.

1.0 (1.6) 3rd Ave. W. 78.2 (125.9)
Jct. Eddie Sargent Pkwy./2nd Ave. W.
Continue traveling North on 3rd Ave. W.

2.0 (3.2) CR 1 Jct. 3rd Ave. W. 77.2 (124.3)
Continue traveling North on CR 1.

9.8 (15.8) Dawson Rd./CR 26 @ CR 1 69.4 (111.7)
Turn East on to Dawson Rd./CR 1 to go the scenic way along the edge of Owen Sound and Colpoy's Bay.
If you prefer, continue following CR 1, it turns West in 1.6 km. (1 mi.) and joins PH 6, 16 km. (10 mi.) further on. It is then an additional 3.2 km. (2 mi.) to Wiarton & the Main Route, using PH 6. Total distance using the direct CR 1/PH 6 Route = 21 km. (13 mi.)

18.2 (29.3) Big Bay Village @ CR 26 61.0 (98.2)
Continue traveling on CR 26.
Great real home made ice cream at the corner store.

29.7 (47.8) PH 6 @ CR 26/Elm St. 49.5 (79.7)
Turn North on to PH 6.
Counterclockwise Georgian Bay cyclotourists can reduce their distance by continuing South here and turning East in 3.2 km. (2 mi.) on to CR 1/Kemble Rd. Follow CR 1 into Owen Sound. Using this direct route it is 11 km. (7 mi.) shorter to go to Owen Sound.

WIARTON

Info.: Bruce Peninsula Tourism, PO Box 269, Wiarton ON N0H 2T0, 519 534-2502. Area code: 519.

Lodging: Phone the lodging for its exact location and directions to it. Motels. B&Bs: Grey Bruce B&B Assoc., PO Box 916, 534-1210; Bayview, RR 6, 534-5013; Bruce Gables, 410 Berford St., 534-0429; Cedarholme, RR 6, 534-3705; Gadd-About, 501 Frank St., 800 354-9078; Hillcrest, 394 Gould St., 534-2262; Maplehurst, 277 Frank St., 534-1210; McIvor House, RR 4, 534-1769; Rosecliffe, 502435 Island View Dr., RR 2, 534-2776; Sally & Leighton's, RR 4, 534-3504; The Green Door, 376 Berford St., 534-4710; The Parke House, 220 Bruce Rd. 9, 534-0922; Thomas, 270 William St., 534-5432.

31.8 (51.2) CR 9 @ PH 6 47.4 (76.3)
Turn East on to CR 9.
Once again you have the choice of using heavily trafficked PH 6 or the more scenic lightly trafficked CR 9.
If you want, continue North on PH 6 all the way to

Tobermory.

48.0 (77.3) CR 29/Lion's Head Rd. @ CR 9/Ferndale Rd. 31.2 (50.2)

Turn West on Ferndale Rd./CR 9 will bring you to the main route to Tobermory via PH 6.
CR 29 will bring you directly into Lion's Head.

LION'S HEAD

Info: Area Code: 519. Postal code: NOH 1W0.
Attractions: Bruce Trail (hiking). Lion's Head Prov. Pk., (day use only.) Rock formations.
Lodging: Motels. B&Bs: 45th Parallel, 21 Main St., 793-3529; Cape Chin Connection, Cape Chin Rd N., RR 4, 888 999-6254; Cat's Pajamas, 64 Main St., 793-3767; Harvest Moon, PH 6, 592-5742; Northwinds, RR 1, 793-4590; Spirit of the Bruce, 672 East Rd., 795-7200; Taylor's, 31 Byron St., Gen. Del., 793-4853. Camping: Heron Point Trailer Pk., Box 275, 519 592-5871; Lakeside Pk., RR 2, 800-463-5514; Lion's Head Beach Pk., Box 310, 793-4090; Rockshore Trailer Pk., Isthmus Bay Rd., Box 197, 793-3326; Whispering Cedars, RR 2, 793-3219. Also see below the entries for Miller Lake Rd. & Dyer's Bay Rd.

50.0 (80.5) PH 6 @ CR 9/Ferndale Rd. 29.2 (47.0)

Turn North on to PH 6.

64.8 (104.3) Dyer's Bay Rd. @ PH 6 14.4 (23.2)

Continue traveling on PH 6. Dyer's Bay Rd. is a dead end road 6 mi. (9.7 km.) long.
Lodging: Dyers Bay Rd. B&Bs: Applewood Inn, 878 Dyers Bay Rd., 795-7552; Moeke's Ankerstee, 479 Dyers Bay Rd., 519 795-7769.
Miller Lake Rd. B&B: Plumica, RR 1, 519 795-7499.

72.5 (116.7) Bruce Peninsula Nat'l Pk. @ PH 6 6.7 (10.8)
Continue traveling on PH 6.
Or turn on to the Park Rd. Bruce Peninsula Nat'l Pk., camping, 596-2263.

79.2 (127.5) Tobermory Ferry @ PH 6 0.0 (0.0)

TOBERMORY

Info.: Tobermory CofC, PO Box 250, Tobermory, ON N0H 2R0, 800 265-3163/519 596-2510, www.tobermory.com. Area code: 519.

Services: Groceries and other retail stores. Local bike routes on the CofC web site.
Transportation: Chi-Cheemaun Ferry, Tobermory Terminal, 596-2510; 4 departures from Tobermory each day during the height of the season. Call to check the current schedule.

Attractions: Fathom Five Nat'l. Pk, PH 6, 596-2263; Bruce Peninsula Nat'l. Pk., PH 6, 596-2263. St. Edmund's Mus., PH 6, 596-2452. Diving around ship wrecks; sailing, canoeing. Bruce Trail (hiking only.)

Lodging: Motels. B&Bs: Bayside, Eagle Rd., 596-2712; Casa Verano, RR 1, 596-2471; Christine's, Elgin St., 596-8014; Cedars & Birches, Water St., 596-2100; Dogwood Point, 97 Eagle Rd. E., 596-2671; Guesthouse, Carlton St., 596-2350; Innisfree, Bay St., 596-8190; Our Nest, Maple Grove Cres., 596-2936; Paddling Gourmet, Bay St., 596-8343; Setting Sails, Eagle Rd., 596-2038; Sunset Bay, 432 Eagle Rd. W., 596-2286; Tobermory Shores, 7 Grant Watson Dr., 596-2010; Vista Hermosa, 119 Eagle Rd., 596-8065. Also see entries above for Miller Lake Rd. & Dyer's Bay Rd.
Camping: Bruce Peninsula Nat'l. Pk., Cyprus Lk., PH 6, 596-2263; Cha Nao Zah TeePee, PH 6, 596-2708; Happy Hearts TT Pk., RR 1, 596-2455; Harmony Acres Camp, RR 1, 596-2735; Land's End Pk., Hay Bay Rd., 596-2523; Tobermory Village, RR 1, 596-2689.

Counter Clockwise Travelers Note

We suggest that you break this segment into two (2) sections, Tobermory to Wiarton/Lion's Head and Wiarton/Lion's Head to Owen Sound.

Clockwise ↓ Read mi. (km.)	**Tobermory to Owen Sound**	Counterclockwise mi. (km.) Read ↑

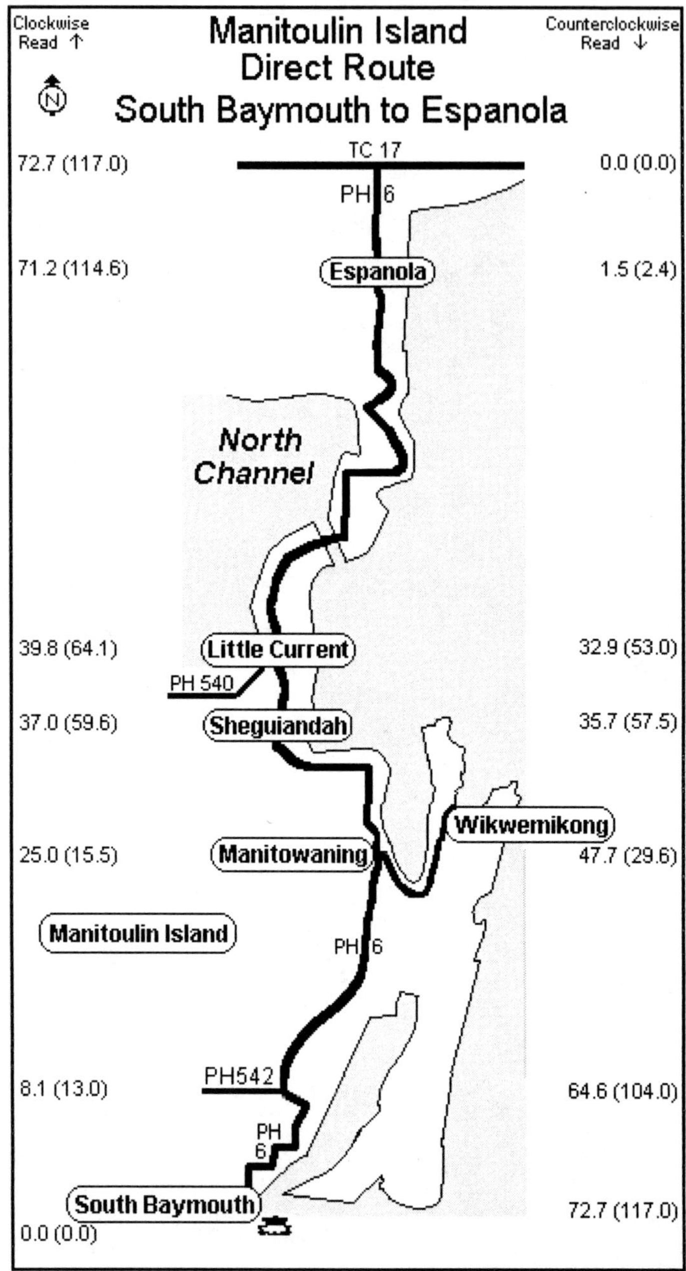
Clockwise Read ↑
Manitoulin Island
Direct Route
South Baymouth to Espanola
Counterclockwise Read ↓
N
TC 17
72.7 (117.0)
0.0 (0.0)
PH 6
71.2 (114.6)
Espanola
1.5 (2.4)
North Channel
39.8 (64.1)
Little Current
32.9 (53.0)
PH 540
37.0 (59.6)
Sheguiandah
35.7 (57.5)
Wikwemikong
25.0 (15.5)
Manitowaning
47.7 (29.6)
Manitoulin Island
PH 6
PH542
8.1 (13.0)
64.6 (104.0)
PH 6
South Baymouth
72.7 (117.0)
0.0 (0.0)

SOUTH BAYMOUTH TO ESPANOLA

Clockwise ↓ Read mi. (km.)	**Manitoulin Island Direct Route South Baymouth to Espanola**	Counterclockwise mi. (km.) Read ↑

Travelers Note

You're on Manitoulin Island. The direct route from the southern edge of the Island to the northern edge is presented here. The pedaling around route, *Manitoulin Island Scenic Loop*, to the western most point on the Island is in the *South Baymouth to Espanola* segment. The Island's ambiance will entice you to use the *Loop*.

Provincial Highway 6 (PH 6) from South Baymouth to Espanola presents no inherent problems for the bicyclist other than a massive long steep hill.

0.0 (0.0) Ferry Terminal @ PH 6 72.5 (116.7)

Travel North on PH 6.
Counterclockwise 'round the Bay cyclotourists, the ferry will arrive soon!

SOUTH BAYMOUTH

Info. & Services: Grocery and other stores. AC: 705. Transportation: Chi-Cheemaun Ferry, South Baymouth Terminal, 859-3161; 4 departures from South Baymouth each day during the season.
Attraction: Little School House & Mus.
Lodging: B&Bs: Gramsi's, 68 Church St., 859-2333; Southbay Guesthouse, 1802 South Bay Rd, 859-2363. Camping: John Budd Mem. Pk., First St., 859-3293; South Bay Resort TT Pk., 21214 PH 6, 859-3106.

8.1 (13.0) Hwy. 542A/542 @ PH 6 64.3 (103.5)

Continue traveling on PH 6 to directly cross the Island. Wanderers wanting to *loop around* turn West on to Hwy. 542 and then use the *Manitoulin Island Scenic Loop* in the *Espanola to South Baymouth Segment.*

25.0 (15.5) Manitowaning Village @ PH 6 47.7 (29.6)

Continue traveling on PH 6.
Turn East here to go to Wikwemikong.

MANITOWANING & WIKWEMIKONG

MANITOWANING: **Attractions:** The Assiginack Mus., 859-3905; S.S. Norisle Herit. Pk.; McLean Pk. Trl.

Lodging: Camping: Camp Bray More, RR 1, 859-3488; Holiday Haven Resort, 152 Holiday Haven Rd., 859-3550; L & J TT Pk. RR 2, 859-3154; Black Rock Resort, 859-3347.

WIKWEMIKONG: **Attraction:** Wikwemikong Bay Marina Mus., 859-2850. **Lodging:** B&B: Baywatch, Murray Hill Rd., 859-2955. Camping: Peltier's TT Pk., 61A61B Cape Smith Rd., 859-3657.

37.0 (59.6) Sheguiandah Hamlet @ PH 6 35.7 (57.5)
Continue traveling on PH 6.

SHEGUIANDAH

Attractions: Howland Centennial Mus., 368-2367; Orr's Mountain, Lewis Twin Peaks Trl.

Lodging: B&B: Lakeview Garden, 859-2042; Whitehaven Resort, 368-2554. Camping: Green Acres TT Pk., PH 6, 368-2428; Batman's Cottages, PH 6, 368-2180.

39.6 (63.8) Hwy. 540 @ PH 6 32.9 (53.0)
Direct cross the Island cyclists travel on PH 6. Counterclockwise wandering cyclists can turn West on to Hwy. 540 and use the *Manitoulin Island Scenic Loop* in the *South Baymouth to Espanola Segment.*

LITTLE CURRENT

Services: Grocery and other retail stores.

Attractions: Gordon's Outdoor Wildlife Mus.

Lodging: B&B: Ruth's, 368-3891; Wedgewood Inn, 31 Worthington St., 368-3876; Nancy's, 368-1253. Camping: On PH 6 at Sheguiandah & Manitowaning.

71.0 (114.3) Barber St. @ Centre St./PH 6 1.5 (2.4)
Continue traveling on PH 6/Centre St. or stop here in Espanola itself.

ESPANOLA

Info.: Area code: 705
Services: Grocery and other retail stores.
Transportation: Greyhound, 134 Barber St., 869-2242. There are three buses a day, in each direction, between Espanola and Sudbury (morning, mid-day, and evening). There are two buses a day, in each direction, (morning and afternoon) between Espanola and Sault Ste. Marie. Call a few days in advance to make certain that the Espanola Greyhound station has bicycle boxes or bags.
If the agent states that bike boxes or bags are not available (According to Greyhound-Canada bike boxes have to be sent from Vancouver.) then ask the agent to have a driver bring bike boxes or bags from the Ontario-Northland ticket office in Sudbury.
Lodging: Motels.

72.5 (116.7) TC 17 @ PH 6 0.0 (0.0)
Turn East on TC (Trans-Canada Hwy.) 17 to go Whitefish, Sudbury and continue 'round Georgian Bay.
Turn West on TC 17 to go to Sault Ste. Marie and 'round Lake Huron.

Caveat

TC 17 is a wretched road for bicyclists to traverse. It is heavily trafficked with wide bodied, long, fast moving vehicles. TC 17 has a negligible gravel shoulder. I reccommend that use the bus to go from Espanola to Whitefish or Sudbury. Many bicyclists do cycle on TC 17 and many wish they took the bus.

Manitoulin Island Direct Route

Clockwise ↓ Read mi. (km.)	**Espanola to South Baymouth**	Counterclockwise mi. (km.) Read ↑

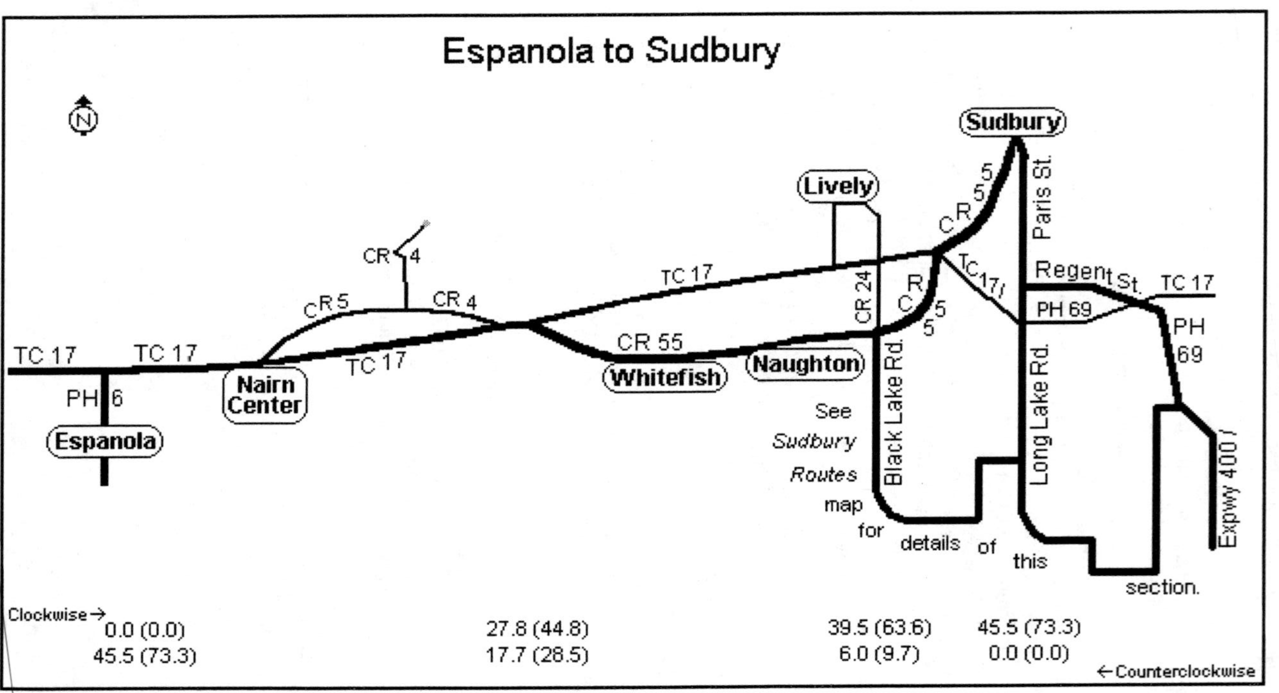
Espanola to Sudbury
TC 17
TC 17
PH 6
Espanola
Nairn Center
CR 5
CR 4
CR 4
TC 17
TC 17
CR 55
Whitefish
Naughton
Lively
CR 24
CR 55
Black Lake Rd.
Sudbury
CR 55
TC 17
Paris St.
Regent St.
TC 17
PH 69
PH 69
Long Lake Rd.
Expwy 400
See Sudbury Routes map for details of this section.
Clockwise→
0.0 (0.0) 45.5 (73.3)
27.8 (44.8) 17.7 (28.5)
39.5 (63.6) 6.0 (9.7)
45.5 (73.3) 0.0 (0.0)
←Counterclockwise

ESPANOLA TO SUDBURY

Clockwise ↓ Read mi. (km.)	**Espanola to Sudbury**	Counterclockwise mi. (km.) Read ↑
00 (0.0)	Barber St. @ Centre St./PH 6	45.5 (73.3)

Travel North on PH 6/Centre St.

ESPANOLA information is in the *South Baymouth to Espanola* segment.

1.5 (2.4)	TC 17 @ PH 6	44.0 (70.8)

Turn East on to TC 17 to go to Sudbury and 'Round Georgian Bay. TC 17 is a heavily trafficked, narrow road with wide bodied vehicles. Use extreme caution. Do not travel on this road when the sun is low in the sky. Motorists will have a hard time discerning a bicyclist from the surrounding environment.

McKERROW: **Lodging:** Motel.

NAIRM CENTRE:(A bit further East on TC 17): **Lodging:** Riverside Cpgd., Birch St., 705 869-2049.

27.8 (44.8)	CR 55 @ TC 17	17.7 (28.5)

Continue traveling on CR 55 or TC 17.

WHITEFISH

Lodging: Motel. Camping: Cedar Grove, CR 55, 705 866-0722; Holiday Beach, CR 55, 705 866-0303; Fairbank Prov. Pk., N. of TC 17, W., 705 866-0530.

39.5 (63.6)	TC 69 @ CR 55/TC 17	6.0 (9.7)

Turn East on to TC 69 and begin to 'round the Bay.

Or travel into downtown Sudbury using TC 17. If you go into Sudbury you'll be able to go directly to TC 69 via CR 80/Paris St. from the heart of Sudbury. It is 7.4 km. (4.6 mi.) from TC 17/Elm St. in the center of Sudbury to TC 69 via CR 80/Paris St.

AZILDA: **Lodging:** Camping: Bayside-Balfour Whitewater Pk., Montee Principale, 705 983-5690.

45.5 (73.3)	CR 80 @ TC 69	0.0 (0.0)

Turn North on to CR 80/Paris St. to go into downtown Sudbury, 7.4 km. (4.6 mi.)

SUDBURY

Info.: Sudbury CVB, 200 Brady St., Sudbury ON P3A 5PA, 705 674-3141, www.city.sudbury.on.ca.
Area code: 705.

Services: All. Bike shop.
Transportation: Sudbury Bus Terminal Ltd., 854 Notre Dame Ave., Greyhound-Canada, 524-9900; Ontario Northland bus.

Attractions: Anderson Farm Mus., RR 24, Lively ON 692-4448; Big Nickel Mine, Lorne St., 522-3700; Copper Cliff Mus., Power St., 705 674-3141; Laurentian Univ. Mus., 251 John St., 674-3271; Science North, Ramsey Lake Rd., 522-3700. Cortina Cruise, Science North Dock, 522-3701.

Lodging: B&Bs: Southbay Guesthouse II, 1802 South Bay Rd., 671-9611; Loonsnest, 5962 Onwatin Lake Rd., 674-9829. Camping: Carol Cpgd., 1989 TC 69 (W. of CR 80/Paris St.), 522-5570; Mine Hill Cpgd., TC 69, 522-5076.

Clockwise ↓ Read mi. (km.)	**Sudbury to Espanola**	Counterclockwise mi. (km.) Read ↑

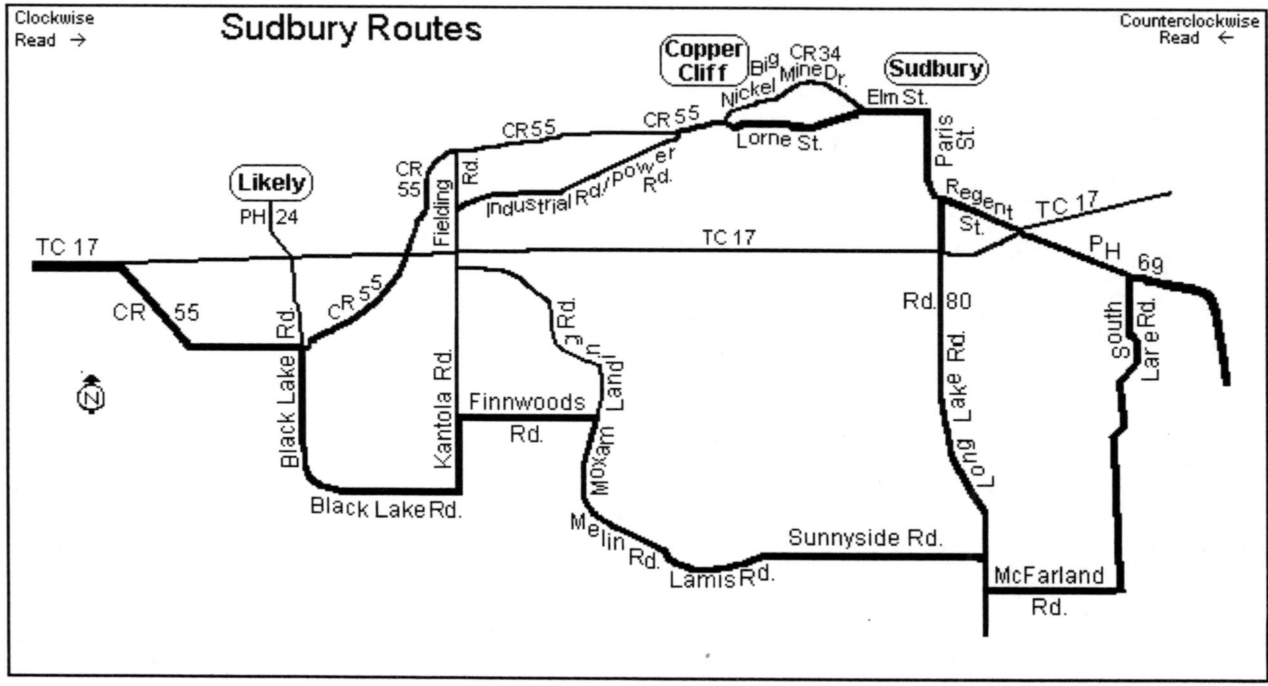
Clockwise Read →
Sudbury Routes
Counterclockwise Read ←
Copper Cliff
Sudbury
Likely
CR34
Big Mine Dr.
Nickel
Elm St.
CR 55
CR55
Lorne St.
Paris St.
CR 55
Fielding Rd.
Industrial Rd./Power Rd.
Regent St.
TC 17
PH 24
TC 17
TC 17
PH 69
CR 55
CR 55
Black Lake Rd.
Kantola Rd.
Finnwoods Rd.
Moxam Landing Rd.
Rd. 80
Long Lake Rd.
South Lare Rd.
Black Lake Rd.
Melin Rd.
Lamis Rd.
Sunnyside Rd.
McFarland Rd.

SUDBURY TO PORT SEVERN

Travelers Note

Trans-Canada Highway 69 (TC 69) is being reclassified as Expwy. 400, between Sudbury and Barrie during the next few years. Bicycles are not permitted on Expwy. 400 series roads.

There are very few roads, parallel to TC 69, which are suitable for bicycle riding. Most of the roads near Georgian Bay and parallel to TC 69 are discontinuous. Don't blame the Ministry of Transportation, it is due to geography. However you can write the Ministry and suggest that they construct a bicycle trail parallel to TC 69/Expwy. 400 for its entire length from Sudbury to Barrie.

During the period of reclassification and reconstruction bicycles are permitted on this road. Extreme caution is advised.

Before you leave Sudbury, check with the Ministry of Transportation to make certain that you will be able to bicycle on Trans-Canada Highway 69 (TC 69) all the way to Parry Sound.

Between Parry Sound and Port Severn TC 69 has been reclassified as Expwy. 400. You will have to take the bus to traverse this section of the route.

If you determine that it is impossible to use TC 69/Expwy. 400, then take Ontario Northland bus from Sudbury to Port Severn; or hitch a ride.

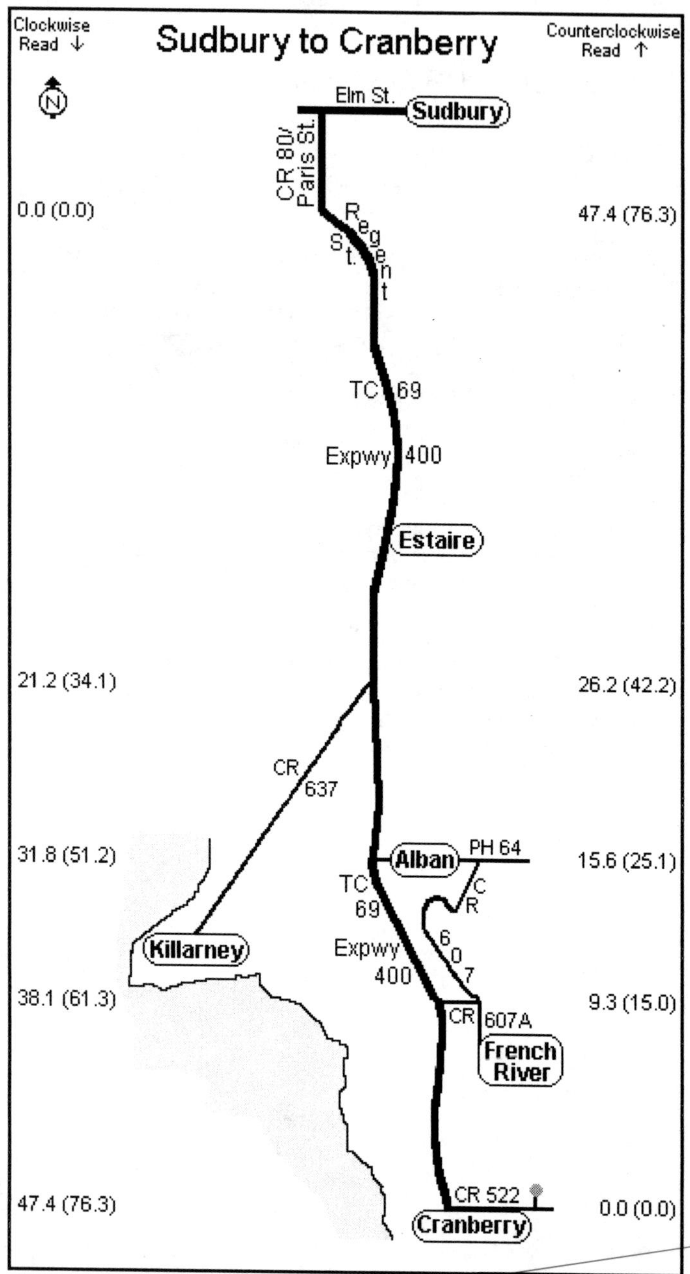
Clockwise
Read ↓
Sudbury to Cranberry
Counterclockwise
Read ↑
N
Elm St.
Sudbury
CR 80/
Paris St.
0.0 (0.0)
47.4 (76.3)
Regent
St.
TC 69
Expwy 400
Estaire
21.2 (34.1)
26.2 (42.2)
CR 637
31.8 (51.2)
Alban
PH 64
15.6 (25.1)
TC 69
CR
Killarney
Expwy 400
607
38.1 (61.3)
9.3 (15.0)
CR 607A
French River
47.4 (76.3)
CR 522
Cranberry
0.0 (0.0)

SUDBURY TO CRANBERRY

Clockwise ↓ Read mi. (km.)	**Sudbury to Cranberry**	Counterclockwise mi. (km.) Read ↑

0.0 (0.0) CR 80/Paris St. @ TC 69 47.4 (76.3)

Travel South on TC 69.
Turn North on to CR 80/Paris St. to go to Sudbury.
For SUDBURY information refer to the *Espanola to Sudbury* segment.
ESTAIRE: Estaire is ~24 km. (15 mi.) from this intersection. **Lodging:** Carol Campsite, 2388 Richard Lake Dr., 705 522-5570; Vacationland Cpgd., Napewassi Lake Rd., 705 695-2177.

21.2 (34.1) CR 637 @ TC 69 26.2 (42.2)

Continue traveling on TC 69.
CR 637 goes to Killarney Village and Killarney Prov. Pk. You will have to return to this intersection after going to the Park. One way distance = ~68 km. (~42 mi.) Lodging: Camping: Killarney Prov. Pk., 705 287-2900. Attraction: The Park; Killarney Mus., Commissioner's St., 705 287-2424.

31.8 (51.2) PH 64 @ TC 69 15.6 (25.1)

Continue traveling on TC 69.
PH 64 goes North to TC 17.
You can take a little diversion by turning East on to PH 64. In 7 km. (4.4 mi.), after going through Alban, turn South on to CR 607. You'll rejoin the TC 69, in about 12 km. (7.5 mi.)

ALBAN

Info.: Area code: 705.
Lodging: Camping: Sportsman's TT Pk., Daoust Lake Rd., (off TC 69 before PH 607), 857-0461; Deer Bay Pk., Golf Course Rd. (in Alban), 857-2543; Schell's Camp & Pk., RR 2 (E. on PH 607 to 607A to Schell's Rd.), 857-2031.

38.1 (61.3) CR 607/607A @ TC 69 9.3 (15.0)

Continue traveling on TC 69.
Turning East on to CR 607 will bring you to French River on CR 607A. See preceding entry for a diversionary route. There are several resorts in French River.
Turning West on to Hartley Bay road will bring you to

French River Prov. Pk., There are no facilities at this Park.

47.4 (76.3) CR 522 @ TC 69 0.0 (0.0)
Continue traveling on TC 69.

CRANBERRY

Info.: Convenience store.
Lodging: Turn East on to CR 522, and ride for 3.2 km. (2 mi.) to go to Grundy Lake Prov. Pk. (Camping), RR 1, Britt ON POG 1AO, 705 383-2286.

Clockwise ↓ Read mi. (km.)	**Cranberry to Sudbury**	Counterclockwise mi. (km.) Read ↑

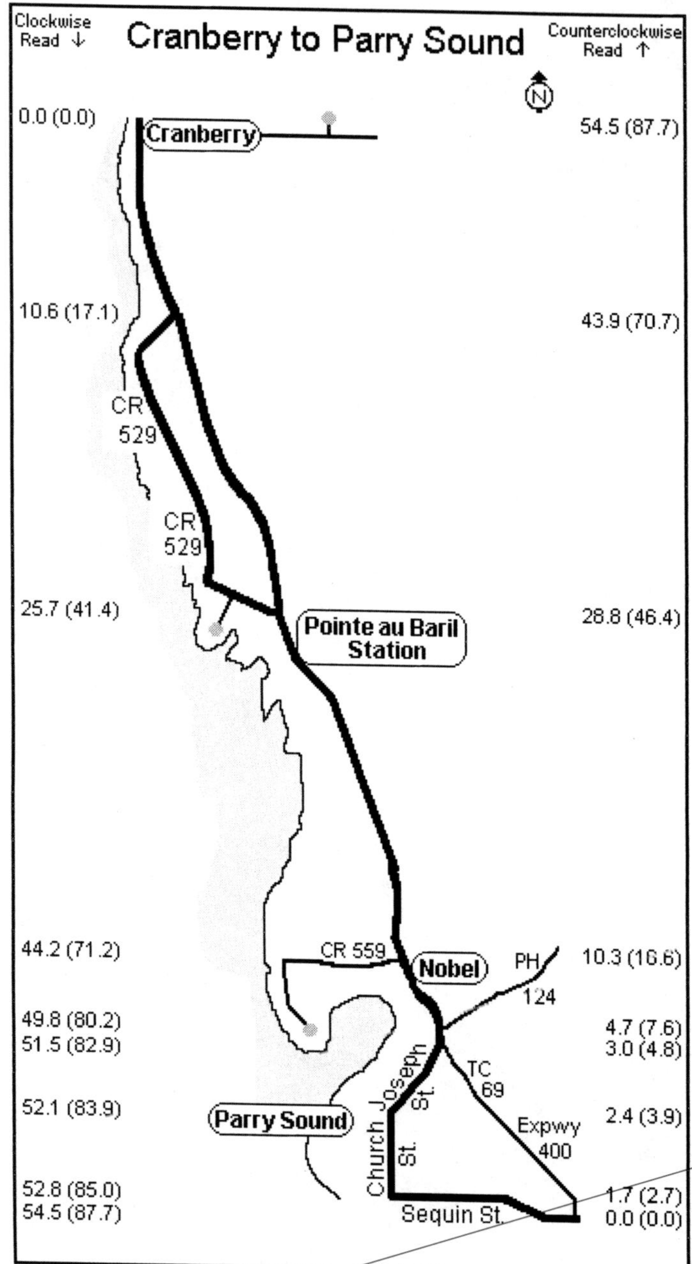
Clockwise Read ↓
Cranberry to Parry Sound
Counterclockwise Read ↑
N
0.0 (0.0)
Cranberry
54.5 (87.7)
10.6 (17.1)
43.9 (70.7)
CR 529
CR 529
25.7 (41.4)
Pointe au Baril Station
28.8 (46.4)
44.2 (71.2)
CR 559
Nobel
PH 124
10.3 (16.6)
49.8 (80.2)
51.5 (82.9)
4.7 (7.6)
3.0 (4.8)
Joseph St.
TC 69
52.1 (83.9)
Parry Sound
Expwy 400
2.4 (3.9)
Church St.
52.8 (85.0)
54.5 (87.7)
Sequin St.
1.7 (2.7)
0.0 (0.0)

CRANBERRY TO PARRY SOUND

Clockwise ↓ Read mi. (km.)	**Cranberry to Parry Sound**	Counterclockwise mi. (km.) Read ↑
0.0 (0.0)	CR 522 @ TC 69	54.5 (87.7)

Continue traveling on TC 69.
CRANBERRY information is in the *Sudbury to Cranberry* segment.

10.6 (17.1)	CR 529 @ TC 69	43.9 (70.7)

Turn Southwest on to CR 529.
Or continue traveling on TC 69.
Sturgeon Bay Prov. Pk. is at the southern end of CR 529, 705 366-2521; Forest Glen Resort, CR 529, 705 366-2841.

25.7 (41.4)	CR 529 @ TC 69	28.8 (46.4)

Turn South on to TC 69.
Counterclockwise cyclotourists can turn Northwest on to CR 529. CR 529 takes you to Sturgeon Bay Prov. Pk. (camping).
Or continue North on TC 69

44.2 (71.2)	CR 559 @ TC 69	10.3 (16.6)

Continue traveling on TC 69 to Parry Sound.
Turn West on to CR 559 for **Lodging**: Dillon Cove Resort, Dillon Rd., 705 342-5431; Killbear Prov. Pk. (camping)., 705 366-2521. It is 21 km. (13 mi.) on CR 559 to the Park.

49.8 (80.2)	Parry Sound Dr./PR 124 @ TC 69	4.7 (7.6)

Turn Southwest on to Parry Sound Dr.

51.5 (82.9)	Joseph St. @ Parry Sound Dr.	3.0 (4.8)

Bear due South on to Joseph St.

52.1 (83.9)	Isabella St. @ Joseph St./Church St.	2.4 (3.9)

Continue traveling South on Church St.

52.8 (85.0)	Seguin St. @ Church St.	1.7 (2.7)

Turn East on to Seguin St.

53.0 (85.3)	Sequin River @ Sequin St./Bowes St.	1.5 (2.4)

Continue traveling on Sequin St./Bowes St.
Seguin St. changes its name to Bowes St. as it crosses the River.

54.5 (87.7) TC 69 @ Bowes St. 0.0 (0.0)

Counterclockwise travelers turn West on to Bowes St. to go into Parry Sound.

PARRY SOUND

Info.: Parry Sound Tourism, 1-A Church St., Parry Sound ON P2A 1Y2, 705 746-4455, www.parrysoundarea.com; Parry Sound Area CofC, 70 Church St., Parry Sound ON P2A 1Y9, 800 461-4261/705 746-4213.

Area code: 705. Postal Code: various.

Services: All. Bike Shop. Scheduled Ontario-Northland bus stop from Sudbury to Barrie,

Attractions: West Parry Sound Mus., Tower Hill Pk., 746-5365; Island Queen Cruises, Gov't. Wharf/Hay St., 746-2311; M. V. Chippewa, 19 Bay St., 746-6064.

Lodging: Motels. B&Bs: Belvedere, 6 Waubeek St., 746-8372; Blackwater Lake, 167 Blackwater Lake Rd., 389-3746; Carson House, 33 Church St., 746-8768; Parry Sound B&B Assoc., Box 21, Parry Sound ON P2A 2X2, 705 746-9305. Camping: Hall's, 20 Mill Lake Rd., 740-5152; Hill Acres, TC 69, 285-4226; Parry Sound KOA, Rankin Lake Rd., 378-2721; Rainbow Camp, North Channel Rd., 898-2356; Richmond Lake Pk., TC 69, 746-2860; Roll in G, Clear Lake Rd., 375-2518. There are additional nearby campgrounds going South on TC 69, they are listed under the appropriate intersection or town in the *Parry Sound to Midland* segment.

Counter Clockwise Travelers Note

You must read the Note at the beginning of the *Sudbury to Port Severn* section.

Clockwise ↓ Read mi. (km.)	**Parry Sound to Cranberry**	Counterclockwise mi. (km.) Read ↑

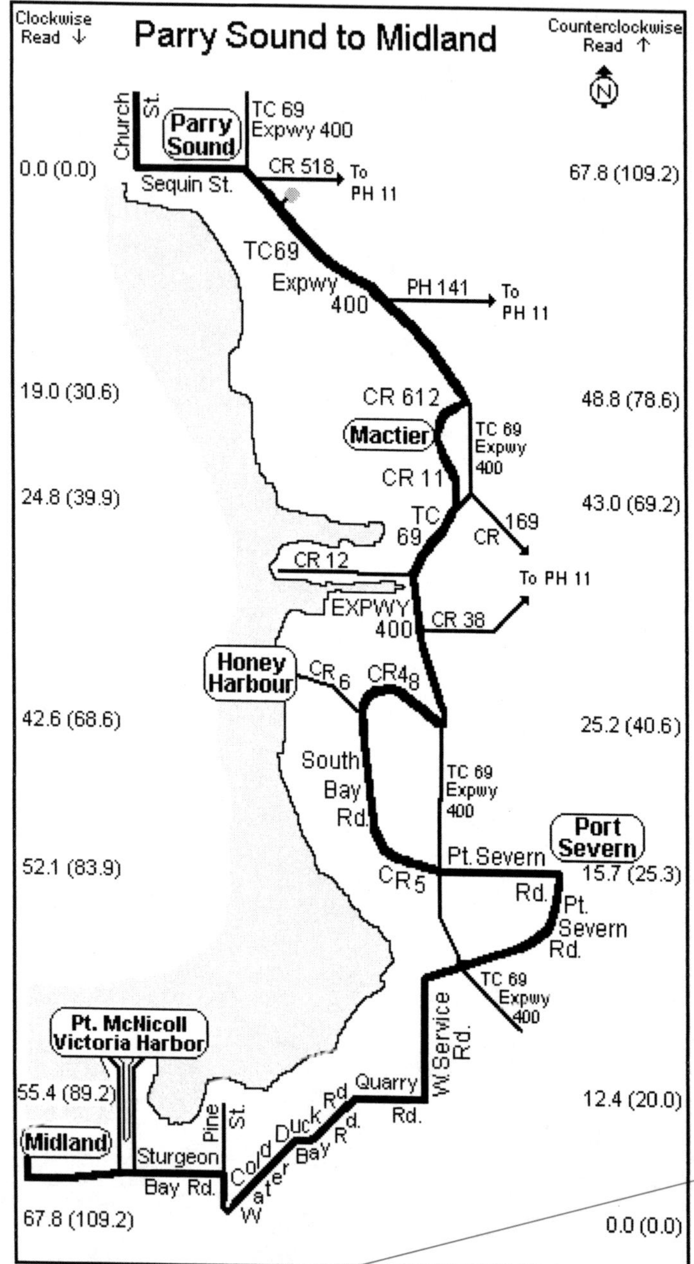
Clockwise Read ↓
Parry Sound to Midland
Counterclockwise Read ↑
N
Church St.
Parry Sound
TC 69 Expwy 400
0.0 (0.0)
Sequin St.
CR 518
To PH 11
67.8 (109.2)
TC69 Expwy 400
PH 141
To PH 11
19.0 (30.6)
CR 612
48.8 (78.6)
Mactier
TC 69 Expwy 400
CR 11
24.8 (39.9)
TC 69
CR 169
43.0 (69.2)
CR 12
To PH 11
EXPWY 400
CR 38
Honey Harbour
CR 6
CR48
42.6 (68.6)
25.2 (40.6)
South Bay Rd.
TC 69 Expwy 400
Port Severn
Pt. Severn Rd.
52.1 (83.9)
CR 5
15.7 (25.3)
Pt. Severn Rd.
TC 69 Expwy 400
W. Service Rd.
Pt. McNicoll Victoria Harbor
55.4 (89.2)
Quarry Rd.
12.4 (20.0)
Pine St.
Cold Duck Rd.
Water Bay Rd.
Midland
Sturgeon Bay Rd.
67.8 (109.2)
0.0 (0.0)

PARRY SOUND TO MIDLAND

Clockwise ↓ Read mi. (km.)	**Parry Sound to Midland**	Counterclockwise mi. (km.) Read ↑

0.0 (0.0) Seguin St. @ Church St. 67.8 (109.2)

Turn East on to Seguin St.
PARRY SOUND information is in the *Cranberry to Parry Sound* segment.

0.2 (0.3) Sequin River @ Sequin St./Bowes St. 67.6 (108.8)

Seguin St. changes its name as it crosses the River.

1.7 (2.7) TC 69 @ Bowes St. 66.1 (106.4)

Turn South on to TC 69.
Counterclockwise travelers turn West on to Bowes St. to go into Parry Sound.

4.2 (6.8) Oastler Prov. Pk. @TC 69 63.6 (102.4)

Continue traveling on TC 69.
Lodging: Camping: Oastler Lake Prov., Pk., TC 69, 378-2401; Trailside Pk., 105 Blue Lake Rd., 8 km. (5 mi.) S. of Parry Sound, 378-2844.

12.2 (19.6) PH 141 @ TC 69 55.6 (89.5)

Continue traveling on TC 69.
PH 141 goes East to PH 11.
Lodging: Area code 705. Camping: A J's, Horseshoe Lake Rd., 378-2762; Horseshoe Lake, Sandy Plains Rd. (off PH 141), 732-4928; Terrawoods on Horseshoe Lake, Horseshoe Lake Rd., Box 17; 378-2762.

19.0 (30.6) CR 612/CR 11 @ TC 69 48.8 (78.6)

Turn Southwest on CR 612/CR 11/High St.
This road crosses a District political boundary and thus the road numbers change. It's 612 at the northern end; CR 11/High St. at the southern end.

MAC TIER

Services: Grocery, restaurants, hardware store.
Transportation: Scheduled stop on Ontario-Northland bus route, 705 375-5111.

24.8 (39.9) CR 11/CR 612 @ TC 69 43.0 (69.2)

Turn on to TC 69 and travel South.
Counterclockwise travelers should turn on to CR 11/

High St. (which becomes CR 612 as it crosses a District boundary.)

29.7 (47.8) CR 12 @ TC 69 38.1 (61.3)
Continue travekubg on TC 69.
CR 12, 21 km. (13 mi.) leads to O'Donnell Point Prov. Pk., a natural environment park, no camping.

33.5 (53.9) CR 38 @ TC 69 34.3 (55.2)
Continue traveling on TC 69.
This is a crucial intersection. You will not be able to bicycle very much further South on TC 69, it becomes Expwy 400 in 6.1 km. (3.8 mi.) The actual distance you have to bicycle on Expwy 400 is only 10.9 km. (6.8 mi.).
Your options are:

1. Wait for the Ontario-Northland bus.
2. Hitch a ride with a passing vehicle.
3. Turn East on to CR 38 and take a round about inland route via Bala to Sturgeon Bay.
4. Take your chances and bicycle on the expressway's shoulder.

The bus or hitch are the preferrable options.

35.8 (57.6) Expwy 400 @ TC 69 32.0 (51.5)
You will have to ride on Expwy. 400 for only 10.9 km. (6.8 mi.) This presents a problem. You will be breaking the law if you go any further South on Expwy. 400.
Info.: Georgian Bay Tsp. Welcome Ctr., 705 538-0817.

42.6 (68.6) CR 48/South Bay Rd. @ Expwy 400, exit 162. 25.2 (40.6)
Exit Expwy 400, on to South Bay Rd./CR 48.
Travel Southwest on CR 48/South Bay Rd.

46.1 (74.2) CR 5 @ CR 48/South Bay Rd. 21.7 (34.9)
Travel South on CR 5.

HONEY HARBOUR & SOUTH BAY

Info.: Area code: 705. Postal code: P0E 1E0
Services: Grocery, hardware store and restaurants in Honey Harbor.
Attraction: Georgian Bay Islands Prov. Pk. Box 28, 756-2415, camping allowed only on the islands.
Lodging: B&Bs: Panacea, 756-2156; Elks Hide-A-Way, 756-2993. Camping: Bayview Marine Resort, 756-2482; Bluewater Resort, 756-2454; Brandy's Island, 756-2132; Dreamers Trailer Pk., 756-8070; Hidden Glen, 756-2675; King's Portage, 756-2323; Picnic Is. Resort, 756-2421.

51.1 (82.3) Expwy. 400 16.7 (26.9)
@ CR 5/Port Severn Rd.

Cross under Expwy. 400.
You'll be on Port Severn Rd. after crossing the Expwy. Travel into Port Severn.

52.1 (83.9) Kelly's Rd./Pt. Severn Rd. 15.7 (25.3)
@ Pt. Severn Rd.

Turn South on Pt. Severn Rd. or Kelly's Rd.

PORT SEVERN

Info.: Tsp. of Georgian Bay, 99 Lone Pine Rd., Port Severn ON L0K 1S0, 800 567-0187/705 538-2337, www.township.georgianbay.on.ca. Area code: 705.
Services: Grocery, restaurants, hardware store.
Transportation: Scheduled stop on Ontario-Northland bus, 538-2941.
Attraction: Lock 45, Trent-Severn Canal.
Lodging: B&Bs: Rawley Lodge, 538-2272; Inn at Christe's Mill, 263 Port Severn Rd., 538-2354.

52.7 (84.8) West Service Rd. 15.1 (24.3)
@ Pt. Severn Rd.

After crossing over Expwy. 400, turn South on to West Service Rd. Use care as you cross over the Expwy. Exit # 153 is just after the overpass.

55.2 (88.9) Quarry Rd./CR 59 12.6 (20.3)
@ West Service Rd.

Turn West on to Quarry Rd./CR 59.

55.4 (89.2) Duck Bay Rd. 12.4 (20.0)
@ Quarry Rd./CR 59

Turn Southwest on to Duck Bay Rd.

56.0 (90.2) Coldwater Rd.. @ Duck Bay Rd. 11.8 (19.0)

Continue traveling Southwest on Coldwater Rd.

56.4 (90.8) Sturgeon Bay Rd./Pine St. @ Coldwater Rd. 11.4 (18.4)

Cross Pine St. on to Sturgeon Bay Rd.

WAUBAUSHENE & COLDWATER

Info.: Coldwater is ~9 km. (5.6 mi.) South of this intersection along Coldwater Rd. Area code: 705.

Attraction: Waubaushene Prov. Pk., Natural Reserve (day use). Gratix Garden Lilies, Coldwater, 835-6794.

Lodging: B&Bs: WAUBAUSHENE: Heritage House, 337 Pine St., 538-1857; Lamplight Inn, 1163 Gratrix Rd, 835-5622. COLDWATER Echoing Hills, 3449 Beechwood Dr., 686-3776; Inn The Woods, 4240 6th Line N., 835-6193.

56.7 (91.3) PH 12/Heritage Dr. @ Sturgeon Bay Rd. 11.1 (17.9)

Turn West on to PH 12/Heritage Dr.

VICTORIA HARBOUR & PORT MCNICOLL

Info: Area code: 705.

Lodging: B&Bs: Canary Towne, 29 Maple St., Victoria Harbour, 534-3523; Mary's Cottage Garden, 601 4th Ave., Port McNicoll, 534-7809. Camping: Victoria Harbour Resort, 10 Winfield Dr., 534-7551.

66.1 (106.4) King St. @ PH 12/Heritage Dr. 1.7 (2.7)

Turn Northwest on to King St.

67.8 (109.2) Yonge St. @ King St. 0.0 (0.0)

MIDLAND

Info.: Midland CofC, 208 King St., Midland ON L4R 3L9, 705 526-7884, www.southerngeorgianbay.com. Area code: 705.

Services: All. Transportation: Georgian Bay Is. Natl. Pk. Water Taxi, Docks, 527-5586.

Attractions: Castle Village, 701 Balm Beach Rd., 526-9683; Huronia Mus., Little Lake Pk., 526-2844; 30,000 Island Cruise, 475 Bay St., 526-0161; Royal Canadian Legion Mus., 422 Gloucester St., 527-8080; Wye Marsh Wildlife Ctr., PH 12 E., 526-7809.

Lodging: B&Bs: A Place For All Seasons, 168 Hummingbird Hill Rd, 835-9948; B&B with the Artists, 431 King St., 526-8102; Beacon Shore on Georgian Bay, 128 Midland Point Rd., 526-5005; For The Birds Nature Studio, 76 Blueberry Marsh Rd., 835-0003; Little Lake Inn, 669 Yonge St., 526-2750; The Victorian Inn, 670

Hugel Ave., 526-4441; Trail's End, 45 Blueberry Marsh Rd., 835-2158. Camping: Bayfort Camp, Ogdens Beach Rd., 526-8704; Smith's Trailer Pk., 736 King St., 526-4339.

Clockwise ↓ Read mi. (km.)	**Midland to Parry Sound**	Counterclockwise mi. (km.) Read ↑

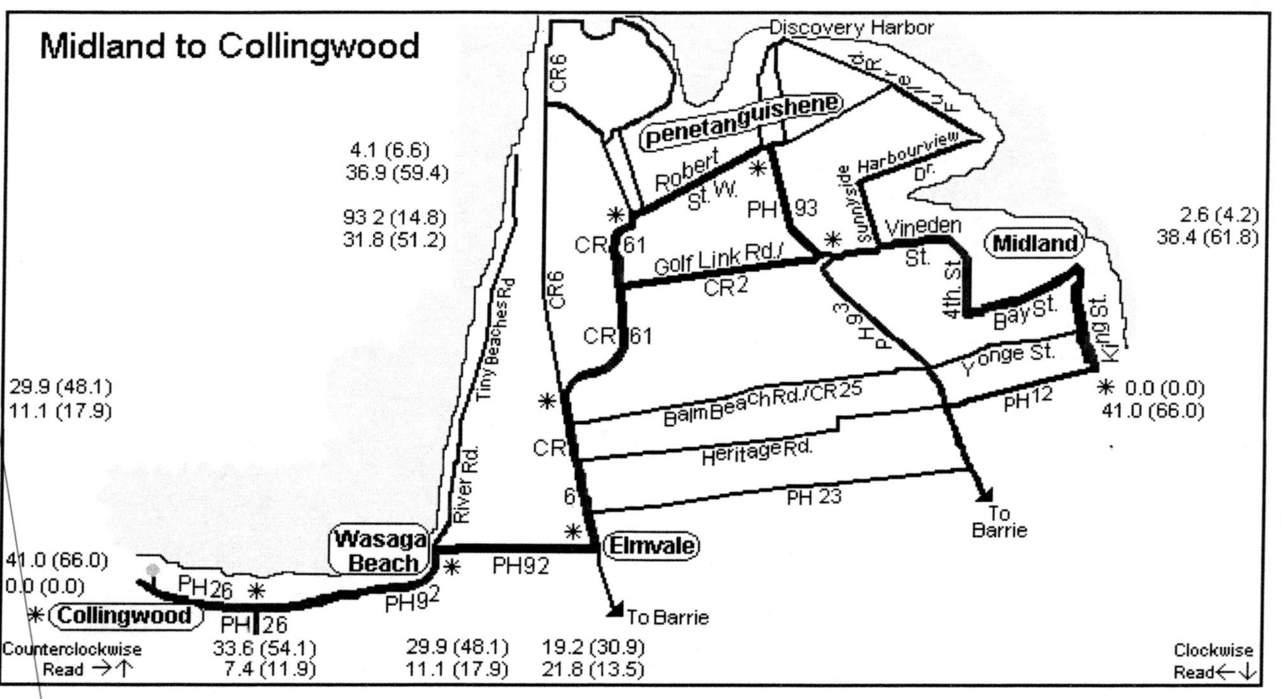
Midland to Collingwood
Discovery Harbor
Fuller Rd.
Penetanguishene
Harbourview Dr.
Sunnyside
Robert St. W.
PH 93
Vineden St.
Midland
4th. St
Bay St.
King St.
Yonge St.
PH12
PH 93
Golf Link Rd./ CR2
CR 61
CR 61
CR6
CR6
Balm Beach Rd./CR25
Heritage Rd.
PH 23
To Barrie
CR 6
Elmvale
To Barrie
PH92
Tiny Beaches Rd
River Rd.
Wasaga Beach
PH92
PH26
PH 26
Collingwood
4.1 (6.6)
36.9 (59.4)
93 2 (14.8)
31.8 (51.2)
2.6 (4.2)
38.4 (61.8)
0.0 (0.0)
41.0 (66.0)
29.9 (48.1)
11.1 (17.9)
41.0 (66.0)
0.0 (0.0)
33.6 (54.1)
7.4 (11.9)
29.9 (48.1)
11.1 (17.9)
19.2 (30.9)
21.8 (13.5)
Counterclockwise
Read →↑
Clockwise
Read ←↓

MIDLAND TO COLLINGWOOD

Clockwise ↓ Read mi. (km.)	Main Route Midland to Collingwood	Counterclockwise mi. (km.) Read ↑

0.0 (0.0) Yonge St. @ King St. 41.0 (66.0)

Travel Northwest on King St.

MIDLAND information is in the *Parry Sound to Midland* segment.

0.4 (0.6) Bay St. @ King St. 40.6 (65.4)

Turn West on Bay St.

0.7 (1.1) 4th St. @ Bay St. 40.3 (64.9)

Turn Northwest on 4th St.

1.2 (1.9) Vinden St./CR 2 @ 4th St. 39.8 (64.1)

Turn West on to Vinden St./CR 2.

2.6 (4.2) CR 93/Penetanguishene Rd. @ Venden St./CR 2 38.4 (61.8)

Turn North on CR 93/Penetanguishene Rd.

Turning South on to CR 93 will bring you to Wyebridge after cycling for 5 km. (3 mi.).

WYEBRIDGE

Info.: Area code: 705.

Attraction: Wye Lake Marsh Prov. Pk., wildlife area.

Lodging: B&Bs: Hackney Horse, 39 Darby Rd., 322-1339; Two Ponds, 7300 CR 93, 526-7673.

4.1 (6.6) Robert St. W. @ CR 93/Penetanguishene Rd. 36.9 (59.4)

Turn South on Robert St. W.

PENETANGUISHENE

Info.: Penetanguishene-Tiny CofC, 2 Main St., Penetanguishene ON L9M, 1T1, 705 549-2232; www.southerngeorgianbay.com. Area code: 705.

Attractions: Discovery Harbour, 93 Jury Dr., 549-8064/ 527-7771; King's Wharf Theatre, 93 Jury Dr., 549-5555; 30,000 Island Cruises, Town Dock, 549-7795; Centennial Mus., 13 Burke St., 549-2150.

Lodging: Motels. B&Bs: Bluenose, 37 Jennings Dr., 549-2964; Canopy of Trees, 124 Farlain Lake Rd. W., 549-1964; Champlain Lodge, 438 Champlain Rd., 549-

3718; Chesham Grove, 72 Church St., 549-3740; McGibbon's By The Bay, 32 Water St., 549-1060; No.1 Jury Drive, 1 Jury Dr., 549-6851; On The Bay, 54 Beck Blvd., 549-6030; Payette House, 27 Church St., 549-6794; Sue's, 121 Fox St., 549-8203. The Burgundy Door, 1281 Methodist Pt. Rd., 533-1696. Camping: Awenda Prov. Pk., 670 Conc 18 E., 549-2231; Lafontaine, 240 Lafontaine Rd. E., 533-2961; Ojibway Landing, 111 Robert St. W., 549-2531.

5.1 (8.2) Champlain Rd. @ Robert St. W. 35.9 (57.8)
Continue traveling West on Robert St. W.
Champlain Rd./Conc. Rd. 17/Kettle's Beach Rd. circles around the Tiny Peninsula ending at Awenda Prov. Pk. It is ~24 km. (15 mi.) from here to Awenda Prov. Pk.
See the *Tiny Peninsula Loop* for a shorter way to go to Awenda Prov. Pk.

5.3 (8.5) CR 26/Lafontaine Rd. @ Robert St. W. 35.7 (57.5)
Travel a bit further on Robert St. W. Actually 1 pedal stroke to CR 61.
Traveling North on CR 26 will bring you to Cedar Pt. or Thunder Beach, at the top of the Peninsula. A signed turn off along CR 26 will bring you to Awenda Prov. Pk.

5.4 (8.7) CR 61 @ Robert St. W. 35.6 (57.3)
Bear Southwest on to CR 61.

Travelers Note
The main *Midland to Collingwood* route continues after the *Tiny Peninsula Loop.*

Main Route
Midland to Collingwood

Clockwise ↓ Read mi. (km.)		Counterclockwise mi. (km.) Read ↑

Clockwise ↓ Read mi. (km.)	**Tiny Peninsula Loop**	Counterclockwise mi. (km.) Read ↑

Travelers Note

This is a loop trip. Gauge your time carefully there are very limited services along the way..
Road designation abbreviations: Conc. = Concession Rd.; CR = County Road.
See PENETANGUISHENE for information.

0.0 (0.0) CR 26/Lafontaine Rd. @ Robert St. W. 22.1 (35.6)

Turn North on CR 26/Lafontaine Rd.

0.1 (0.2) MacAvalley Rd. @ CR 26/Lafontaine Rd. 22.0 (35.4)

Continue traveling on CR 26.
Traveling N. on MacAvalley Rd., Conc. Rd. 16 & Awenda Pk. Rd. for ~9 mi. (~14.5 km.) brings you to the Park.

2.2 (3.5) Conc. Rd. 16 E. @ CR 26 19.9 (32.0)

CR 26/Lafontaine Rd. turns West here, follow it!
Traveling E. on Conc. Rd. 16 E. brings you to Pk. Rd.

4.2 (6.8) CR 6 @ CR 26 17.9 (28.8)

Continue traveling CR 26/Conc. Rd. 16 W.
Turning North on CR 6 will bring you to Thunder Beach, center top of the Peninsula in 2.4 km. (1.5 mi.)
Turning South on CR 6 will bring you back to the *Main Route, Midland to Collingwood.*

6.1 (9.8) Cedar Pt. Rd. @ CR 26/Conc. Rd. 16 E. 16.0 (25.8)

Turn North on CR 26/Cedar Pt. Rd.

LAFONTAINE

Services: Convenience store.
Lodging: Camping: Lafontaine Cpgd., 240 Lafontaine Rd. E., 705 533-2961.

7.9 (12.7) Conc. Rd. 18 W. @ CR 26/Cedar Pt. Rd. 14.2 (22.9)

CR 26/Cedar Pt. Rd. goes West along Conc. Rd. 18 W. from this point.

8.9 (14.3) CR 26/Conc. Rd. 18 W. @ CR 26/Cedar Pt. Rd. 13.2 (21.3)

Turn North on to CR 26/Cedar Pt. Rd.

10.9 (17.5) Cedar Pt. 11.2 (18.0)
North Shore Rd. is discontinuous.
Pop a wheelie and do a 180.

11.9 (19.2) Conc. Rd. 18 W. 10.2 (16.4)
@ CR 26/Cedar Pt. Rd.
Turn East on Conc. Rd. 18.

13.7 (22.1) Cedar Pt. Rd./CR 26 8.4 (13.5)
@ Conc. Rd. 18 W./CR 26
Turn South on CR 26/Cedar Pt. Rd.

15.6 (25.1) CR 26/Lafontaine Rd./ 6.5 (10.5)
16 Conc. Rd.
@ Cedar Pt. Rd./CR 26
Turn East on to Lafontaine Rd./CR 26
LAFONTAINE: **Services:** Local stores, some lodging.

17.6 (28.3) CR 6 @ CR 26/Lafontaine Rd. 4.5 (7.2)
Turn South on to CR 6.

22.1 (35.6) CR 61/Conc. Rd. 11 E. @ CR 6 0.0 (0.0)
Continue traveling South on CR 6/King St.
The *Main Route, Midland to Collingwood* junctions here with the *Tiny Peninsula Loop*.

Clockwise ↓ Read mi.	**Tiny Peninsula Loop**	Counterclockwise mi. (km.) Read ↑

Clockwise ↓ Read mi. (km.)	**Main Route, continued Midland to Collingwood**	Counterclockwise mi. (km.) Read ↑

Counterclockwise Travelers Note

The *Main Route, Midland to Collingwood* continues after the *Tiny Peninsula Loop.*

5.4 (8.7) CR 61 @ Robert St. W. 35.6 (57.3)

Bear Southwest on to CR 61.

6.9 (11.1) Golf Link Rd. @ CR 61 34.1 (54.9)

Bear Southwest on to CR 61 which also takes the nom d'plume of Conc. Rd. 11 E./CR 61.

9.2 (14.8) CR 6/King St. @ CR 61/Conc. Rd. 11 E. 31.8 (51.2)

Turn South on to CR 6/King St.

10.2 (16.4) CR 25/Balm Beach Rd. @ CR 6 30.8 (49.6)

Continue traveling on CR 6/King St.
CR 25 goes directly into/from Midland to CR 6.

16.2 (26.1) CR 23 @ CR 6 25.8 (41.5)

Continue traveling South on CR 6.

19.2 (30.9) PH 92 @ CR 6 19.8 (31.8)

Turn West on to PH 92.
ELMVALE

24.2 (39.0) River Rd. E./PH 92 @ PH /92 16.8 (27.0)

Turn Southwest on River Rd./PH 92. Just pedal along the shore!

26.9 (43.3) Main St./Bridge @ River Rd. E. 14.1 (22.7)

Turn towards the Bay and cross the bridge to ride on the sand bar.
Or Continue on PH 92.

WASAGA BEACH

Info.: Tourist Info., Wasaga Beach CofC, PO Box 394, 550 River Rd. W., Wasaga Beach ON L0L 2P0, 705 429-2247, www.wasagainfo.com; Town of Wasaga Beach, Box 110, 30 Lewis St., Wasaga Beach ON L0L 2P0, 705 429-3844; www.wasaga-beach.on.ca. Area code: 705.

Services: All.

Attractions: Chomps Shark Mus., 20 Main St., 429-2564; Nottawasaga Valley Cons. Auth., 429-1479.

Lodging: Motels. B&Bs: Roost Country Retreat, 8405

Nottawasaga 33/34 Sd. Rd., RR #1, 445-9715. Camping: Bell's Maple Pk., 97 Bell's Park Rd., 429-4144; Cedar Grove Pk., 429-2134; Gateway, 429-5862; Holiday Pk., 236 Main St., 429-5816; Jacques Landing, 1873 Klondike Pk. at Powerline Rd., 429-3028; Jell-E-Bean Pk., 121 PH 26, RR 4, 429-5418; Morest Cpgd., 289 River Rd. E., 429-3606; Sunshine Pk., 604 River Rd. W., 429-2334; Toney's Holiday Pk., 140 Main St., 429-5816; Wasaga Dunes, CR 29, 322-3130; Wasaga Pines, PH 92, 322-2727.

27.0 (43.5) Mosley St. @ Bridge 14.0 (22.5)
Turn West on Mosley St.

29.9 (48.1) Mosley St./PH 92 Jct. Mosley St. 11.1 (17.9)
Continue traveling on to Mosley St./PH 92.

31.5 (50.7) 45th St. N. @ Mosley St./PH 92 9.5 (15.3)
Turn towards the Lake on to 45th St. N.
You can turn towards the Lake on any of the side streets. Or continue traveling on Mosley St./PH 92. The distances are same.

31.8 (51.2) Shore Ln. @ 45th St. N. 9.2 (14.8)
Turn West on to Shore Ln.

33.3 (53.6) Greenock St. @ Shore Ln. 7.7 (12.4)
Travel due West on to Greenock St.
Shore Ln. turns towards the Lake and then dead ends.

33.6 (54.1) PH 26/Hume St. @ W Greenock Rd. 7.4 (11.9)
Travel due West on to PH 26.
The County and Provincial roads going South and East-West from the Lake are in a grid pattern. You can make your own loop tours of the area. Here's an example.

Travelers Note

The *Main Route Midland to Collingwood* continues after the *Stayner-Creemore Loop*.

Main Route, continued
Midland to Collingwood

Clockwise ↓ Read mi. (km.) | Counterclockwise mi. (km.) Read ↑

Clockwise ↓ Read mi. (km.)	**Stayner-Creemore Loop**	Counterclockwise mi. (km.) Read ↑

0.0 (0.0) PH 26 @ River Rd. 21.8 (35.1)

Turn South on to PH 26.

3.2 (5.5) CR 42/CR 91 @ PH 26 18.6 (29.9)

Continue traveling South on CR 42.

PH 26 turns East here. You could take it to CR 7/Townline Rd. and then turn North to go back to the Lake Huron shore.

STAYNER

Attraction: A&D Bird Seed Petting Zoo, 7535 PH 26, 428-2465.

Lodging: B&Bs: Donet, 221 Louisa St., 428-3812; Wolves' Crossing, RR 2, 428-5250.

8.8 (14.2) CR 9 @ CR 42 13.0 (20.9)

Turn West on to CR 9. Cashtown Corners.

9.4 (15.1) Fairgrounds Rd. @ CR 9 12.4 (20.0)

Continue traveling West on CR 9.

CREEMORE

Attraction: Creemore Springs Brewery Ltd., 139 Mill St., 466-2240.

Lodging: B&Bs: Cedar Pond, 36920 Sideroad 12/13 (off Airport Rd.), 466-5065; Edenstone, RR 4, 466-3564.

10.0 (16.1) 6th Line Rd. @ CR 9 11.8 (19.0)

Turn North on to 6th Line Rd.

21.8 (35.1) PH 26 @ 6th Line Rd. 0.0 (0.0)

Hey! You're back at the shore. And only 6 km. (3.7 mi.) from your staring point.

Clockwise ↓ Read mi. (km.)	**Stayner-Creemore Loop**	Counterclockwise mi. (km.) Read ↑

Counter Clockwise Traveler Note

The *Main Collingwood to Midland Route* continues after the *Stayner-Creemore Loop.*

Clockwise ↓ Read mi. (km.)	**Main Route, continued** **Midland to Collingwood**	Counterclockwise mi. (km.) Read ↑
39.6 (63.8)	Pretty River Pkwy./PH 26 @ PH 26/Hume St.	1.4 (2.3)

Turn towards the Lake on to Pretty River Pkwy./PH 26.

40.4 (65.0)	Huron St./PH 26 @ Hume St./PH 26	0.6 (1.0)

Turn West on to Huron St.

41.0 (66.0)	Huronontario St./PH 24 @ PH 26/Huron St./1st St.	0.0 (0.0)

COLLINGWOOD

Info.: Georgian Triangle Tourist Assoc., 19 Mountain Rd., Unit 3B, Collingwood ON L9Y 4M2, 705 445-7722; www.georgiantriangle.org; Town of Collingwood, 97 Hurontario St., 705 445-1030; Collingwood ON L9Y 3Z5, www.town.collingwood.on.ca. Area code: 705.

Services: All. Bike shops and rentals. Mt. bike trails.

Attractions: Black History & Cultural Mus., PH 26 W., 445-0201; Bygone Days Mus., 6th St. W., 445-4316; Classic Aircraft, Airport Rd., 445-7545; Collingwood Mus., Memorial Pk., 445-4811; Theatre Collingwood, 444-6376; Scenic Caves Nature Pres. Prov. Pk., Scenic Caves Rd., 446-0256. Canoe & sail boat rentals. Charter fishing boats.

Lodging: Georgian Triangle Lodging Assoc., 601 First St., 445-0748. Motels. B&Bs: Aspen Lodge, 111 Tyrolean Lane, 446-0259; Cedar Chest, 216 Cedar St., 790-2507; Edelweiss, 1 Plater St., 445-0639; Haus Sol, RR 3, 445-3340; Joseph Lawrence House, 492 Huronontario St., 445-7132; Pedulla's Mountainside, 109 Carmichael Cres., 445-7307; Poplar Country Inn, CR 124, 445-9592; Silver Creek Gardens, 49 Silvercreek Dr., 445-6637; The Mountains, 10 Craigmore Cres., 445-0015; Trillium Place, 135 Third St., 444-7207. Camping: Craigleith Prov. Pk., PH 26, 12 km. (7.5 mi.) W. of Collingwood, 445-4467.

Clockwise ↓ Read mi. (km.)	**Main Route** **Collingwood to Midland**	Counterclockwise mi. (km.) Read ↑

STOP

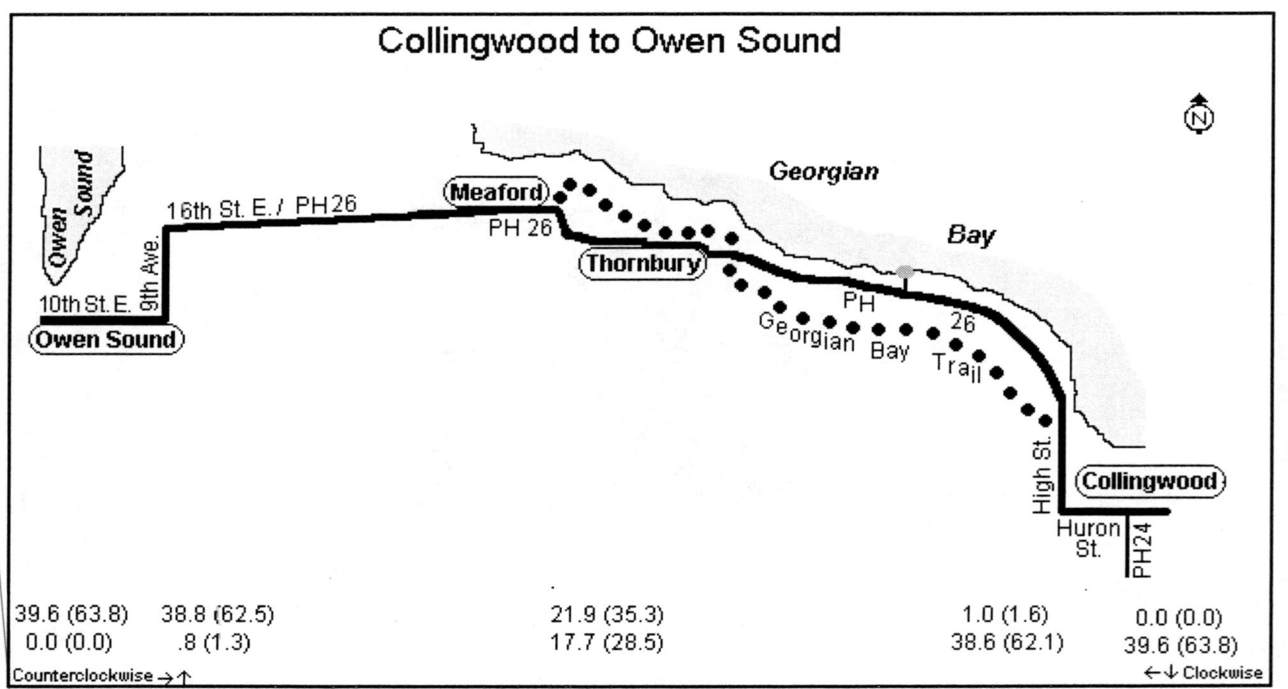
Collingwood to Owen Sound
N
Owen Sound
16th St. E. / PH 26
Meaford
PH 26
Thornbury
Georgian
Bay
PH
26
Georgian Bay Trail
10th St. E.
9th Ave.
Owen Sound
High St.
Collingwood
Huron St.
PH24
39.6 (63.8)
0.0 (0.0)
38.8 (62.5)
.8 (1.3)
21.9 (35.3)
17.7 (28.5)
1.0 (1.6)
38.6 (62.1)
0.0 (0.0)
39.6 (63.8)
Counterclockwise
Clockwise

COLLINGWOOD TO OWEN SOUND

Clockwise ↓ Read mi. (km.)	**Collingwood to Owen Sound**	Counterclockwise mi. (km.) Read ↑
0.0 (0.0)	Hurontario St./PH 24 @ PH 26/Huron St./1st St.	39.6 (63.8)

Travel West on 1st St.
COLLINGWOOD information is in the *Midland to Collingwood* segment.

0.8 (1.3)	High St./PH 26 @ PH 26/1st St.	38.8 (62.5)

Turn North on to High St./PH 26.
In other words, follow PH 26.

1.0 (1.6)	Georgian Trail @ High St./PH 26	38.6 (62.1)

Turn West on to the Georgian Bay Trail.
Or Continue traveling on PH 26. The distance to Meaford is about the same either way you go.
Camping: It's another 10.5 km. (6.5 mi.) to Craighleigh Prov. Pk., at the lakeshore, 705 445-4467.

20.8 (33.5)	PH 26/Sykes St. @ Georgian Trail)	18.8 (30.3

Turn Northwest on to PH 26/Sykes St.

21.9 (35.3)	Nelson St. @ Sykes St./PH 26	17.7 (28.5)

Continue traveling West on PH 26 through Meaford.

MEAFORD

Info.: Municipality of Meaford, 12 Nelson St. Ext., Meaford ON N4L 1A1, 519 538-1060, www.meaford.com; Meaford CofC, Box 4836, Meaford ON N4L 1X6, 519 538-1640. Area code: 519.

Services: All.

Attractions: Georgian Theatre Festival, Meaford Opera House, 12 Nelson St. E., 538-3569; Meaford Mus., Bayfield St., 538-1060.

Lodging: Motels. B&Bs: Ash-Berry Hill, RR 4, 538-2760; Belina House, Old Mall Rd., RR 4, 538-3536; Ben Bow Inn, 78 Bridge St., 538-4232; Blackberry Hill, RR 1, 538-3643; Carroll's Country Inn, RR 2, 538-1077; Chestnut Lane Farm, RR 2, 538-1445; Franro Farm, RR 2, 538-4597; Irish Mountain, RR 1, 538-2803; Minniehill Creek Farm, 25671 Grey Rd. 40, 538-1646; Rocklyn Inn, RR 2, 538-5992. Camping: Memorial Municipal Pk., Grant Ave., 538-2530; Fairview Trailer Pk., 538-2631.

38.5 (62.0) PH 6/10/9th Ave. E. @ PH 26/16th St. E. 1.1 (1.8)
Turn South on 9th Ave.

38.8 (62.5) 10th St. E. @ 9th Ave. E. 0.8 (1.3)
Turn West on to 10th St. E.

39.6 (63.8) Inner Harbor Walkway @ 10th St. W. 0.0 (0.0)
Yup! You've done it! Rounded Georgian Bay.
OWEN SOUND information is in the *Owen Sound to Tobermory* segment.

Clockwise ↓ Read mi. (km.)	**Owen Sound to Collingwood**	Counterclockwise mi. (km.) Read ↑

'Round the Sound you went!

BIBLIOGRAPHY

Blocksma, Mary. The Fourth Coast. New York: Penguin Books. 1995.

Cantor, George. The Great Lakes Guide Book: Lake Huron and Eastern Lake Michigan. Ann Arbor MI: University of Michigan Press. 1985.

DeHaan, Vici. State Parks of the Midwest: America's Heartland. Boulder CO: Cordillera Press. 1993.

DeHarpporte, Dean. Northeast and Great Lakes Wind Atlas. New York: Van Nostrand Reinhold, 1983.

Eichenlaub, Val L. Weather and Climate of the Great Lakes Region. Notre Dame IN: University of Notre Dame Press. 1979

Environment Canada, United States Environmental Protection Agency, Brock University and Northwestern University. The Great Lakes: An Environmental Atlas and Resource Book.

Toronto ON and Chicago IL: Environment Canada and United States Environmental Protection Agency. 1987.

Freedman, Eric. Great Lakes, Great National Forests. Lansing MI: Thunder Bay Press. 1995.

Johnson, Clifton, 1865-1940. Highways and Byways of the Great Lakes, New ed. New York, The Macmillan company. 1913.

Phillips, D. W. and J. A. W. McCulloch. The Climate of the Great Lakes Basin. Toronto: Information Canada. 1972.

Roberts, Bruce and Ray Jones. Eastern Great Lakes lighthouses: Ontario, Erie, and Huron. Philadelphia PA: Chelsea House Publishers. 1999.

Robertson, James Alexander and K. D. Card. Geology and scenery: north shore of Lake Huron Region. Toronto: Ontario Ministry of Natural Resources, Division of Mines. 1972.

Wells, Kenneth McNeill. Cruising the North Channel. Toronto: Kingswood House. 1960.

Winckler, Suzanne. The Smithsonian Guide to Historic America: The Great Lakes States. New York: Stewart, Tabori & Chang. 1989.

APPENDIX

Contents

CREDITS

Kamnitzer, Steven. Toronto, ON. Photographs.

Kellogg, Janis. Kelloggraphy. 3487 E. Sturgeon Valley Rd. Vanderbilt, MI 49795. Cover, title page, pgs. 49, 67, 74, 136.

Stricos, Bob. Schenectady NY. Photographs.

Ostendorph, Richard. Chagrin Falls, OH. Photographs.

Ostermeir, Bob, Mentor, OH. Photographs.

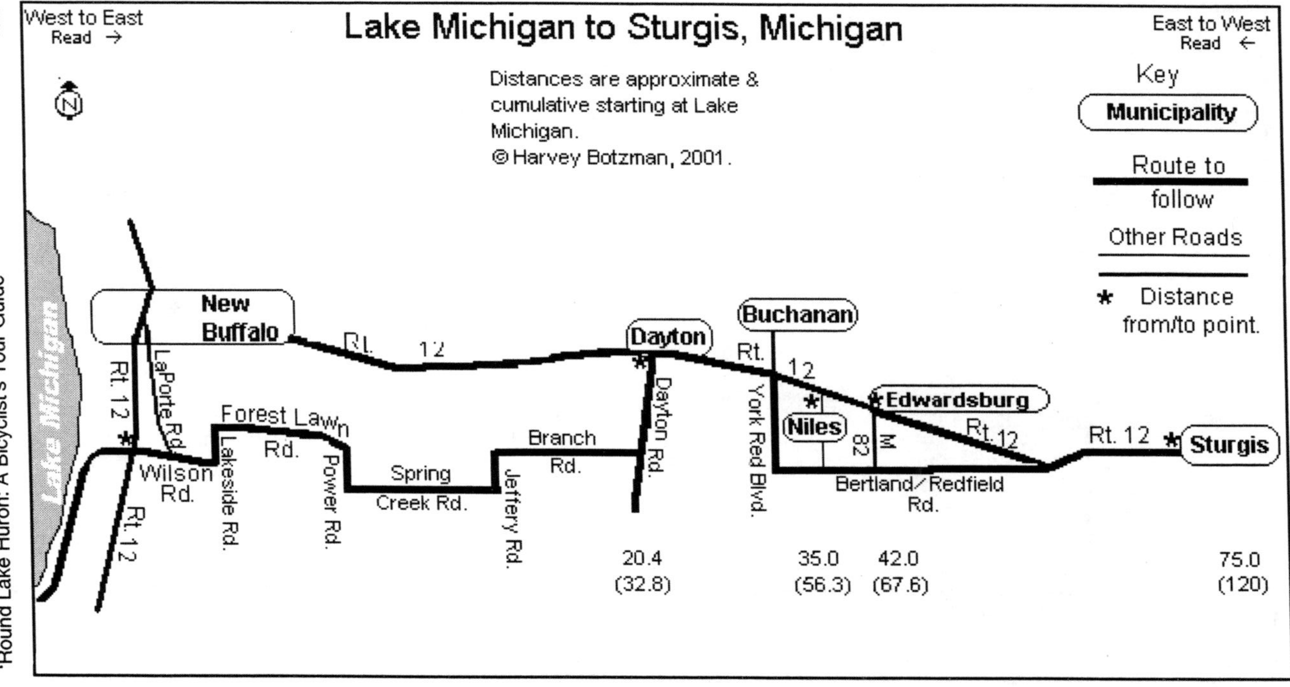
West to East Read →
Lake Michigan to Sturgis, Michigan
East to West Read ←
N
Distances are approximate & cumulative starting at Lake Michigan.
© Harvey Botzman, 2001.
Key
Municipality
Route to follow
Other Roads
* Distance from/to point.
Lake Michigan
New Buffalo
Rt. 12
LaPorte Rd.
Wilson Rd.
Rt. 12
Forest Lawn Rd.
Lakeside Rd.
Power Rd.
Spring Creek Rd.
Jeffery Rd.
Branch Rd.
Rt. 12
Dayton
Dayton Rd.
Buchanan
Rt. 12
York Red Blvd.
Niles
M 82
Edwardsburg
Rt. 12
Bertland/Redfield Rd.
Rt. 12
Sturgis
20.4
(32.8)
35.0
(56.3)
42.0
(67.6)
75.0
(120)

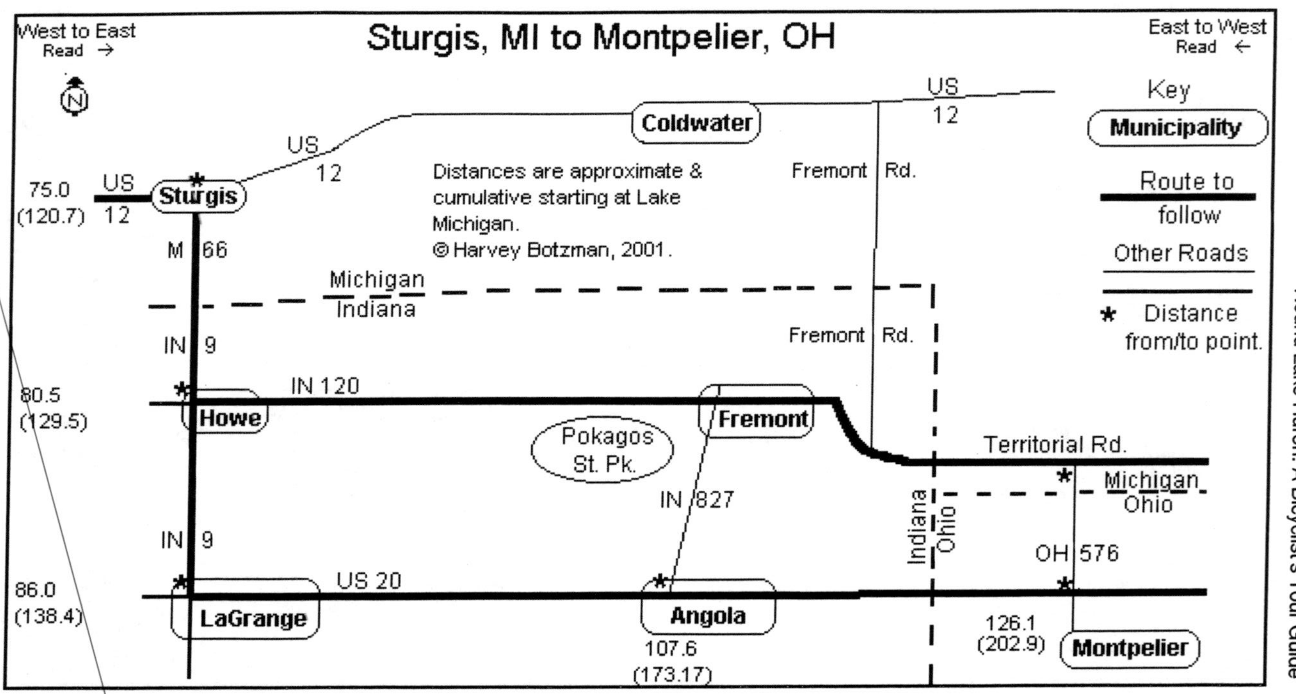

Sturgis, MI to Montpelier, OH
West to East Read →
East to West Read ←
Key
Municipality
Route to follow
Other Roads
* Distance from/to point.
Distances are approximate & cumulative starting at Lake Michigan.
© Harvey Botzman, 2001.
Sturgis
Coldwater
Howe
Fremont
LaGrange
Angola
Montpelier
Pokagos St. Pk.
US 12
M 66
IN 9
IN 120
US 20
IN 827
OH 576
Fremont Rd.
Territorial Rd.
Michigan
Indiana
Ohio
75.0 (120.7)
80.5 (129.5)
86.0 (138.4)
107.6 (173.17)
126.1 (202.9)

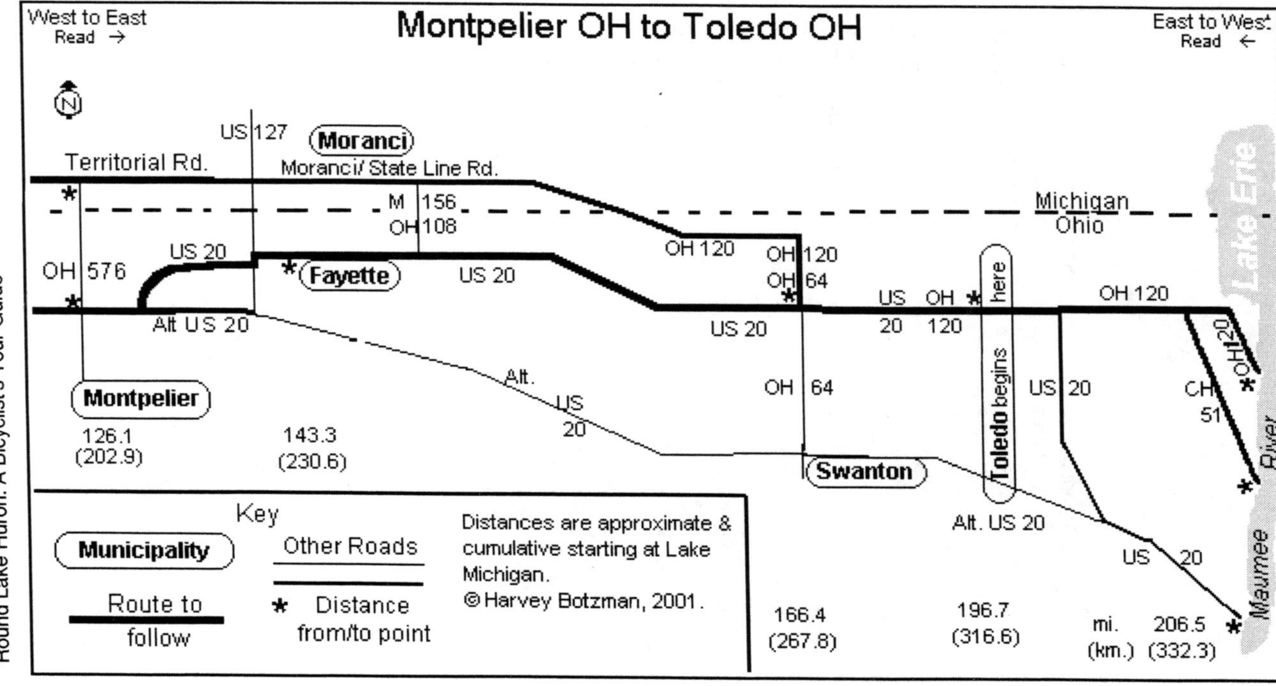
Montpelier OH to Toledo OH
West to East
Read →
East to West
Read ←
US 127
Moranci
Territorial Rd.
Moranci/ State Line Rd.
M 156
OH 108
Michigan
Ohio
US 20
OH 576
Fayette
US 20
OH 120
OH 120
OH 64
US OH
20 120
here
OH 120
Alt US 20
US 20
Alt.
US
20
OH 64
Toledo begins
US 20
CH 51
OH 120
Montpelier
126.1
(202.9)
143.3
(230.6)
Swanton
Lake Erie
River
Maumee
Alt. US 20
US 20
Key
Municipality
Other Roads
Route to follow
* Distance from/to point
Distances are approximate & cumulative starting at Lake Michigan.
© Harvey Botzman, 2001.
166.4
(267.8)
196.7
(316.6)
mi. 206.5
(km.) (332.3)

EQUIPMENT LISTS

✓ Clothing
- ❍ Cycling Short
- ❍ Cycling Shorts
- ❍ Cycling Shorts
- ❍ Cycling Gloves
- ❍ Off Cycling Shorts
- ❍ Tee Shirts
- ❍ Tee Shirts
- ❍ Socks #_____
- ❍ Short Socks #_____
- ❍ Underwear
- ❍ Jacket
- ❍ Sweater/Fleece top
- ❍ Dress pants
- ❍ Long (thermal) Tights
- ❍ Jeans
- ❍ Rain Gear
- ❍ Shoes
  - ❍ Cycling
  - ❍ Off-cycling
- ❍ Dress
- ❍ Blouse #_____
- ❍ Shirt #_____
- ❍ Wicking base layer
- ❍ Bathing Suit
- ❍ Scarf (*do rag*)
- ❍ Belt
- ❍ Clothes Pins
- ❍ Sewing Kit
- ❍ Hat
- ❍ Other _______________
- ❍ Other _______________

✓ Tools
- ❍ Combination tool
- ❍ Patch Kit
- ❍ Screwdriver(s)
  - ❍ Philips
    - ❍ # 0
    - ❍ # 1
    - ❍ # 2
  - ❍ Flat
    - ❍ 5mm/ 3/8 in
    - ❍ 8mm/ 5/8 in
- ❍ Wrenches
  Hex, Open, Box
  or Sockets
    - ❍ 4mm-H O B S
    - ❍ 5mm-H O B S
    - ❍ 6mm-H O B S
    - ❍ 8mm-H O B S
    - ❍ 9mm-H O B S
    - ❍ 10mm-H O B S
- ❍ 11mm-H O B S
    - ❍ 12mm-H O B S
    - ❍ 13mm-H O B S
    - ❍ 14mm-H O B S
    - ❍ Other______
- ❍ Pliers
- ❍ Vise Grips
    - ❍ 3in
    - ❍ 5in
- ❍ Cone Wrenches
- ❍ Screws
- ❍ Freewheel Remover
- ❍ Crank Remover
- ❍ Electrical Tape

EQUIPMENT LISTS

✓ Bicycle

- ❍ Rear Rack
- ❍ Front Rack
- ❍ Low Riders
- ❍ Rear Panniers
- ❍ Handlebar Bag
- ❍ Front Light
- ❍ Rear Flashing Red
- ❍ Light Other Color
- ❍ Wiring for Lights
- ❍ Generator
- ❍ Batteries
- ❍ Extra Batteries
- ❍ Cables
  - ❍ Brake
  - ❍ Gears
- ❍ Other__________
- ❍ Special Screws
- ❍ Special Screws
- ❍ Cyclometer
- ❍ Bungie Cords #_____
- ❍ Other _______
- ❍ ____________
- ❍ ____________
- ❍ ____________
- ❍ ____________
- ❍ ____________
- ❍ ____________
- ❍ ____________

✓ Personal

- ❍ Watch
- ❍ Towel
- ❍ Sunglasses
- ❍ Helmet
- ❍ First Aid Kit
- ❍ Soap
- ❍ Tooth Brush
- ❍ Tooth Paste
- ❍ Cosmetics
- ❍ 2nd pair of Eyeglasses
- ❍ Shaving Equipment
- ❍ Medical Prescriptions
- ❍ Eyeglass Prescription
- ❍ Contact Lens Solutions
- ❍ Journal
- ❍ Citizenship ID
- ❍ Pen
- ❍ Stamps
- ❍ Sun Screen
- ❍ Medicine
- ❍ Calculator
- ❍ Flashlight
- ❍ 25¢ (for phone)
- ❍ Credit Cards
- ❍ Passport & Visas
- ❍ Tickets
- ❍ Maps
- ❍ Camera & Film
- ❍ Photographs (self)

EQUIPMENT LISTS

✓ Camping
- ❍ Tent
  - ❍ Tent stakes
  - ❍ Tent Poles
  - ❍ Ground cloth
- ❍ Rope (3m/10ft)
- ❍ Sleeping Bag
- ❍ Mattress
- ❍ Day pack
- ❍ H_20 Purifier/Filter
- ❍ Toilet Paper
- ❍ Candle
- ❍ Flashlight
- ❍ Other
- ❍ ____________
- ❍ ____________

✓ Cooking
- ❍ Cup
- ❍ Pot (Cook Set)
- ❍ Knife
- ❍ Fork
- ❍ Spoon
- ❍ Can
- ❍ Opener/Cork Screw
- ❍ Stove
  - ❍ Fuel Bottle
  - ❍ Fuel
  - ❍ Matches
  - ❍ Pre-Starter
- ❍ Stove Repair Kit
- ❍ Swiss Army Knife
- ❍ Wire (2m/2yds)
- ❍ Other ___________

✓ Food
- ❍ Pasta
- ❍ Cereal
- ❍ Rice
- ❍ Dried Milk
- ❍ Fruit
- ❍ Cookies
- ❍ Snacks
- ❍ Other _______
- ❍ ____________
- ❍ ____________

LESS IS MORE
LESS IS MORE

- ❍ Peanut Butter
- ❍ Oil or fat
- ❍ Vegetables ______
- ❍ Vegetables ______
- ❍ Vegetables ______
- ❍ Other ___________
- ❍ ________________
- ❍ ________________
- ❍ ________________
- ❍ ________________

LESS IS MORE
LESS IS MORE

COMMENTS

I appreciate your comments. Please feel free to add comments.

Dates you toured _______________.

Which chapters or information did you find most useful in:

Tour Guide: ____

- ❍ Tour Preparation
- ❍ The Route
- ❍ Distance Information
- ❍ Lodging Information
- ❍ Municipal Information
- ❍ Other: ____________________

Lodging Recommendations

Attractions Recommendations

Restaurant/Bakery/Grocery Recommendations

Route Recommendations

Other Comments:

Your Name: ________________________________

Your Address: ________________________________

City, State/Prov., Zip/PC: ________________________

E-mail: ________________________________

The name of a friend who might be interested in receiving our brochure:

Name: ________________________________

Address: ________________________________

City, State/Prov., Zip/PC: ________________________

E-mail: ________________________________

We do not sell or rent our mailing list.

Please return this Comment Form to:
Cyclotour Guide Books, PO Box 10585, Rochester, NY 14610

Thanks, Harvey

SURVEY FORM

One of the most significant problems facing bicycling advocates is the the lack of data on cyclotourism and cyclotourists. It is almost impossible to make a case for improving roadway and general bicycle touring conditions unless cycling advocates have data on bicycle tourists.

This Survey is anonymous. You do not have to provide your name, etc. and I will not compare this Form to the *Comment Form*. That's why there are two separate forms.

I have tried to make this Survey Form easy for you to complete. Check the boxes or fill in the spaces, almost all of which are on the right side of the page. Sorry lefties!

Tour of ____

How many people were in your touring party? _______

Demographic data of cyclotourists

Your age? __________ Sex? _______
Spouse's age? __________ Sex? _______
Child's age? __________ Sex? _______
Child's age? __________ Sex? _______
Friend's age? __________ Sex? _______
Friend's age? __________ Sex? _______
Friend's age? __________ Sex? _______

Your approximate per annum income range:

❍ US $ ❍ CAN $ ❍ EURO ∈ ❍ Other _____

Teenager on allowance? ❍
College Student? ❍
Below US$20,000 ❍
US $20,001 - $30,000 ❍
US $30,001 - $40,000 ❍
US $40,001 - $50,000 ❍
US $50,001 + ❍

Enough of this demographic stuff but It is important for presenting a case for better bicycling conditions.

What was the total distance you toured? _______________ mi.

The average daily distance you traveled? _______________ mi.

Did you tour in segments? _______________ How many? ____

Average amount of money expended each day, per person?
In ❍ US $ ❍ CAN $ ❍ EURO ∈ ❍ Other _____

Less than US$10.00 ❍
US $10.01 - 15.00 ❍
US $15.01 - 25.00 ❍
US $25.01 - 35.00 ❍
US $35.01 - 45.00 ❍
US $45.01 - 55.00 ❍
US $55.01 - 65.00 ❍
US $65.01 - 75.00 ❍
US $75.01 - 85.00 ❍
Over US $85.01 ❍

Average Amount of money expended each day for these items:

In ❍ US $ ❍ CAN $ ❍ EURO ∈ ❍ Other _____

Amount	Lodging	Food, incl. snacks	Enterainment Attractions	Misc.
< $5.00				
$5.01-10.00				
$10.01-20.00				
$20.01-25.00				
$25.01 +				

How did you cyclotour? General description.

Loaded touring? ❍
Camping & mainly eating in restaurants? ❍
Sagwagon camping? ❍
❍ B&Bs ❍ Motels & preparing own meals? ❍
❍ B&Bs ❍ Motels & eating in restaurants? ❍
Other: ______________________________ ❍

Feel free & you are encouraged to add other comments or data:

Please return this form to: Cyclotour Guide Books, PO Box, 10585, Rochester, NY 14610. Thanks, Harvey.

Cyclotour Expense Log

Date	Odometer	Destination	Brkfast	Lunch	Dinner	Groceries	Snacks	Lodging	Bicycle	Misc.	Daily Total	Running Total
Total												

Cyclotour Expense Log

Date	Odometer	Destination	Brkfast	Lunch	Dinner	Groceries	Snacks	Lodging	Bicycle	Misc.	Daily Total	Running Total
Total												

INDEX

ORDER FORM

I want a great experience bicycle touring.

In addition to our bicycle tour guides, Cyclotour Guide Books distributes hard to find bicycle tour guides and maps for New Zealand, the French Canal System (also a waterway guide), crossing North American, and Massachusetts. These wonderful bicycle tour guides are described in full detail on our web site, www.cyclotour.com.

You can order any Cyclotour Guide Books or other bicycling guides books/maps directly from our web site.

We answer bicycle touring questions cheerfully.

Please send me the books I have checked.
All prices are in US $.

____	'Round Lake Ontario: A Bicyclist's Tour Guide	$24.95
____	'Round Lake Erie: A Bicyclist's Tour Guide	$24.95
____	'Round Lake Michigan: A Bicyclist's Tour Guide	$24.95
____	'Round Lake Huron: A Bicyclist's Tour Guide	$24.95
____	'Round Lake Superior: A Bicyclist's Tour Guide	$24.95
____	Erie Canal Bicyclist & Hiker Tour Guide	$24.95
____	Finger Lakes Bicyclist's Tour Guide	$24.95
____	Long Distance Bicycle Touring Primer	$19.95

Sub total: ________

+ Per order shipping charge: + **$5.00**

TOTAL:________

Name: ____

Street: ____

City/St./Prov./Zip/PC ________________________________

Send your US funds check or money order to:	Cyclotour Guide Books PO Box 10585 Rochester NY 14610-0585
Email your order to:	cyclotour@cyclotour.com
Telephone or fax your order to:	585 244-6157
Order directly from our web site::	www.cyclotour.com